Words and Deeds in Renaissance Rome

Trials before the Papal Magistrates

The social historian, searching for the basis of a culture, often turns to a study of ordinary people. Perhaps one of the most revealing places to find them is in a court of law. In this presentation of nine criminal trials of sixteenth-century Rome (1540–75), where magistrates kept verbatim records, Thomas and Elizabeth Cohen paint a lively portrait of a society, one that is reminiscent of Boccaccio. These stories, however, are true.

Each trial transcript is followed by an essay that interprets the beliefs, codes, everyday speech, and personal transactions of a world that is radically different from our own. The people on trial include assassins, a spell-caster, an exorcist, an adulterous wife, several courtesans, and the peasant cast of a bawdy, sacrilegious play. Out of their often poignant troubles, and their machinations, comes a vivid revelation of not only the tumultuous street life of Rome but also rituals of honour, the power and weakness of women, and the realities of social and economic hierarchies.

Like *cinéma-vérité, Words and Deeds in Renaissance Rome* gives us an intimate glimpse of a people and their world.

Thomas V. Cohen and **Elizabeth S. Cohen** are members of the Department of History and of the Division of Humanities, York University.

Words and Deeds in Renaissance Rome: Trials before the Papal Magistrates

THOMAS V. COHEN AND
ELIZABETH S. COHEN

UNIVERSITY OF TORONTO PRESS
Toronto Buffalo London

© University of Toronto Press Incorporated 1993
Toronto Buffalo London
Printed in Canada

Reprinted 2000, 2005

ISBN 0-8020-2825-x (cloth)
ISBN 0-8020-7699-8 (paper)

∞

Printed on acid-free paper

Canadian Cataloguing in Publication Data
Cohen, Thomas V. (Thomas Vance), 1942–
Words and deeds in Renaissance Rome

Includes bibliographical references and index.
ISBN 0-8020-2825-x (bound) ISBN 0-8020-7699-8 (pbk.)

1. Trials – Rome.   2. Justice, Administration of
(Roman law).   3. Rome (Italy) – History – 1420-1798.
I. Cohen, Elizabeth S. (Elizabeth Storr), 1946–.
II. Title.

KJA2700.C64 1993   347.45'63207   C93-093599-3

University of Toronto Press acknowledges the financial assistance to its
publishing program of the Canada Council for the Arts and the Ontario Arts
Council.

University of Toronto Press acknowledges the financial support for its publishing activities of the Government of Canada through the Book Publishing
Industry Development Program (BPIDP).

For our teachers,
especially R.V.C., R.J.S., T.K.R., and N.Z.D.

Contents

Preface

❦

This is a book of nine trials from late Renaissance Rome. They are only a few of the many thousands that still survive, bound in fat, dusty volumes in the state archive of that city. That Roman collection, in its turn, is but one of dozens like it in Italy and elsewhere. So why print these? Not because they are famous or important trials. On the contrary, in the large, they record forgotten deeds and misdeeds of obscure men and women. Rather, we print them because, among the dozens we have seen, they stand out for their colour, their language, their clarity of plot, their general interest for the study of history, language, social structures, values, beliefs, and patterns of behaviour. They paint a picture of their time at once lively and telling. Although sometimes piquant or surprising in their turns of phrase and story, these trials conjure a vision of Italian life confirmed by other judicial records and by the literature of the time.

We have tried for unity of place and time. Most of the trials come from Rome itself; a few reach into its hinterland in central Italy. As for time, most date from a narrow span of years, the last two years of the pontificate of Paul IV (1558–9) and the first months of that of his successor, Pius IV. They all reflect a particular society at a particular historical moment during the passage from the Renaissance to the Catholic Reformation. The several trials may thus be read to comment on one another. Two cases break the unity of time: 'The Abbot's Assassins' (1542) and 'The Village Play' (1574). This last, unlike the others, is here precisely because it is anomalous. The story of an amateur theatrical on trial, it charts in fascinating ways the foggy borderlands of literacy and written culture.

This book grew out of our use of such trials in the classroom. It is designed, therefore, for teachers and students, but, at the same time, for the pleasure of other readers drawn to exploring a colourful past, in particular, that of Italy in the Renaissance. Our goal is at once to instruct, to entertain, and to kindle interest in a lively social world profoundly different from our own. Thus, the commentaries are intended to help cut a path through the thickets of testimony. We suggest lines of inquiry, but hope to leave the readers room to construct their own interpretations. We do not proffer a critical edition or a definitive scholarly analysis. Those who would like to see a formal and more thorough treatment may consult our articles, listed in the bibliography.

This book benefited from much generous support. York University, the American Council of Learned Societies, the National Endowment for the Humanities, and the American Academy in Rome provided grants. The staff of the Archivio di Stato in Rome, especially Donato Tamblè, gave much help. Welcome advice came from many scholars. Special thanks go to Linda Carroll, Laurie Nussdorfer, Riccardo Bassani, and Irene Polverini Fosi. Claudio Gori Giorgi provided invaluable logistical aid. Prudence Tracy, of University of Toronto Press, encouraged us from the start; her colleagues graciously followed through with the project. The enthusiastic interest of dozens of York University undergraduates contributed energy that helped bring this book into being. Among them, Elizabeth Petruccelli, Raffaele Girardo, and Linda Traverso earned special mention for their long and skilful labours upon some of these manuscripts. On the homefront, William Cohen and Julie Cohen long suffered distracted parents and often sacrificed familiar haunts and computer time; their goodwill is gratefully remembered.

T.V.C. and E.S.C.
Rome, 1992

Glossary

Auditore Here, a judge of the governor's court

Baiocco Small Roman coin, rated at one-tenth of a giulio

Bando Any decree. The governor, among others, could issue bandi.

Bargello Sheriff. Each Roman court had its policemen and its bargello, who commanded them. The bargello we meet in these trials headed the police of the governor, the biggest force in Rome.

Campidoglio The Capitoline hill and, by extension, the communal government of Rome

Caporione An urban magistrate who had authority in a Roman district called a rione (region)

Castellan A local official in charge of a castle. He was often responsible for defence and public order.

Fiscale In full, *procuratore fiscale*, the prosecutor of the governor's court. He was so called because the court was a department of the fisc, or Camera Apostolica, the papal treasury.

Giulio A Roman silver coin, in theory ten baiocchi

Lieutenant in Criminal Matters The presiding magistrate in most trials before the governor's court. He sat in for the governor, who himself heard only a few cases.

Madonna Title for a respectable woman, below signora

Maestro Title of address reserved for artisans who were masters of their own establishments

Messer (Sometimes contracted as *ser*.) Title of address above maestro and below signore, appropriate to notaries, lawyers, and other men of substance

Notary Official whose job it was to create and to keep copies of documents of public record. The court of the governor had its own notaries.

Podestà The chief magistrate of a town

Quattrino A small coin; quattrini, generic small change

Rione A district of Roman municipal administration

Scudo A Roman gold coin, eleven giulii in value

Signora Title of address of a noblewoman, but also used as a common noun by the servants for the lady of the house

Signore Title of address for noblemen, and also for the judges of the court. Often contracted to *signor'*. Somewhat more formal than *signore* was *Vostra Signoria*, which we have translated as 'your Lordship.'

Vicario A cardinal, the pope's deputy for the pastoral care of the city of Rome. His tribunal's jurisdiction overlapped that of the governor's court.

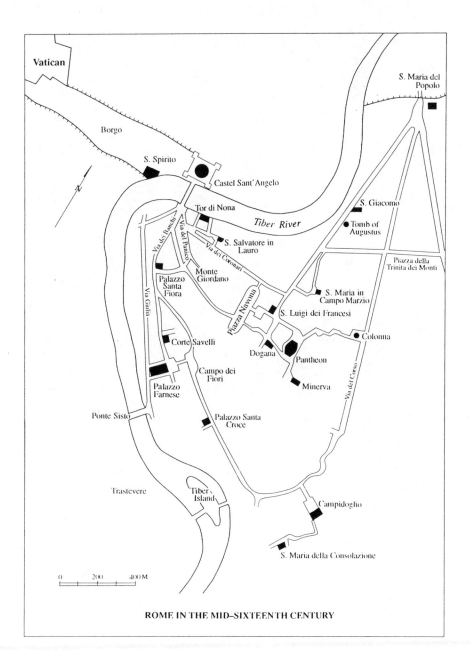

Vatican

Borgo

S. Spirito

N

Castel Sant'Angelo

Tor di Nona

Tiber River

S. Maria del
Popolo

S. Giacomo

Tomb of
Augustus

S. Salvatore in
Lauro

Via dei Banchi

Via del Panico

Via dei Coronari

Piazza della
Trinita dei Monti

Monte
Giordano

Palazzo
Santa
Fiora

Via Giulia

Piazza Navona

S. Maria in
Campo Marzio

S. Luigi dei Francesi

Corte Savelli

Dogana

Colonna

Pantheon

Campo dei
Fiori

Minerva

Via del Corso

Palazzo
Farnese

Ponte Sisto

Palazzo Santa
Croce

Trastevere

Tiber
Island

Campidoglio

S. Maria della Consolazione

0   200   400 M

ROME IN THE MID–SIXTEENTH CENTURY

Nicholas Van Aelst, Conclave for the Election of Paul V (detail) (1605).
An icon of the Vacant See, the caporione and his band of citizens arresting
evil-doers by night

Polidoro Caldara di Caravaggio, Women Sewing (c. 1525). A rare glimpse of domestic life from sixteenth-century Rome

Israel Silvestre, The Madonna of the Popolo (ca. 1645). Though the obelisk is new since Maddalena came to see an exorcism, the scene is little changed. At left is the Porta del Popolo, the gate for the great roads to the north.

Etienne Du Pérac, Forum with the Arch of Septimius Severus (ca. 1574). Arch and Senate house, monuments of the ancient forum, are overgrown, reused as fort and church, and half-engulfed in risen ground.

Antoine Lafréry, Castel Sant'Angelo (ca. 1570). The great papal fortress, residence, and prison

Henrik Van Cleve, Colosseum (ca. 1570). The ancient monument was well outside the settled zone.

Anton Van Den Wyngaerde, Panorama of Rome (detail) (ca. 1543). The view east from the high ground behind Trastevere, with the Tiber and the densely settled zone below Santa Maria d'Aracoeli (right).

Etienne Du Pérac, Rome from the roof of the Cancelleria palace (ca. 1570).
A pigeon's view of jumbled roofs and countless chimneys. At the end of the
Renaissance, Rome still had its motley gothic skyline of belfreys and towers.

Words and Deeds in Renaissance Rome

libri uecchi

Introduction

To many modern readers, the trials in this book will seem strange and sometimes shocking. In them, one finds a murderous abbot, a shoemaker exorcist, a housewife and her maid who tell the future with beans, a lord who strips his debtor naked, a prostitute who mixes sex and magic, and various other characters who behave in surprising ways. One might think that these legal records present not the late Renaissance but a mere rogues' gallery of Roman curiosities. It is better not to dismiss them, however, for in large and small these trials do indeed represent their world in countless ways. Despite their striking features, they are neither odd nor rare. The records of the papal courts are full of such unexpected behaviour. Furthermore, oddities aside, these trials depict behaviour embedded in the normal, for in them the rhythms of speech, the patterns of belief and action, are all faithful to their world. Letters, diaries, *novelle*, and plays confirm the trials' image of mid-sixteenth-century Italian life.

What the trials reveal, however, is a culture not high but vernacular. As in anthropology, so here 'culture' sums up the values and habits of judgment, perception, and expression that give shape and colour to a particular social world. We prefer 'vernacular' to the usual 'popular,' which implies – falsely – that the rich and powerful did not share the culture of the mass. Rather, from day to day, the élite did business, made love and war, greeted, gossiped, and quarrelled by codes and habits that had much in common with those that governed their inferiors. Therefore, vernacular culture nourished the high culture of arts and letters that the élites consumed and patronized and did much to shape it. Thus, in these Roman trials, one seizes not the lovely flower of the Renaissance, but its lowly roots. But this botanical metaphor can mislead, for the traffic of influence went both ways. It was also the lot of high culture, then as always, to feed vernacular traditions. Thus, for instance, these trials show how folk magic took much of its vocabulary and ritual from the official liturgy of the church. So, too, street life could purloin forms from the crafts of state. Thus, a servant bearing a love-message to her mistress could announce she was coming on an 'embassy.' The law, the church, the state, the stage, the printing-house both gave to the culture of the populace and took from it.

The best route into the vernacular culture of sixteenth-century Italy, or of most other European countries of the time, is through the records of the courts. As did few other offices, tribunals wrote down and saved what ordinary people really said. Thus, in Rome, the notary, an official record-keeper, had to take verbatim notes of every testimony. Thanks to him, we can hear the lost voices of some of those many men, and even more women, who could not or did not write. Because such trials show the whole of Italian society, not just its literate peaks and uplands, they illustrate both the gaps and the connections between high and low cultures.

Among historians, of late, there has been a stampede into the dossiers of justice. The past few years have seen lively books about the once-forgotten commoners in Italy, England, France, Germany, the Netherlands, and Spain. Novels, and even a few films have felt the impact of the enterprise. Much of this writing attempts a 'cultural history,' which incorporates some of the interests of sociology, anthropology, and literary theory. By offering up a sample of raw materials, and by glossing them, this book of trials aims to illustrate the pleasures and dilemmas of such research.

Like all trials, these here are tales of deviance, for, as ever, it was infraction of the rules that haled a case before the magistrates. But how then, one might ask, can quirky stories about the unusual, chosen for their rich narrative and lively detail, illustrate general truths? This fair question deserves a four-pronged answer. For one thing, by negation, all deviance outlines the boundaries of the normal; to explore its impact helps to chart the rules it broached. For another, even those who broke some rules observed most others. Thus, the abnormal is couched in the normal. And, third, many who testified were only witnesses, not partners to a crime. Fourth, it would be wrong to see even the guilty as 'criminals,' set apart by their defective natures. Today, the term has become a noun, a stigmatizing tag at home in journalism, sociology, politics, and law. In the sixteenth century, however, 'criminal' was still just an adjective labelling acts, not persons. Thus, unless they had offended God, those accused of crimes were often not in theory or fact distinguished by their deeds; they were just ordinary people who had overstepped a line.

In sixteenth-century Italy, 'criminal' transgression became all the more likely, in the course of quite ordinary social dealings, because the very borders of the illegal were in flux. The zone of the forbidden widened fast as an expanding state and an ambitious, consolidating church, both zealous for order, worked to criminalize all sorts of behaviour that had hitherto seemed legitimate or tolerable. Soothsaying, love magic, folk cosmology, sharp-tongued talk, and all sorts of vengeful mayhem only gradually, under the pressure of the authorities, took on the name of 'crime.' In the sixteenth century, however, there was still a chasm between the law's aspirations and its grasp. Weakly policed, the state made up in harshness what it lacked in efficient thoroughness. Unable to catch the many, it made examples of the few. Thus, the 'deviants' here on trial were more often than not just unlucky to have been caught doing what countless others did.

Reading a good trial is much like throwing back heavy shutters to open a window on the past. The effect is dazzling. Just as a Renaissance painting is much like a window frame, through which the beholder discerns a natural scene in all its bright colour, life, depth, and fine detail, so a court case can portray a moment at once sharply bounded and rich in texture, movement, and complexity. But, as with paintings, with trials we must observe with cautious, educated eyes. For no Renaissance painting, not even a Flemish townscape, was photographic in ambition or effect. Rather, the artist's brush strokes followed conventions set by style, symbolic vocabulary, and political or intellectual program. Much the same was true of testimony in court. The industry of the faithful notary does indeed afford us a very accurate transcription of words said before the magistrate. But the truth behind those words is another matter. Suspects and witnesses had every reason to shape their versions of an event to fit the politics of the moment, for the stakes were often high. So, in many ways, a tale told before the court was like a work of art. It too had its conventions of style and subject and it too had its program. To work back from testimony to the true act of conspiracy, abduction, seduction, bewitchment, or affront takes something of a detective's canny science. Thus, to a degree, the modern reader joins forces with the inquisitive magistrate of some four hundred years ago. Both judge and historian seek the truth behind appearances. But, unlike the court official, who goes home to dinner, wine, and gossip, we must stay outside the past, quizzically peering in.

There is a delightful children's book, in which, at the stroke of midnight, a doll, a mouse, and a stuffed bear awake, drink tea together, and climb into the painting above the mantle piece. There they find a rowboat, which they board and ride downstream and out of sight to lively adventures. We readers of trials can seize no such magic moments. Rather, we are tightly hemmed by the frame of our documents. In this, we differ from the anthropologist, an intruder into an unfamiliar world, who can climb in and wander around, trespassing on negotiations, feasts, and ceremonies, to make friends and allies, to buy and give and gossip. The itinerant anthropologist, by asking questions and engaging the inhabitants, can, like the mouse, the doll, and bear, test the host society. We anthropologizing historians, by contrast, can do no such thing. Only the magistrate, long ago, could ask his questions, which only sometimes jibe with ours; our hands and tongues are tied, for we can only observe the answers. We cannot check on what witnesses say, because their obscurity makes them very hard to trace in books and archives. Thus, 'what you see is what you get!' as salesfolk sometimes say. That is, what we can learn comes from the trial itself, which we must read closely, for we have little else to go on.

Many anthropologists, when first in the field, suffer a kind of double vision. On the one hand, the world on which they have intruded strikes them as so unfamiliar in its customs, images, and beliefs as to seem almost bizarre, as if beyond comprehension. On the other hand, beneath all their strangeness, its denizens seem so human, so much like anyone else. The anthropologist's task is to achieve a kind of middle ground, where the strangeness makes analytical and intuitive sense. Likewise, we social historians, in reading vivid documents such as these trials, walk a narrow causeway. On one side yawns an abyss of bafflement, while on the other side there gapes a chasm of complacency. For, in the latter case, it is so easy to say, 'So Ottavia is a teenaged girl who falls in love with an older man! So she has spats with her mother and then decides to run away from home! What's so strange about that? It happens all the time!' Indeed it does, but we must go on to ask what she then does about those facts and how her words and actions reflect the opportunities and restrictions her particular culture sets around her. Not to pose that question is to read history in the spirit of much bad historical fiction, which only drapes people just like us in quaint costumes.

AN EXAMPLE OF A TRIAL

As an exercise in interpretation, let us take a trial and read it. What follows is the story of a moment that at first glance will seem either bizarre or simply brutish. But, pondering it, one can attain that middle ground, from which it seems at once strange and somehow comprehensible. Understanding its unspoken rules, we learn a little about how real people could operate within the boundaries of conventions of a world whose differences from ours one can discern and portray.

In June 1560, Giacobo Malatesta, a noble of an ancient line, appeared before magistrates in the papal fortress of Castel Sant'Angelo in Rome. They asked him if he had beaten a woman named Marta. He answered, no, that he had not, unless you can call sexual intercourse a beating. He chose a coarse word to name the act. And had he beaten one of his servants with stirrup-thongs? He was just joking, he retorted. And had Marta been there when he beat two servants with a switch? After several more questions in such a vein, Malatesta suddenly tried to take the interrogation in hand, saying that he knew what the real matter was. He volunteered this tale.

When the pope was at war, Malatesta said, he was in charge of a regiment of five hundred foot. Then, a man named 'The Hatter' had cheated him of money that he, Malatesta, had laid out for pay. When peace came, the Duke of Paliano, a papal nephew, a commander in the war, and in effect a minister of state, wrote a letter patent saying that, to get back misappropriated pay, all the feudatories of the State of the Church could seize cheaters, arrest them, and take them to Rome. Malatesta told the court that he had tried to arrest the Hatter in Cesenatico, a small coastal town near Cesena and Rimini. But the governor in Cesena, a papal official, would do nothing. Malatesta went home to a palace of his near Cesena and there learned that the Hatter had loaded a boat with some cargo and was about to take it to Venice for Easter. So he sent one of his servants to the governor, asking him to stop the boat and to jail the man for two or three days. But the governor wrote the *podestà*, a local official in little Cesenatico, ordering him to free the man. The podestà forwarded a copy of the governor's letter to Giacobo, saying that the baron had to let his debtor go in peace. From here on, we quote. Malatesta told the court:

I let him know by letter or by word of mouth – I am not sure which – that if he [the podestà] could not hold him in accord with his honour, and he had to obey the governor of Cesena, he should let him go. And he should do what he thought right, because I didn't want to see him suffer for it. And, because I thought he was going to let him go, I mounted one of my big horses, with only a sword on the bow of the saddle, which is always attached there. I went off alone toward Cesenatico without waiting for any others of my men to mount. I told them where I was going. I went to the bridge there, at Cesenatico, where I thought the Hatter would have to pass by to go off to Cesena.

So, near there, I met up with him, and riding up to him, I asked the Hatter if he intended to give me my money, of which he had cheated me. He answered that he had served me more than the money I had given him was worth. I said, the money that I had *lent* him, and that I wanted him to give it back. And I said that if he had served, he should be paid by the pope, and that I too hadn't been paid, while he had gone off with half pay.

Then he said: 'Signore, you know I haven't the means. You know I served five pay-stints to scoundrels, and so I haven't been paid. Let me go to Venice so that I can pay you.'

Then I said to him: 'The money I lent you, I lent you from my own funds and I want you to give it to me. And if you have served the pope, get yourself paid, because I must have mine. Or give me a pledge.'

And he said: 'Let me go to Venice so I can pay you.'

I answered: 'Give me a pledge so I can let you go.'

He said : 'I don't have it.'

I said: 'Come with me if you don't have it.'

He came and said: 'Lead me where you wish.'

So I took him into a meadow of mine about two arquebus shots away from Cesenatico. In the meadow, I told him to take off his clothes, because, if he had neither money nor a pledge, I wanted his clothes. He answered me, commending himself with his sword in his hand, in its scabbard, saying: 'Signore, do not make me get undressed. It is too great a shame upon me.'

And I said to him: 'Off with your clothes! I want you to get undressed.'

And I urged my horse in his direction and put my hand on the handle of the sword that was attached to the bow of the saddle.

And he was afraid and said: 'Signore, I'll undress. Don't hit me!'

And I said: 'Don't be afraid I'm going to hit you. I want your clothes. I don't want to attack you.'

He threw his sword upon the ground and began to undress. I made him move away from his sword and stayed to watch him take off his clothes. So he stripped down to his doublet and turned to beseech me not to make him strip further. I said I wanted him to go down to the shirt. So, as he took off his clothes, he gave me everything. He threw each thing on the ground. And, because he had two shirts on, the way people do when they go on a trip, he wanted to give me only one of them.

And I said to him: 'Pull off the other one too.'

So, when he was all naked, he begged me not to let him go naked, for the shame of it.

I told him: 'Go to Cesena and tell the governor that he should get you dressed again. Because you will find your clothes impounded there for my money. And, if you still owe me money, they will be given to me. Otherwise, your clothes will be given to you.'

So I dismounted and took the clothes that were on the ground and made myself a bundle of them. And I got back up on my horse and went off. And he, naked, went away across that meadow and there was a big wind blowing. And, as I was riding with those clothes toward my palace, I met one of my squires and another man on horseback. I gave him the clothing and he carried them to my palace. That very evening I sent those clothes to Cesena by the hand of signore Aurelio to have them impounded by the court at my instance. I did this because the governor had not wished to do me justice or get me a pledge. That fellow was going to Venice and I would never have been able to have my money.

So ends that scene. The trial record goes on for only a few more pages. There, Malatesta tells that the Hatter had lodged a grievance with the marchese of Montebello, a papal nephew who had commanded forces in the recent war. Hearing of it, Malatesta had grabbed his debtor by the chest and berated him. Then, in Holy Week, at the request of the Hatter, a preacher of the Augustinian order had come begging pardon for him and asking that the debt be forgiven. Malatesta had assented and the Hatter had knelt before him and then gone to tell the Marchese that his ill reports had been untrue. At that point in the tale, the court sent the prisoner back to his place of confinement 'with a mind to continue.' When, another day, Malatesta returned, the court inquired a little further about the story of the Hatter and then swerved off to other acts of lordly thuggery. The trial has no clear focus.

One cannot easily lodge this story in a larger tale. We do not know how much it had to do with the real reasons for Malatesta's imprisonment. Although he professed belief that it was central, he could well have dragged it like the proverbial red herring across his trail to divert magistrates in pursuit of something grave. Certainly, news sheets of the time aver he had bludgeoned the insalubrious cardinal del Monte in a quarrel over a prostitute. Thus, we have a self-serving narrative, which we cannot check against the Hatter's version. Is it truth or fable, or something half-way in-between? Most likely, it is this last. But if so, how to read it and come out the wiser? Only by being willing to see the truth in lies. Like an anthropologist, who hears from informants all sorts of fabulation, we must recognize that a good fiction, to be believed or even politely swallowed as a white lie, must bear verisimilitude. The sceptical Italian magistrates were forever grumbling at a squirming witness, 'Non è verosimile!' that is, 'It is not truth-like!'; or, as we would say, 'It is not plausible!' Verisimilitude – resemblance to the truth – is central to a successful lie. So, even if lordly Giacobo Malatesta never stripped the Hatter of his shirts, the scene must embody cultural truth.

Like so many Renaissance encounters, this one had much in common with a work of art. Like art, life too, at crucial moments, often followed clear rules of presentation. Here, in the meadow near Cesenatico, we have a well-shaped scene with a clear beginning, a clear end, and a well-balanced rhythm. The encounter, as retold, had a formal, almost a ceremonious quality. It almost looks like literature. And with good reason too, for, after all, here on paper is not an event but the story of an event, which must have followed the contours of the narratives of the day. But the moment itself may too have had its aesthetic cast, for lifelike art and artful life assuredly fed off one another; that is, people shaped their deeds under the influence of tales they had heard. But, beyond that, social custom itself encouraged drama. Here, as often elsewhere, in stories and in the happenings behind them, appears that taste for theatricality that pervaded the vernacular culture of Renaissance Italy.

Malatesta's private drama proclaims the bullying and swagger that go with rightful lordship. The baron makes no apologies. He depicts himself as a local lord, a feudatory of the pope, who acts out his prerogatives by cowing and humiliating a social inferior who will not do his will. He wants to be seen as the master of the scene. It is he who releases the local podestà from any obligation to his powerful neighbour, himself, and it is he who acts alone, without those henchman he leaves at his palace. They reappear in the tale only when the central scene has come to a close. Then, properly, they do the office of carrying the clothing-pledge back home. Face to face with the hapless Hatter, Malatesta and his horse lord it over the adversary. Every word and gesture, in the telling, flaunts his mastery.

The central transaction in Malatesta's meadow is a ritual of shaming. It has, at first glance, a double meaning, affirming at once Malatesta's pride and right and power and his debtor's complete abasement. In fact, however, those two meanings are at heart one, for one man's shaming, his loss of honour, is at the same moment his adversary's commensurate gain. As a shaming ritual, the stripping of the Hatter echoes countless ceremonies, both public and private, in the Europe of that time. Like most shamings, this deed was a calculated affront. Like many, it worked with what we might call symbols, had their meaning not been taken so concretely by the people of the time. Such a world had a keen eye for clothing, for dress did not merely betoken a man's or a woman's social position; rather, it even embodied it. Thus, to strip the Hatter of his clothes was not only to lay on shame but also to peel off the honour that went with social place. So, although at first glance the confrontation in the meadow might seem to have pitted two individuals, one of them aggrieved, the other stubborn and then afraid, looking more closely, we find that it was more a reckoning between social persons: a lord who enacted lordship and a merchant who inclined before it. This was less a psychological than a social drama.

The stripping of the Hatter did more than enact the lord's proud anger and his debtor's humiliation. There was in fact yet a third reading of the deed, clear, one suspects, to Malatesta, to the court, and to the governor of Cesena. That third reading was the main one. For, in fact, the real butt of Giacobo's ire was not the lowly merchant, who had bilked him of five hundred scudi, for so great a noble only a middling sum. Rather, it was the real adversary, the governor, the pope's minion, who had balked his lordly will. A social inferior, agent of a centralizing state that looked askance at wilful barons, the governor had refused a just request, citing the forms of law. Malatesta's riposte, an attack on the hapless merchant, was an act of aggression by indirection, by displacement as psychologists would call it. Did the governor dare to think he could deny the lord rightful legal process? Never! What he had not received, Malatesta would take with his own hands. The pledge! Note the odd formalism, the account of the careful wrapping, the tale of who carried the bundle to the Malatesta palace, the use of a *signore*, that is, a man of rank, as an emissary to deliver it to the governor's palace in Cesena. Note too, in the end, the formal declaration to the Hatter to the effect that his clothes had now become a pledge, in hock against his debt. Malatesta was acting out a sham judicial procedure. The play, again, was Renaissance. Its target was the governor and the state that loomed behind him.

This tale of the lord and his debtor thus illustrates many aspects of the life of its time. The same is of course true of all the trials in this book. In the relations between Malatesta and the podestà we see matter for political science, the study of institutions and the state. In the play of social distance between lord and commoner, we see the stuff of sociology. In the signs and symbols that shaped the stripping, we see details that would attract a cultural anthropologist, avid student of the vocabulary of codes of behaviour. In the artful shape of the tale and of the event itself is meat for the historian of literature. Thus, like all the others, this trial invites many kinds of reading and research. And, like all the others, it makes much richer sense if one dissects it with the help of several disciplines. Thus, let us survey briefly what the political science, the sociology, the anthropology, and the literary study of the past, all of them historical sciences, would say about the time and place in which these trials occurred.

ROME AS A POLITY

Let us begin with the political science of Rome, the capital city of a most unusual domain. In its institutions, the town was in some ways typical of its place and time, and in others odd. At its centre was the pope, at once the spiritual leader and chief administrator of Catholic Christendom and the prince of a middling Italian state. His principality straddled the peninsula. The Papal State had a goodly area, but much of it was rough terrain, backward, unproductive, and feebly governed. Only in the Romagna – around Bologna – and on the

Adriatic coast did the State of the Church rule over prosperous cities. The pope was a paradoxical prince, in his prestige, with the German Emperor, brightest in the firmament, in his real power, often a star of lesser magnitude. His office was elective. It almost always came to him late in life. As a consequence, his reign was usually brief and his capacity to effect real change correspondingly slim. Discontinuity was the bane of the Papal State. Each new election brought to bear on the college of cardinals the pressures of every interest group, and especially of the two great powers, France and Spain, that wrestled one another for hegemony in Italy. As pope succeeded pope, policy could veer wildly, favouring first the one and then the other kingdom.

Around the pope was a constellation of princely courts. In nestling in his own court, the pope was like other monarchs of his age. Renaissance princes, the pope among them, were richer and stronger than their medieval predecessors. As a consequence, courtiers swarmed around them like so many yellow-jackets around a pot of jam, for the monarch was the font of offices, commissions, nominations, recommendations, titles, grants, loans, gifts, contracts, pardons, reprieves, privileges, exemptions, titles, invitations, well-kept secrets, and honeyed smiles. So the state spat out to the perfumed few what it had sucked up from the sweating many. The pope and other princes were thus the centres of a barter system, which passed out wealth, power, and prestige, not gratis, but in exchange for political support. The autocrat was not of course the only giver; rather, he gave to a few who gave to many others, many of whom themselves gave yet again. Because loyalty, or at least its semblance, flowed up those channels down which came good things, the Roman court, like its counterparts, became the centre of pyramids of patronage. These were cemented by the values of the time, which saw the bond of patron and client not as venal and demeaning to the latter but as normal and even right. In Rome, patronage was everywhere, not only in the arts, but in all political life.

But why was the pope, as we have said, at the centre of a constellation? Because many of the cardinals, with their wealth, their palaces, their powerful connections with other states, were in effect princes too. They, and the great barons of the countryside, who had their city palaces, and the ambassadors of the major states, were lesser poles of attraction, nodal points in the circulation of bartered political goods. These lesser courts had their alliances and their feuds, all of which could shift as pope succeeded pope. Many centres made for complex politics. In several of our trials we will see how Romans could at times take advantage of confusion about where first obligations lay.

Alongside this swirl of patronage was a large officialdom, a zone of rules and procedures. The church, the state, and the lesser lords all boasted staffs of judges, notaries and scribes, treasurers, collectors, bursars, purchasing agents, overseers of men and lands and revenues. In theory, these officials were servants of impartial government. In fact, however, the boundary between bureaucrats and courtiers was vague and easily traversed, for public posts could be sold, traded, or given. It was an open question, in this city where, often, public office was a gift a patron gave his client, whether a magistrate could be just.

In the mid-sixteenth century, the power of the Papal State grew weaker with every mile from Rome. The back country remained largely feudal, under the sway of lords much like Giacobo Malatesta, who could tyrannize over their peasants and thumb their noses at the pope's rag-tag constabulary. Much of the hinterland was wild, mountainous to the south and east, malarial and half-deserted to the north and west. The records of the governor's court abound with tales of brigandage, inter-village feuding, defiance of authority, and savage violence, both noble and plebian. Popes of the sixteenth century tried time and again, with only mixed success, to bring the *campagna*, the countryside, to heel. The semi-independence of local lords, the insularity of the villages, and the rough terrain often combined with the brevity of the popes' rule to bring their work to naught. The porous Neapolitan frontier, half-encircling the Papal State, offered outlaws easy asylum and subverted the peace of the borderlands. We will see how, in one of our trials, Bernardino the Spanish music master almost succeeded in spiriting his Ottavia across this frontier.

Though tamer than the countryside, Rome was itself no easy town to rule. It was a violent place. The docket of the governor's court brimmed with insults and blows, stabbings, shootings, brawls, and riots. There were many reasons for this mayhem. In Italy and, indeed, in all of Mediterranean Europe, for reasons discussed below, codes of values fostered violent words and deeds. But Rome was special, for reasons at once political and social. As for politics, the instability and diffuseness of power both permitted and encouraged the use of force. Urban thuggery, like war, can be an extension of politics, and in Rome it often was. Those pyramids of patrons and clients could bring to bear not only the good they could do their members, but also the harm they could do their enemies. The unsteady hand of the state and the unreliability of public justice encouraged men and, sometimes, women, singly and in coalition, to take matters into their own hands. Society, like the polity, was labile. Rome, far more than most big towns, was a place of strangers. Natives were in the minority. Lombards, Venetians, Tuscans, Neapolitans, Spaniards, Frenchmen, Germans, Flemings, and Slavs filled the streets and piazze, taverns, lodging houses, and palaces. Some were immigrants, but many only passers through, on the trail of divine grace, trade, work, or political advantage. With each passing lord or prelate came a train of servants, retainers, and hangers-on. Most of these were male and few were married. Rome was a city of loose men, and loose women, in the latter case in two senses of the term. Loosely tethered to their protectors, but not much pegged down by neighbourhood, kin group, or professional association, these outsiders were often quick to fly to violence. Not all rough deeds were theirs, but they did much to set the tone.

To this violence, the state responded, in Rome as everywhere, with repression. The Roman authorities shared with all European princes the urge to quash unruliness, be it of deed or word. Between the fifteenth and the eighteenth centuries, indeed, authorities much tamed the whole continent. Not only bloodshed, but language, architecture, festivity, speculative thought, religious belief and practice, even warfare came, ever so slowly, to conform to the models and commands of the capital city and its rulers. The perennial ambition of monarchs to establish order was far older than the Renaissance, but now, thanks to gunpowder, the printing press, bureaucratic structures, and new ideas about rightful power, stronger means were there. But the domestication of the social landscape was a slow business, especially in a backward polity like Rome. In our period, it was just beginning.

THE MACHINERY OF JUSTICE

Political weakness cast a shadow, harshness. Like all monarchs of the time, the popes strove to squelch the endemic violence enshrined in custom by criminalizing it. To this end, they needed an apparatus of repression. But their instruments were frail. Recruited from the dregs of Rome, their police, the *sbirri*, were as like to run as fight. Scorned and hated as spies and bullies, they could not easily face down their social betters, or even cow their equals. *Signori* barred the door even to the *bargello*, the sheriff, and villagers rose up to rout his men. So malefactors were hard to catch. Therefore, when the authorities succeeded in apprehending one, they laid on a heavy hand. Punishments were stern. Heavy fines, banishments, and sentences to row the galleys were common, though sometimes not enforced in full. Although Rome's governor had two prisons, Corte Savelli and Tor di Nona, he used them to hold malefactors before a trial, not to punish afterwards. Rather, the state rid itself of undesirables through exile, galley stints, or execution. Nevertheless, the real goal of the frequent hangings and the occasional burnings and dismemberments was to set an example. A good public execution, with its penitential pomp, was a piece of edifying theatre. It at once execrated crime and glorified the majesty of the law and the mercy of God, who received the soul of any victim displaying the gifts of faith and contrition. Men, women, and children came in throngs to see the show.

In its struggle to keep the peace, Rome relied on several courts of law. The most important were three: that of the vicar, who was the pope's delegated overseer of the churches of Rome; that of the senator, a papal appointee who inherited the old communal authority; and that of the governor. It is this last whose trials appear in this collection. The boundaries between the competences of these magistrates were blurred. Nevertheless, the sixteenth century buoyed the governor, for he belonged not to the church or the city, but to the state itself, and the popes used him in their campaign to consolidate power. Thus, capital crimes and treason came to the governor's tribunal, as did cases from other cities; his was a court of last appeal. At the same time, his judges heard many cases of lighter import and the record books of his police swarm with tales of thefts, insults, brawling, swearing, gambling, and other misdemeanours that seldom provoked a formal trial.

The governor's court followed inquisitorial rules that tilted against a suspect. It did so with good intentions, for it saw its mission as the chastisement of crime. At the same time, like the Roman Inquisition, this lay tribunal had a deep respect for procedure that, to a degree, protected the accused. Most Italian courts, both secular and ecclesiastical, followed a version of the law of ancient Rome revived and modified in the Middle Ages. This code dictated that a judge could convict only if he had telling evidence from more than one witness or a confession from the suspect. Hungry for such evidence, a criminal court functioned as an investigative body, for there were no detectives. It took denunciations and testimony and kept them secret. It brought suspects before the prosecutor and examined them without counsel, telling them neither of what they were accused nor who had said what about them. It recorded every word of these depositions. The tribunal did on occasion stage a *confrontatio*, in which it brought a suspect face to face with a witness. It did this not to permit cross-examination, but rather to see if the testifiers had the nerve to stick to their stories. Thus, the magistrates pressed hard in pursuit of condemnations. Yet, by their own lights, they were fair-minded and scrupulous; we should not see them as sadistic or fanatical. The initial, investigative hearings we see here, the so-called *processi per informazione*, were not the whole trial. Only at this preliminary stage did the suspect have no notice of charges and no counsel present. Later, both prosecution and defence would make their arguments before the judge. Then, the accused might have a lawyer. To prepare a case, the defendant and the advocate could use a transcript of the investigative hearings, though with the names of witnesses deleted.

The procedures of the initial hearing shape our transcripts. The records show that the officers of the court moved around the city to take depositions. They gathered many testimonies in the prisons, but took others in the houses of the sheriff, of notaries, and of private persons. It was the presence of the court's own notary, always duly recorded, that gave the record official standing. At times, in less grave matters, the notary conducted the interrogation on his own. When, however, a senior court official, a prosecutor (*procuratore fiscale*), or a judge (*auditore* or *luogotenente*) or, in gravest matters, the governor himself was there, the notary fell silent and let him speak. The clerk recorded the Italian voice of the court only in a Latin summary, but was punctilious to transcribe verbatim, or nearly so, the answers of suspects and witnesses, noting down not only words but, sometimes, gestures, sighs, and tears. The document was usually careful to distinguish mere witnesses from the accused. At the beginning of each testimony, it laid out the setting, the date, the names of officials present, and the identity of the person testifying. At the end, it almost always concluded with the record of the precautions taken to assure the integrity of the trial, showing witnesses to have been sworn to silence and suspects to have been shut away either *in secretis* or *ad largam*. The latter was a freer form of imprisonment, with easier access to outsiders. When the court finished with suspects, it released them under caution or placed them in the public part of the jail [ad largam], where they might consult a lawyer, to prepare their defence within a few stipulated days.

The later stages of the trial are harder to reconstruct. The next phase, the trial for judgment, seldom leaves a trace, for lawyers' briefs had less legal standing than did these notarized records of testimony. Pleas were, therefore, less likely to be preserved in public hands. Those that do appear, though valuable for the history of forensic thought, are in general far less interesting to social historians than are the original depositions. Legal argument, which places details more in the context of the law than in that of social practice, rends the fabric of testimony. The eventual sentence, if ever emitted, was kept in a separate set of records that, for Rome, is very incomplete. Such sentences as do survive are useful for indicating whom the judges chose to believe. They are, however, too conventional in their rhetoric and too veiled in their explanations to give much sense of judicial reasoning. Furthermore, it is hard to be sure they were carried out; the weakness of the Roman state and the very political nature of its justice argue against taking their harsh terms as proof of a suspect's eventual fate.

When no confession came forth, the court not rarely tortured, sometimes more than once. To early modern lawyers, torture, like a medieval ordeal, tested the truth of utterances. Thus, on occasion, courts tortured not only suspects but also their accusers. Torture was more likely when crimes were graver; many trials had none at all. It was usually witnesses and suspects of low condition who fell victim. Those who had honour could stake it against their word; those who lacked it had instead to put their bodies in jeopardy to vouch for truth. Because a lawyer could challenge a confession on the grounds that torture had been too long and too severe, the magistrates applied it cautiously. To validate their findings, they brought the accused back the next day to ratify the confession. Torture certainly hurt. The court bound men's hands behind their backs and lifted them by a rope tied to the wrists. To women, if it did not use the *corda*, it sometimes applied thumb-screws. But, in this court, milder than some, the sessions were usually brief; they lasted, according to the precise notary, perhaps a 'quarter' or a 'third' of an hour. Solicitude and punctilio tempered the court's brutality.

Though torture was a blunt instrument, it was not a useless one. It could elicit a true confession. This, almost certainly, it did in the case of the music teacher, Bernardino. Also, resistance could validate a just claim to innocence. Danese, the necromancer, who stuck to his story under torture, may consequently have had an easier time before the judge. On the other hand, the guilty could tough it out. 'I've been up and down a dozen times. Better to go up and down than swing,' said a murderer in a trial not included here. Notoriously, too, the innocent could confess falsehoods to escape the pain. Torture was a very imperfect method of inquiry. But, for lack of a detective force, it was often the best tool the court had. The magistrates were practised in its application and often, it seems to us, with it found the truth.

To interpret the words in these trials, one must always keep in mind the circumstances that surrounded a deposition. Though men and women spoke volubly, they did not speak freely, for they knew well that they were in court. As witnesses, they were in multiple jeopardy, subject on the one hand to the court's punishments for crime and perjury and on the other to retaliation from those they hurt by what they said. Though one testified in camera, under oath to silence, one never knew what words might leak. Besides, the transcript given the accused could, even with the names deleted, betray the speaker. Especially where the state was weak, many rewards and penalties remained in private hands. Romans quite often took revenge, which offered a sort of extralegal justice. That is one reason why so many chose cautious perjury.

Testimony, therefore, was a very political form of speech, which one must read with caution. These trials, designed for information, not for judgment, are documents prepared by and for the prosecution. That fact much marks them. We must never forget that the line of questioning was in the hands of the magistrates. The suspects and the witnesses of course controlled their answers, but only within constraints set by the procedures of the court itself, by the categories of legal thought, and by the wider circumstances of the crime and its investigation. All testimony reflected the politics of the moment. Like the witnesses and suspects, who might well choose their words with care, we too should try to keep in mind the risks and gains at hand. Thus, though law had its rules and reasons, its majestic autonomy was a fiction. Although the courts strove to provide an independent alternative to the rough justice of the streets, in fact, social politics often captured the machinery of the law. Not rarely, as they pursued their quarrels, Romans used the courts, even more than we do now, as instruments of suasion or chastisement. For instance, as in Bernardino's trial, a suit for rape might be a ploy to snag a husband or extort a dowry. Malatesta's purported assault on the cardinal nowhere appears in his interrogation. Thus, larger undertakings that one can often but surmise could embroil a trial. To understand what hemmed witnesses and their words, we must therefore try to picture the larger politics of their immediate position.

Roman life was intensely political. This does not mean that Romans were all engaged in affairs of state; rather, those habits that marked statecraft shaped smaller matters too. Like princes and courtiers, the gentlemen, the masters and mistresses of houses, the artisans, servants, soldiers and whores, alone and in concert, made and broke their alliances. Like princes, they campaigned, bribed and threatened, conspired and betrayed. By slanderous words and hurtful deeds, they could make guerrilla war on one another. Living politically, Romans had a well-honed sense of tactics that they could bring to bear, as we shall see in our trials, on courtship and seduction, on their relations with their spouses and their patrons, on their dealings with the devil, and, of course, on their conduct before the magistrates.

ROME AS A SOCIETY

As a society, Rome shared many of the traits of other cities of early modern Europe. In the pope's city, as elsewhere, stasis and flux combined in complex ways. In all of Europe, social hierarchies were more sharply defined than they are today. Family, wealth, power, occupation, gender, and personal inclination and capacity both defined social place and tended to preserve it. At the same time, people did in fact move about, both in space and in society. The sixteenth century, far more than the two more rigid ones that followed it, permitted movement but, at the same time, strove to channel and contain it. Under all regimes, one great barrier to self-determination was the quirky nature of public power. In the absence of a predictable, even-handed, over-arching state, from which all men and women could hope for equal services and the law's protection, Europeans had to seek shelter in more local associations. But solidarities took their tolls. Beneficiaries of their support had complex obligations, many of which hemmed the will and deterred mobility. Like other Europeans of their time, Romans so much lived as members of collective groups that, to a large measure, they defined themselves less as individuals than as social persons, members of their families, their professions, their neighbourhoods, their classes. We have seen this mental habit already in Giacobo Malatesta, who played out his offended lordship in his meadow.

While it shared common European structures, Rome, as a society, had its own distinguishing marks. As we have seen already, it was a notoriously unstable polity and a very fluid world, a town of migrants. Most people came from somewhere else. This transience undercut the very social institutions that Romans needed as counterweights to an unsteady state. Still, solidarities were very much present. There were formal groups: guilds, professional bodies, learned academies, and pious confraternities. For many there was family, both narrow and extended. In addition, Romans could build informal networks upon god-kinship, friendship, and pragmatic interest. Not only men, but also the more house-bound women, could weave webs of alliance across the city. Close to home was the neighbourhood, where men and, especially, the women, vigilant at their windows and strident in their comments, could act as the eyes and the voice of public morality. Often, in a trial, one meets the remark, 'All the neighbourhood holds him to be a person of good (or bad) repute.' The trial of Bernardino shows such a character witness, who vouches for the reputation of the girl who runs away.

Vertical alliances connected with these horizontal solidarities. Any society where the few monopolized power, prestige, and information invited patronage. The institution pervaded Renaissance Italy and flourished in the orbit of its courts. In Rome, where there were many courts and where other solidarities often had less hold, the patron-client bond was especially prominent. Vertical alliances were useful in a world where trust was rare and fitful. Masters and mistresses joined forces with their servants, lords with their peasants, courtiers with their clients. Thus, hierarchy did not beget social segregation; on the contrary, it could foster strongly felt connections. These bonds could be formal or tacit. Seldom did pacts and ceremonies seal them. They could last a lifetime or only weeks or days. They were fragile; betrayal was a constant theme, a widespread fear, a not uncommon fact. Despite all their informality and their frequent abuse and instability, these links were of immense importance to the conduct of daily life. The young servant in the Secret Pigeon trial who hesitated to testify, he said, 'because he has eaten the bread' of his former master was improvising an appeal to the duties of good clientage.

Patron and client were bound together by obligations to mutual protection. In theory and, to a degree, in fact, they shared one another's welfare and one another's vulnerability. Paolo di Grassi's hurt and rage when his henchman is shot expresses not only fellow-feeling, but also social role, for Paolo has been wounded in his patronage.

These alliances across barriers of status were no sign of a democratic spirit. Rather, to the contrary, like all of Italy, Roman society was very stratified. Men and women had a keen sense of precedence. It appeared in their language, where titles of address and respectful flourishes bore witness to pride and deference. A *signore* was more than a *gentilhuomo*, who outranked a *messer* (or, more briskly, *ser*). That last title attached to notaries, lawyers, officials, and solid merchants. Next in line came *maestro*, master, the title of an independent artisan. Peasants, journeymen, and labourers went without any honorific. For women, *signora* outranked *madonna*, that last a title accorded to most wives and widows and to prosperous courtesans. All of these distinctions were rough, for a man or woman's title could vary from moment to moment. Rank also appeared in family names. The wealthy tended to have a lineage name, while the humble went by patronymic or place name. Thus peasants and artisans would be called Pietro di Paolo da Verona: 'Pietro son of Paolo from Verona.'

Likewise, the play of pronouns mirrored status. English has lost its 'thou,' but Italian, then as now, used *tu* for intimates and inferiors, much as we use first names. The counterpart was the formal *voi*, with which the poor Hatter parried the haughty *tu* of his tormentor. Modern English is too democratic to catch the plain distinction; in this book we have resorted to a capitalized 'You' for *voi*. Like formal titles, so too pronouns could shift with circumstances. Thus, Ottavia, reminding Bernardino of her love for him, drops down to *tu* only to return to *voi* when she recounts her hurt and anger. Above *voi* on the ladder of respect were deferential flourishes only newly current, 'Your Lordship,' 'Excellency,' and the like.

Much of the culture of daily life in Rome revolved around the expression and the negotiation of status. The sensitivities that shaped language determined much else besides. As for the Hatter, so for everyone, clothing proclaimed the man and woman. So too did weapons, retainers, horses, carriages, houses, chapels, coats of arms, and conspicuous patronage of arts and letters. Romans, like other Italians, were forever acting out their position in the world. Social station was tightly bound to honour, a central preoccupation of most

Romans. We will have to return to honour when we discuss the social values of the city. Honour and status did not rest with the individual alone. Rather, they were shared and contagious. Men and women partook of the honour of those solidarities to which they looked for social definition. Thus, family, profession, home-town, and patrons all combined to mark and to secure one's rank and place.

THE SOCIAL VALUES OF THE CITY

Just as, in discussing Rome's polity, we found we had to describe its society, so in depicting the society, we have had to intrude on matters usually in the preserve of the anthropologist. For these matters of behaviour, of habits of doing business, and of viewing one's neighbours are the meat of anthropology. So too are value systems such as the honour ethic and so too, in some of its aspects, is religion. Let us turn first to the all-important issue of honour and then to its rival, Christian charity, which vied with it to shape behaviour.

Romans were not alone in paying heed to honour. Honour ethics of various kinds have long flourished in many parts of the world. Conspicuous among Mediterranean peoples, both Christian and Muslim, honour codes have much figured in the history and the anthropology of the zone. Indeed, especially in the mountains, they are still alive today. Furthermore, elsewhere in Renaissance Europe, the military classes, and some others too, lived by similar strictures. Although they vary greatly in the conduct they evoke, as value systems, all these codes share at least one thing, a preoccupation with shame. The obverse of honour, shame is at once a psychological and a social state; it is the perception and the expression of collective disapproval. Honour, by contrast, is approbation. Thus, an undiluted honour ethic differs sharply from an ethic based on guilt, for guilt hearkens to the inner voice of conscience, shame to that of the community. An honour ethic diverges, too, from the less agonistic, less charged habits of social recognition that seem present almost everywhere. Though honour is good repute, not all good repute is honour. Honour is reputation contested in the public sphere.

What then gave honour? In Rome, the answer much depended on social station, age, and gender. Some things were common. Membership in an honoured and honourable collectivity conferred honour. Thus, to a degree one shared the honour, above all, of one's family, and also of one's city, patron, household, friends, and colleagues. That holy trinity of sociology, the three determinants of social status – wealth, power, and prestige – gave honour. So did the social skill to display them well for, within bounds, ostentation won less blame than approbation. Other skills as well gave honour. So, for instance, a knowledge of the courtesies and rules of social conduct was honourable, as were learning, eloquence, and the consumption and production of art. Both patronage and clientship gave honour. While the patron garnered praise for generosity and for protection bestowed on dependents and revelled in their loyal adulation, the client gained security and basked in the glow of greatness. Such reciprocity shows best with artists and writers, who flourished in a culture of honour. They repaid their patrons, to whom they sold or dedicated works, in the reflected glory their productions won, for a handsome painting, statue, gem, or tapestry honoured both the maker and the owner. Military skills, too, conferred honour; a gentleman studied swordplay and horsemanship for lustre as well as for safety in the street and on the field of battle.

Honour depended as well on moral virtue. Different strictures lay on men and on women. It is sometimes said, with some exaggeration, that a man's honour hung on what he did, and a woman's on what she did not do. In fact, by her beauty, clothing, industry, wit, modesty, and social grace, a woman could win honour for herself and for her menfolk. But, far greater than all the good she could do was the harm she brought if she trespassed against the rules of sexual conduct. She owed virginity before marriage, continence after. But men wore no such bridle. Thus, even toward the bottom of the social scale, where other forms of honour counted little, fathers, brothers, and husbands often strove to protect themselves from the harm that could befall them through their women. We will see this well in the story of Agostino Bonamore and his flawed bride and in that of Bernardino, the music teacher, and his restless pupil, Ottavia. Yet, for women, chastity was not the sole virtue. For them, as for men, though in different measure, probity, fidelity, courage, industry, honesty, and generosity all fed honour, while their absence diminished it.

Romans regarded honour as a scarce commodity; there was never enough to go around. In that way, it was like wealth and like land, from which, ultimately, most wealth came. That sense of shortage tinged honour with anxiety, for it was easily lost and often only strenuously regained. Renaissance honour, thus, was more precarious than modern good repute. Often, one man's loss was another's gain, as if honour, like matter and momentum, could be conserved. Thus, men were forever trying to filch honour from one another. Women sometimes did this too, but less avidly, and often in self-defence. Indeed, a man of honour had to be seen to be willing to protect it from theft.

How did one steal another's honour? The ways were manifold. One could assault his body. One could trick or ridicule him or balk his will in public. With luck and skill, one might breach the chastity of his women. Very often, one tried to offer a challenge to which he dared not reply or 'gave him the lie,' that is, accused him with impunity of a falsehood. Such actions often demanded retribution. Though a man had to suffer quietly abuse from his betters and might ignore it from his underlings, he had to parry what came from equals.

Attacks on honour targeted many facets of the social self. The man of standing had to guard the integrity of his house and its inmates, as well as that of his own body. Romans bent on affront burnt doors, broke shutters, and threw stones and paint and excrement at windows. They festooned doorways with insulting horns, lewd pictures, and scurrilous sheets of doggerel. For example, in one trial here, Paolo di Grassi affixes bawdy verses to the portal of a jilted courtesan. Other assaults on honour took aim at the body. Any attack was costly, but those to the face and head, where honour lay, were most keenly felt. Romans stole hats, pulled beards, scratched, cut and bashed faces. Accordingly, laws recognized such insults and imposed much higher penalties for facial wounds, especially if they left a lasting scar. Romans could also attack surrogates for the face, vandalizing portraits, or sketching defamatory caricatures, often bedecked with the cuckold's horns. Because honour was forever open to assault on so many fronts, its owner lived at constant risk of losing it.

Honour, therefore, was a source of jeopardy, one of several that were central to exchanges involving trust. Surprisingly, precisely because that jeopardy was a liability, it was at the same time an asset. Honour was a liability in so far as one had always to be taking steps to protect it. But, at the same time, as a hostage, it gave social credit. Against the prevailing insecurity, Italians were quick to ask for all sorts of hostages and pledges, men or goods placed in jeopardy, which one stood to forfeit if one misbehaved. Like a hostage, honour could be offered up to stake a claim for credibility, for a liar lost honour. The man or woman with little honour, having less to lose, thus earned less trust and, in court, more often had to suffer torture. In both court and world, low status, weakness, and desperation moved Italians to invoke the wrath of God as yet another risk that vouched for honesty. In Italian eyes, truth was assured by jeopardy, be it to soul, or to body or, best of all, to honour.

Honour mandated not only defence of one's person, house, and family, but also, to a lesser degree, of one's other solidarities. Thus, the honour ethic underpinned those coalitions that gave protection, for it assured that they could summon help to protect their own. Thus, paradoxically, honour promoted both safety and danger, safety within and danger without the bounds of alliances. Honour steeled the mettle of family, clientele, guild, city, and other groups as well, to defend their own repute, welfare, and security, and to champion the good of all their members, often at the expense of rivals.

The defence of honour thus could quickly kindle private war. As insult rebutted insult and blow answered blow, the parties could fall into a *vendetta*, a running exchange of vengeful deeds. As the complex lines of solidarity running through the city and its hinterland drew in allies, a conflict might leap, like a restless forest fire, in unforeseen directions. The honour code held that one should besmirch and maim and kill for love and loyalty, not money. A mercenary agent of a vendetta was a vile *assassino*. At least, that was the theory. The practice was more nuanced, as our story about the abbot of San Galgano shows. There, the abbot and bishop who instigated the killing blended the customary blandishments about loyalty and gratitude to patrons with more venal subsidies and promises of places in the cavalry. Between the assassins and the friends, kinsmen and retainers, and the aggrieved themselves, Rome was full of men bent on scorn and violence. To keep the peace, the state wielded its police and courts.

At the same time, alongside the state, society itself strove to contain the mayhem. Thus, mediation and arbitration were deeply rooted in custom. Italians, male and female, rich and poor, knew how to play the go-between, the essential messenger who could buffer pride while bearing placatory tidings from face to wounded face. Just as there were semi-formal rituals to commence hostilities, so there were rites of pacification and reconciliation. Thus, the *caporione*, a lesser magistrate, in his attempts to soothe the rage of Paolo di Grassi, was enacting a role both he and the choleric gentleman knew well. The same is true of the preacher who reconciled Giacobo Malatesta with the Hatter and of the kinsman of the murderous in-laws who visited the stricken Agostino Bonamore in his sick-bed to buy him off.

So far, we have discussed the honour ethic as if it alone dictated the comportment of the Romans. But, also, in their morality, all of them, unless Jews, were Christians, and profoundly so. But, though men and women professed and practised both, on many points the honour ethic and Christian values in theory contradicted one another. Where honour turned on shame and the opinions of others, Christian ethics hinged on guilt and the sting of conscience, the echo of the voice of God. Where honour demanded anger and swift, violent retribution, Christianity preached mild forgiveness. Where honour praised wealth and ostentatious pride, Christianity lauded poverty and humility. Where honour was particularistic, demanding love and loyalty for the denizens of one's solidarities, Christianity was universalistic, holding all mankind as brothers. They seem the very antithesis, yet the two codes nestled snugly in many Roman breasts. In fact, there were some points of convergence, for honourable generosity approached Christian charity in effect, if not in motive, and both codes praised chastity in women, though they agreed much less about the men. About honesty, courage, loyalty, and other virtues they said much in common. But the differences were stark and legion. How did Romans live with such contradictory sets of ethics? This is a hard question. Part of the answer is that ethics are not systems of logical instructions like computer programs. Rather, nuanced and flexible, they apply differently, if at all, according to time and setting. Thus, our murderous abbot and our pious whore who went to hear the orphans sing ought not to jolt us when we meet them in the trials, for both obeyed the dictates of the moment. After all, though morality sets some of the costs and rewards of social action, it seldom dictates choice. Romans, like most people, wielding their values as well as following them, sometimes picked their principles to fit their needs. They also could blend them in inventive ways or tolerate inconsistency. Both religion and lay ethics were malleable.

RELIGION

The Christianity of sixteenth-century Romans differed sharply from the religion most moderns know or practise. It had two intense concerns: salvation and divine providence. In this it was true to its medieval roots. Salvation was no easy matter. Doctrine insisted on the corruption of the unaided soul. Though virtuous deeds and pious devotions might help, only the sacraments had power to assure redemption and well-being in heaven. Providence was God's more immediate protection against the hardships of this world: the storms at sea, the floods and droughts, the wars and famines, the attacks by thugs and bandits, the killing epidemics that with horrid regularity cut a swath through towns and villages, and the myriad other ills of an insecure life. Providence manifested God's justice, for he dealt out safety as a reward for virtue but withheld it as a wage of sin. Catastrophes thus attested to vice. So, religion afforded a bulwark against a looming double menace, to Romans' earthly bodies and to their souls. Its prayers, its ceremonies, and its urgings to a life of virtue could serve a double end, mundane safety and celestial bliss.

Not all supernatural power came straight from a Catholic God. Much of his capacity to chastise and to guard, Romans believed, he had delegated to the Madonna and to the many saints. Consequently, providential power was scattered broadcast across heaven, earth, and cityscape. It lay thickest, of course, in the holy places, in the liturgical furnishings, the bread, the wine, the statues and paintings, and, above all, in the abundant relics in the churches of the city. But any Christian might have access to it through images and amulets at home or on his person, or through prayer alone. The saints were far more than paragons of virtue; they were strong, active divine persons who were quick to fend for the mortals who supplicated help. Although they dwelt in heaven, on earth they made their presence felt. Not all supernatural agents, however, were holy and benign; even closer at hand were the saints' malignant antitheses, the demons, a scourge of sinners, who could flit unseen among the people and take possession of their bodies. Thus, the supernatural was at everybody's elbow.

The clergy had the easiest access to the divine realm. Those of them who were ordained priests shared in St Peter's powers to bind and loose on earth and in heaven. The sacraments were theirs alone and their prayers, and those of monks and nuns and hermits, had greater power than those of the laity. Though they tried hard for control, as they had for centuries, the clergy could boast no monopoly over the conduits of prayer and grace and aid; the supernatural was just too abundant. Vows and consecration set the churchmen apart as a separate order. A clerical culture marked their words and bearing, their dress and deeds. But the world was ever blurring the boundaries between church and lay society. For one thing, lay values and concerns percolated through the clergy. Thus, to give an example from our trials, the bishop of Ancona and the abbot of San Galgano plotted vendetta to assuage their honour; when they did so, they acted as lay lords, not as clerics. On the other hand, the laity could appropriate the ways of the clergy. Self-made lay saints and self-appointed prophets often attracted popular devotion. Such borrowings sometimes led to scandal. The exorcist cobbler, Danese, appears in a trial because he ran afoul of the law in attempting to do a churchman's work. In another trial, not published here, prostitutes upset their neighbours by begging and by visiting their clients camouflaged in the robes of Franciscan third-order nuns. In law, the lines were sharp and clear; in fact, they blurred.

When they made contact with the supernatural, the Christian laity often brought to their dealings that same keen sense of politics that informed their commerce with one another. There was more than a name in common between a patron saint and a patron. Both were special friends and allies who could put in a good word in high places. One commended oneself to both. Both did favours, gave protection, and received grateful recognition. In both cases, there was reciprocity. To a patron, one gave deference, praise, services, and gifts; to a saint, one proffered deference, prayers, services, offerings, and, if one could afford it, a handsome chapel. But it was not only with the holy that one might make a deal. Danese, the cobbler-exorcist, tried, he tells the court, both to do business with the devil and to double-cross him. Thus, one could treat a supernatural enemy much as one could treat one of flesh and blood. This readiness to bargain pervaded not only religion but also Roman magic, which mingled prayers and charms and potions in rituals designed to conjure up love and luck and to damage others. This magic was shot through with religion. To distinguish between the official cult and forbidden practices was the harder because both relied on prayer and invocation and both used ritual to seek supernatural help.

Church and state alike, nevertheless, did all they could both to draw a boundary and to suppress what was beyond the pale. As with social violence, so with folk religion and magic, the authorities of the sixteenth century were keen to quell what they had not wrought. Rulers wanted a monopoly on violence and a monopoly on access to the divine. The shattering blow of the Reformation had put Catholic institutions on edge. Their response, increasingly, in mid-century, was to control, to suppress, or at least to harness popular devotions.

Paul IV (1555-9), pope at the time of most of these trials, marked an acceleration of the movement toward ecclesiastical autocracy. It was he who penned the Jews into a ghetto, who published the Roman Index of Forbidden Books, who fostered the Roman Inquisition. He was zealous to police the morals of clergy and laity alike. His papacy marks the beginning of a Counter-Reformation culture of intellectual caution and surveillance that smothered the Renaissance. Much of the campaign to control beliefs, practices, and lay morality fell to the Inquisition itself. Though in some cities the records of the Inquisition are open to historians, those in Rome remain tightly shut. Fortunately for modern readers, other tribunals, the governor's among them, shouldered some of the burden of policing religion. The investigation of the harmless carnival play in Aspra (1574) is symptomatic of the repression that was to reshape much of European culture.

COURT TESTIMONY AS ART

These trials, as we have said, reflect not only a polity and a society, but also a literary culture. It might seem strange to say so, for many of the suspects and witnesses were illiterate, and others, although they read for work or worship, must have seldom turned to books for pleasure. Most Romans, even if they did read, could never master the bookish culture of the élite, which at once scorned their ways and, more and more, strove to curb and reform them. But, even if as lowly outsiders, most Romans took lively part in the world of writing. For not all literature appeared in print. Italy in the sixteenth century produced plays and short stories that took matter and energy from spoken culture and that, through performances, readings, and retellings, must have repaid the debt in kind. This interplay between written and spoken culture is more easily surmised than proven, for, trials aside, the illiterate have left few records of their thoughts. But the exchange had to have been there. Certainly, our trials have much in common with the literature and drama of the period. Like it, they dwell on codes of conduct and their violation. Both often deal with breaches of the sexual norms. Both swarm with scoundrels and their victims, the dupes who, falling prey to trickery, lose their honour. Betrayal, therefore, is in both a central theme. In all these matters, art more resembled life than the reverse.

But, as we saw in Malatesta's narrative of the stripping of the Hatter, not only narrative, but life itself could also imitate art. That is, Malatesta's deed, as he recounted it, had a dramatic shape worthy of the page or stage. We will find the same literary quality in other stories, for instance, in Agostino Bonamore's account of his near-murder, in madonna Giulia's history of her seduction, or in Chierico's relation of his life with Paolo di Grassi. As we have noted, we cannot separate the aesthetics of the tale from those of the deed itself, for only the tale is in our hands. Nevertheless, real life clearly had its own artistry; Romans had an acute sense of the drama of the moment. In a world bound by codes of honour and piety, where one spent much energy in the enactment of a social persona, and correspondingly little in delving for an inner self, daily life became a ceremonious, artful affair. Even impetuous rage had its script.

At the same time, life, as it appears in trials, was of course not literature. Renaissance short stories and plays have a neatness that sets them off. They have a single author, a single set of goals. They begin, they peak, they end with closure. No strings dangle. Trials, by contrast, have competing authors and cross purposes. They often trail off into irresolution. Or they can circle back on themselves, or stall, or ramble off into weed patches of trivia. Unlike art, trials, like life, abound with loose pieces. We see much we cannot use, and at the same time, many crucial bits are missing. The manuscripts themselves are old and battered. Many are incomplete. To make things worse, as a student complained, 'The worms always eat the punch line.' Thus, a trial is a bit like a badly packaged jigsaw puzzle, with three of these pieces and four of those and none of dozens more. That fact is at once the bane and the joy of the historian.

HOW TO READ THESE TEXTS

The analogy with jigsaw puzzles is only half-correct, for it implies that there is a single right way to reconstruct 'the picture.' In truth, a trial is more like a set of fragments of a jigsaw hologram. That is, 'the picture' rebuilt will much depend on the point of view. Thus, readers will have their own interests, questions, and lines of investigation. Any approach, however individual, will at the same time feel the impress of shared habits of explanation and narration drawn from the reader's culture. Like the past, like life itself, these trials have no single lesson. Nevertheless, some questions clamour for attention. One, of course, is what really happened, out in the streets and houses. There are always things one can never know; at times one arrives at best only at a guess or a brace of meaty hypotheses. Another issue is the trial itself. What were the court, the witnesses, the suspects trying to do? These first queries touch on matters that concerned the magistrates and witnesses directly.

Yet a modern inquiry need not parallel the court's. All sorts of less obvious questions of interest to historians of politics, of society, of culture, and of language can seek answers in these documents. Students of macro-politics can investigate the state's tactics and techniques of repression. Those who prefer micro-politics can explore the balance of power between individuals. What, if anything, curbed an overweening lord? What power had a servant over her guilty mistress? How did one parry a bullying kinsman's lie? Students of society can investigate rules of conduct, their use, and their transgression. How did loss of virginity change the relations between a girl and her family? What privileges did one garner if one had a devil in one's body? How did a prostitute take on some of the social traits of men? There are, as well, countless issues of culture and mentality. These trials illustrate the scruples of an assassin, the political doctrines of a Roman gentleman, the dramatic sense of some rural actors, the piety of a lay exorcist, the faith in magic of a courtesan. The transcripts also show the symbolism of affronting faces, bodies, clothing, and houses by fire and dirt, words and gestures. For the student of language these trials display expostulation, supplication, description, and artful dodging, to mention some, all conditioned by station, gender, and immediate situation. The list could go on and on.

Nevertheless, the materials printed here allow only a first rough sketch of an answer to such questions. To explore further, one could mine the many thousand surviving trials of the governor's tribunal and the countless others of other Italian courts and then, for comparison's sake, go on to England, Spain, Russia, France, or Germany. Most of this archival realm is still terra incognita. There are few maps or guidebooks to the terrain. Often, the explorer must hack out the path. Surprises abound; the destination may be unsure, but the voyage is lively and rewarding.

A NOTE FOR TEACHERS AND STUDENTS

This book grew out of classroom work. Students of ours by the hundreds have read trials with us. We owe many observations to lively interchange with them. Some who know Italian have transcribed trials from the manuscripts and translated them for use in class. A few have even gone to Italy, though undergraduates, and rummaged up new ones. Whatever the nature of the engagement, the training has been rich. By joining in the messy work of discovery, like the budding archaeologists who trowel and scrub the rubble of the past, students have come to appreciate how history writing comes about. As one once said, 'Now I understand where footnotes come from!'

Trials like these not only teach the epistemology of inquiry; they also bring the past to life. We have taken them, with interesting results, to secondary and middle schools, and even to a class of ten-year-olds. One technique that often stirs up interest is to re-enact a trial. Singly or in groups, students can prepare for the occasion. The suspects must work out for themselves what they really did, what they want to hide, why it should remain hidden. Magistrates must learn where the crime resides and must scan the evidence, looking for the implausibilities and inconsistencies in testimony with which to beat a suspect down. If one wishes, the court may be allowed a resort to imaginary 'torture' on the unrealistic condition that, then, the suspect must tell the truth. Torture-questions must be very limited in number; otherwise the magistrates and witnesses will lack incentive to be astute. This re-creation of the past is incomplete. Among other things, it combines the techniques of a trial of inquiry with the goals of a trial of judgment. Furthermore, the past is really dead and gone; our resuscitation is illusory. A teacher can, in fact, turn this incapacity to pedagogical advantage, by pointing out just where we moderns must guess and grope. In the end, the goal is not only to know the past, but, more important, to understand just how it is that we know it.

A NOTE ON THE TRANSLATION

In the trials all Latin in the original appears in italics, all Italian in normal type. Witnesses, on swearing in, are named in boldface. We have not abridged. Thus, '[...]' marks an illegible passage. To aid the reader, we have added punctuation, which is sparse in the original, and have modernized the fluid spelling of sixteenth-century Italian names. Italian time-keeping counted hours from sundown. The second hour of the night was around seven PM at mid-winter, around eleven PM at mid-summer. We have translated such expressions to the modern usage, which counts from noon and midnight.

Spade e saette

CHAPTER ONE

The Abbot's Assassins

THE TRIAL

[Two servants of a family of noble churchmen testify about their masters, the Bishop of Ancona, formerly Archbishop of Amalfi, and his son, the Abbot of San Galgano. They claim that the two nobles, who reside in Rome, have commissioned the henchmen to kill a peasant up in the Sienese countryside. Although this fragment has no surviving context, it seems likely that the masters are under investigation for this and, perhaps, other crimes.]

[1542][1]
Examined in the palace of cardinal Salviati[2] before the reverend lord Alfonso Vercelli, lieutenant in criminal matters, and before me, the notary: **Francesco di Biagio di Cortona.**

He was asked to tell the whole story from beginning to end.

HE ANSWERED: This past January, I was in the service of the Bishop of Ancona, who is also Archbishop of Melfi, and of the Lord Abbot of San Galgano, his son, a Sienese.[3] They live in Rome, in rione Ponte, next to the house of the Altoviti.[4] I had gone to be their servant through my connections with Bino, alias il Corvatto, my companion, who about eight years earlier had been in the service of the bishop and of his son, the abbot. They asked us, not once, but twenty times, or more than a hundred, could we please discharge a burden to their honour. They said that their house would never let us down and that, as for the bread that we ate, we would still be eating it in the future. But we should serve their house by discharging its debt of honour. That is, we should find six or eight other companions, so as to be eight or ten in all, or six at least, and go kill some peasants, a whole household of them, who had inflicted stabbings and wounds on the lord abbot. The abbot told us to kill them all and, if we couldn't kill them, to burn the house and anything else we could.

Because we were their servants, we agreed to go and do the job, but for no reward. So my companion Corvatto found one Giorgino the Perugian, called 'il Riccio,'[5] and one Thomasso from Ferrara, and one other, whose name I don't know.

So all five of us left Rome the fifth of last January. The lord abbot gave us three horses and twenty gold scudi for expenses and mail shirts, hidden sleeves of mail, swords, wheel-locks, and javelins. We went on horseback – Corvatto, Giorgino, and I – and Thomasso and that other one went on foot. We went off towards Siena, where we had to do the job in a place called la Staggia,[6] three miles this side of Siena. Corvatto and I were the only ones there because the two of them on foot couldn't keep up with us and Giorgino's horse was no good. So Corvatto and I went up a road. Down it came one of those peasants we were to kill. He was carrying hay to Siena; Corvatto recognized him because he had the telling marks. As soon as he arrived, Corvatto and I were on him; we killed him there in that road with the javelins. It was about eight in the morning. When we had done the job, we fled, and in our flight our capes and a dagger fell off. We headed for Montepulciano[7] and stayed there a day and a night to rest our horses, which were blown. There we found Giorgino, who had stayed behind because his horse was no good. From there, because we were short of money, we sent Giorgino to Rome to tell the bishop and the lord abbot both that we had done the job and that we were short of cash. He decided to send Giorgino back a few days later with eighteen gold scudi. We had already pawned the chain-mail shirts and the sleeves to cover our expenses, so we got them out of hock with that money and went to Cortona, and from Cortona to Città di Castello.[8] All told, we were about a month getting back to Rome. We came to the house of a woman here in the Borgo,[9] where we lay low for three days. We sent Giorgino to call the abbot. He came with his brothers and other soldiers, one of whom was the friar soldier of Città di Castello. When the abbot came to talk, we were in the house of signore Alessandro Vitelli.[10] So we handed over to him the horses, the bucklers, the sleeves, but the shirts and the swords he left us willingly, out of regard for an enmity we had.[11]

He was asked if the reverend bishop and his son, the lord abbot, had asked him and Corvatto to commit any other crime.

HE ANSWERED: Signore, before we left Rome to do the job, the bishop and the abbot told us, 'Go do this and, when you come back, we want you to do some other jobs of greater importance.' So, when we got back and we went to their house, they told us, both of them, that they wanted us to do this other job they had told us about earlier. I asked them to tell us what they wanted us to do, because we had to know, since we were the ones who had to do it. They said they wanted us to kill one messer Niccolò di Ser Gardi, a Sienese, who is here in Rome. If we did it, they would have us put into the light cavalry guard, or set us up in Città di Castello, or in Ancona, or wherever we wanted, and their house would never fail us, and that afterwards they would give us a pair of horses each to get into the guards.[12] We told them that they should let us think it over and that we would tell them that evening. So in the evening we told them that we didn't want to do anything, for we were not assassins, and said that what we had done was enough to discharge their honour. When they saw that we did not want to take them up on it, they took to hating us and ever since they have been trying to do us harm.

*In the same matter was examined: **Bino**, son of the late Geronimo from Campo in the district of Perugia, alias **il Corvatto**, witness for the information of the court who said as follows. And first he was asked about the matters above. What does he know, and could he narrate the event in order.*

HE ANSWERED: Signore, I will tell you. I had been in the service of the Bishop of Ancona, also Archbishop of Melfi, and of the Abbot of San Galgano, his son, for about eight years. They had brought me up since I was a little boy. It's true that when I needed money I went off to the wars, but when the wars were over I came back to stay with them. So, last year, when the abbot went to Siena to do [...], he happened to have a quarrel with some peasants. They stabbed both him and some others who were with him. When he came back home, he told of this and began to talk about how he wanted to have a vendetta against them.

When we were back in Rome, he wanted me to go back there, along with up to ten others, to kill them and, once I had done what he wanted, to do some other thing. 'What other thing?' I asked. He said that next he wanted us to kill messer Niccolò di Ser Gardi, the

Sienese. I asked him why he wanted to kill messer Niccolò. He told me, 'Enough! Do the other things!'

One day I went [to him][13] and he didn't want to give me a hearing. I told him that it didn't seem to me right that we should kill messer Niccolò. Rather, we should lament such a thing. He said to me, 'Well, that's the way it is. Don't get yourself mixed up in it any more. I want you to do the other job.'

So, when he took me to show me the house of those peasants, three of whom were not too far off, working the land, the abbot said, 'Look at them there. Those are the ones.' And he asked me, 'Do you have it in you to recognize them again?' I looked at them and said I did. One of those peasants had a red beard.

So, when we were back in Rome, he and the bishop called me and Francesco di Cortona and told us that they wanted us to go do this business of killing those peasants. It is true that the bishop said to us that he would have wished us not to kill them, but rather disfigure and lame[14] them, cut off their ears and hands, or the arms, so that people could see it and know it, but the abbot said that he wanted us to kill them, and if we couldn't kill them, to burn their houses. I told the lord abbot that I in no way wanted to go inside their house because there were a lot of them and we could get killed.

He told me to find six or eight other companions to go with us to do the job. I said that it should be understood that we were never to go inside their house. He said yes, and that we should kill them, and that I should find the men, while he would provide the money, arms, and mounts. So I found a fellow named Giorgino di Perugia and a Tomasso di Ferrara and one other. I asked the lord abbot how many horses he had provided us with. He told us six and sent us to a stables on the piazza of the Duke.[15] There he sent me three horses, one of which I didn't like. I told him that, for a job like the one they wanted done, that horse was no good. He said it was. So he sent us mail shirts, hidden mail sleeves, guns, swords and javelins, and twenty scudi in gold for expenses.

I told him that twenty scudi in gold would not be enough for the expenses of three horses and five men, especially because it could be many days before we came back. He told me to take them, because, if we fell short, we could pawn the weapons and anything else. So, the fifth of January, we left Rome, Francesco, Giorgino, Tomasso, and I. Francesco, Giorgino, and I were on horseback and those other two on foot. Along the route, the two on foot fell behind, and Giorgino complained his horse was blown. I offered him mine, and I would have taken his, but he didn't want to do it. Then I knew that he hadn't pluck enough, so I told him to turn back and wait for Francesco and me at Montepulciano. So Francesco and I went on. That evening we stayed at an inn. When the innkeeper saw such beautiful horses, he asked us where we were going and who we were with. I said we were light cavalry and that we were with a signore [...].[16] And, in the evening, I told the innkeeper, please, in the morning to call us early because we had to make a long trip the next day. He called us three hours before daybreak. Right away we gave the horses grain and mounted and went to the house of the peasants and it wasn't yet daylight.

I told Francesco to stay with his horse and watch what I did; wherever I went, he should come too. I put myself in a certain place to see if anyone went in or out of the house. As I watched, I saw coming out one of the peasants the lord abbot had shown me, those who had hit him, whom we were to kill. He wanted to load some straw. So I kept watching where he wanted to go. I saw him heading toward Siena. So I spurred my horse and gave Francesco a sign to come. We caught up with him at a ditch. As soon as that peasant saw me, he recognized me and tried to flee. I told Francesco, 'Hit him!' Francesco hit him with his javelin next to the ear, in the temple, and threw him to the ground, and I came up and struck him in the chest with my javelin. We killed him and then we took flight and went to Montepulciano, where we rested both us and the horses, which were exhausted.

There we found Giorgino. We sent him to Rome to the bishop and the abbot to have them send us more money because we were short of it. Giorgino set off and Francesco and I went to Cortona and then to Perugia. There, for lack of money, we pawned the mail shirts, the sleeves, and the swords. Then Giorgino arrived, bearing eighteen scudi in gold, though the abbot told me when we got back that he had sent twenty-three. So we got the mail shirts out of hock and then came to Rome. We stayed two nights in the house of a woman here in the Borgo and then went to the house of signore Alessandro Vitelli.

We sent Giorgino to call the abbot. He came, accompanied by his brothers and some soldiers. When we told him the job we had done, he told me it was too bad we hadn't killed the others. I said it hadn't been possible and that he should get us money. He said that just now he hadn't any money, but that he was expecting three hundred scudi, and that in the meantime we should pawn something and redeem it later.

Then, one evening, having gone to their house, we spoke with the bishop. He told us to find a rented room wherever we like, and he would pay for the whole of it. So we found one by Pozzo Bianco,[17] and I told him that the mistress wanted two scudi a month. He told us to take it and, so as to eat, to pawn something, because he was going to give us money. So we pawned a mail shirt. While we were living there, we used to go to his house. Sometimes the abbot said to me that he wanted me and Francesco to do that other job of killing that messer Niccolò di Ser Gardi. And I said that it was not right to do it because he was a gentleman and he [Niccolò] had done him [the abbot] no great harm. This is what he said: 'Well, if you do it, our house will never fail you in anything.' In the end, after many pleadings, we decided not to do it. And so, when they saw that we didn't want to kill messer Niccolò, they began to wish us ill. The abbot ordered us to give back the arms we owed him. Then I sent word that his lordship should send me a safe-conduct for this deed, as he had promised before I did it. So he sent me a safe-conduct of the Chamberlain. I was covered by it ten days ago as of yesterday when I was arrested here in the Borgo and examined and I confessed.

But the bishop had informed me through a little window of the prison I was in that I should stand fast, for he would help me with the pope, and I saw that, sometimes, he himself passed that way and gave me the nod to stand fast and to say nothing about how they had put me up to the deed, and said he'd have me freed. So, in the end, this morning, when I was examined I told them I had killed the man I killed because he had wounded my master, but I didn't say that they had made me do all those things they asked me to. I always said that I had done it on my own, and so, by using the safe conduct, they got me out.[18]

THE COMMENTARY

A good story often has a refrain, some theme, or situation, or phase that again and again returns, which, by its variations, gives at once consistency and shape to the narration. The tale of murder in this trial, by such a measure, is a tale well told. Indeed, were it not so grim, it might even be funny, for the two killers, and especially the second, Corvatto, have an ironic sense of theme. Their refrain is blundering. True, the pair do manage to kill one of their several intended victims, but, from start to finish and beyond, almost everything goes wrong. Their tale of botched vendetta is artful, but it is not intended to delight. Rather, the tellers craft it for the court to serve the politics of the moment. This is canny special pleading. Even if less than wholly true, the tale is instructive; it shows many facets of Italian life. In it one sees not only the mayhem sometimes attendant on the code of honour, but also the penetration of the church by lay ethics and the complex bonds between patron and client.

The churchmen in question, the Bishop of Ancona and the Abbot of San Galgano, clearly have taken the cloth without shedding the raiments of nobility. The father, Gieronimo Vitelli-Ghianderone, has been a high cleric, in the sense that he enjoys the titles, income, and prerogatives of a prelate. From 1519 to 1530 he was archbishop, not of the eastern town of Melfi, as his henchmen mistakenly say, but of Amalfi, on the west coast south of Naples. In their mouths, his title outlives the office. Then, from 1530 to 1538, he held a see in Tuscany, in Massa Marittima. In 1538, he transferred to Ancona. From 1534 to 1538, before passing it to his son, Giovanni Andrea, he held San Galgano, a rich Cistercian monastery in the country south of Siena. As absentee abbots, the two have milked the abbey, leaving the running of the place to a delegate. As their name indicates, these churchmen belong to the Vitelli clan, a family who have ruled Città di Castello and who serve the State of the Church. Alessandro Vitelli, in whose house the assassins parley with their masters, has recently commanded the papal army. Kin connections thus explain why Francesco and il Corvatto run to hide in Città di Castello. The feudal ethics of a proud noble house inspire the sanguinary commands of the bishop and his abbot son.

The killers' story is a fragment, not a trial. It is filed, by accident, with papers in the same hand belonging to a vast case of more than six hundred pages, a ponderous investigation of another murder in quite another countryside. The tale's isolation poses problems, for there are only two witnesses who tell almost the same story. Without a second point of view, one has no standpoint from which to triangulate their narrative or to test its accuracy. Furthermore, since the rest of the trial is lost, one cannot reconstruct the purposes of the court. Clearly, Francesco and il Corvatto are not under immediate investigation, for they appear as witnesses 'for the information of the court.' Someone else is the target. That does not, however, mean that the two men are out of danger. Their stories thus may be part apology. Very likely, they are also an attack on the bishop and the abbot. In maligning their former patrons for failing their dependents, the two men may serve the court as much as they serve themselves. As attack and apology, the story has a double burden, the misdeed itself and bad patronage. Whatever the gravity of the former wrong, it is the latter that crowds the foreground.

These stories show that a patron cannot deal with his client as would a tyrant with his subject or a boss with his employee. Rather, their relations are more political, for the patron's authority is complex and only indirect. Thus, a killing, like any enterprise, is a matter for negotiation; to arrange, support, and recompense a killing is a matter of some delicacy. To have his way, the patron must operate politically, using gifts and promises and, perhaps, threats and harm to clinch a deal. Therefore, one can apply to these arrangements for a killing the kind of analysis usually reserved for the machinations of princes. Like men of state, the abbot and the bishop bring to their bargaining liabilities and assets. These are worth reviewing; just what were they trying to do and how are they going about doing it? That is, as il Corvatto and Francesco tell the tale, how much do the patrons wield their wealth, their power, or their prestige as instruments of inducement or persuasion? Where might falls short, right often makes good the lack. So these prelates call on moral codes to strengthen their hands with their servitors. Their repeated talk of food, care, protection, and advancement just as much evokes an ethic of largess and obligation that binds lords and underlings to mutual help as, too, it dangles material inducements. Gift-giving, after all, observes a complex and polyvalent code. Meanwhile, although unequal partners to the bargaining, the underlings are not without their own resources, both political and moral. After all, if they are not lying to the court, they do spurn the second bloody deed. As with the patrons, so with the clients, one can look to values, ends, and assets to see why they might kill the peasant and then, at some cost to themselves, spare the townsman, messer Niccolò di Ser Gardi.

As a testimonial to bad patronage, this story is a moral document. Yet its ethics are nowhere Christian; there is not a whiff of sin. Rather, the wrongs transgress against the social code of honour. Thus, compunctions have no tinge of pity; the tellers shed no tears for the dead peasant. Nor do they foresee shedding any for the Sienese man of worth they might have killed. His death would have offended not

Christian compassion, but a social sense of propriety. For the servitors, the killing is not the central moral issue. Rather the burden of their argument is an indictment of the archbishop, and especially of the abbot, not because they instigate murder, but because time and again they let their henchmen down with false promises and half-measures, and then, in the end, they turn against them. According to il Riccio and il Corvatto, the abbot first offends in being stingy. He is slow to give those very things most tightly bound with honour in the eyes of fighting men: good soldiers, good horses, arms, and gold. That was why he botches his vendetta. The abbot and the bishop, as figured here, are not competent, nor, as we have seen, are they generous, just, or faithful. In all these shortcomings, they have offended honour. At the end of his testimony, il Corvatto claims to have remained loyal to his patrons while in prison, taking all the blame for the killing on himself. But at the same time, casting responsibility on their shoulders, he sells them out. One might well ask to what extent his tale of their betrayal of him explains, rationalizes, or justifies his own betrayal of his former patrons.

CHAPTER TWO

Paolo di Grassi
and His Courtesans

THE FIRST TRIAL,
CONCERNING THE BURNING OF LUCREZIA'S DOOR

[On the night of 15–16 May, someone has burned the door of a courtesan named Pasqua the Paduan. The court suspects a rival prostitute, Camilla the Skinny, who has just quarrelled with Pasqua. The court arrests and interrogates her, two cronies of her lover, Paolo di Grassi, and his servant. On 17 May, the court releases the henchmen, Chierico and Dario, under caution. But, on 18 May, Camilla and the servant, Giorgio, remain in jail, under investigation. On the 17th and 18th, the court also summons as witnesses three of Camilla's friends, another prostitute and two gentlemen.]

16 May 1559
Arraigned in person in Tor di Nona before the magnificent lord Gasparo Arsillo, auditore, and me, the notary, in the presence of the magnificent lord Tommaso Mancino, substitute fiscale: **Gabriele di Giorgio di Correggio**, *who swore and touched [the scriptures] and said as follows.*

He was asked if he knows or presumes to know the cause of his arrest and his present examination.

HE ANSWERED: I don't know why I'm in jail. I'm with messer Paolo di Grassi. And this morning I was in the house of Camilla the Sienese.[1] My master, messer Paolo, was there and so were Chierico and the Abbot, two companions of messer Paolo. The watch came and arrested signora Camilla and me and took us to jail.

And the lord asked why was it that he alone was arrested along with Camilla, and not those others.

HE ANSWERED: I can't think of any reason at all. They asked about Camilla's servant. They were told that he had left the evening before and wasn't there, so they took me.

He was asked for how long he had been serving signor Paolo.

HE ANSWERED: I got the job on the second of this month and I have been there ever since.

And the lord asked in what ways he served signore Paolo.

HE ANSWERED: I serve him by going at his stirrup, and at table, and in the bedchamber, the way one serves a master.

He was asked whether, in the time he has been serving signore Paolo, he has been in the houses of any courtesans, and of which ones.

HE ANSWERED: These past days I have been serving messer Paolo, I have never gone to the houses of any courtesans, except those of signora Camilla the Sienese, Giulia the Neapolitan, and one Beatrice who lives behind San Luigi, and I don't know if she is a courtesan or not.² *Adding to a question of the lord*: I have only been in Beatrice's house once. The same is true of Giulia's house. In Camilla's house I have been every day, because my master sleeps there every night.

He was asked to say where he was [...] yesterday from morning to night.

HE ANSWERED: My master rode off on horseback around noon and went to amuse himself. I accompanied him as his groom. He went into the house of that Beatrice, where he stayed a while. He came back. *Adding on his own*: I made a mistake. It was Saturday that he was at Beatrice's house. Sunday I was always at Camilla's house, except that my master went off on horseback for a while to find signore Paolo Giordano.³ But whether or not he found him I don't know. I was holding the horse. He came back to Camilla's place in the evening and didn't come out of the house again. Yesterday [...] I was in Camilla's house for a while, for they were playing kick-ball in front of it. Then my master rode off and I went with him. He came back to Camilla's house in the evening and I came back there almost at the same moment, for I had gone out to buy meat and pigeons.

And the lord asked if, after that, he left Camilla's house and where he went.

HE ANSWERED: I stayed in Camilla's house until half past eight at night, more likely later than earlier, and then I went off to my master's house to sleep.

His Lordship asked to what person or persons of his master's house he had spoken.

HE ANSWERED: They had all gone to sleep. I went to the serving woman, Santa. I fetched the light. At that point, along came the other two who stay in our house, that is, Chierico and the Abbot, and they asked me what was up with the others. I told them that everybody had gone to sleep. These were the first people I talked to.

He was asked whether, when he left Camilla's house, she saw him leave. And what was she doing at that point?

HE ANSWERED: I thought she saw me when I left, because she was in the room and she had finished playing with the Abbot. *Adding on his own*: Chierico, the Abbot, and I all left together, and the fellow from the stables too.

He was asked where Chierico, the Abbot, and the stable boy went, and if he arrived first at his master's house and fetched the light before they came.

HE ANSWERED: We went by the direct way. And before we arrived at the house of [cardinal] Pacheco, I went up ahead thinking that the door might be locked, but I found it open. *Adding to a question of his Lordship*: Chierico and the Abbot were away for a quarter of an hour, or a little less, before they came home.

He was asked how far his house is from the house of the most illustrious [cardinal] Pacheco, where he left Chierico and the Abbot.

HE ANSWERED: My master lives on the Piazza della Dogana.[4]

And the lord said that a trip like that does not take a quarter of an hour.

HE ANSWERED: They were a little while coming, but where they went and what they did I do not know.

He was asked why they went without a light, given that it was prohibited by the ordinances to go without a light.

HE ANSWERED: We went without a light. I don't know about ordinances. I was as You see me, just like this, without arms. Chierico had a sword because he is a soldier and he always carries it. The

Abbot was unarmed and they didn't have a light either.

He was asked who owned that big lantern that was carried to Camilla's house.

HE ANSWERED: As for me, signore, I have not seen any big lantern, nor a small lantern either.

He was asked whether, when he was at Camilla's house, he had spoken with the serving women or serving boys.

HE ANSWERED: Signore, yes, I chat. One doesn't talk about serious matters.

He was asked whether he knows that Camilla had any courtesan who was her enemy. And who was she? Or any other enemy, and who was she?

HE ANSWERED: I know that a certain Paula the courtesan, who came to stay here in these [Easter] holidays – and I don't know where she is from – is her friend. But if anyone wishes her ill, I do not know it. I don't get involved in the affairs of my masters.

He was asked if, last Saturday, he was at Camilla's house. And what was he there for?

HE ANSWERED: Signore, I wasn't there, either with my master or without him. My master slept at home Saturday evening.

He was asked if he heard Camilla say anything to Paolo about a courtesan. And which one was she?

HE ANSWERED: Signore, no, for it's my habit not to wait around where they are.

He was asked whether, at the request of Camilla or of one of her servants, he went to buy anything yesterday.

HE ANSWERED: Signore, I didn't go to buy anything except food for my master. *Adding to a question of his Lordship*: At the spice shop all I bought was some pepper to stuff a duck at my master's request.[5]

He was asked at what hour of the evening he left Camilla's house, and whether he was alone or in company.

HE ANSWERED: It was half past eight in the evening, more likely later. I left together with those others, that is, the ones I told you about.

He was asked what Camilla was doing yesterday evening when he left her house.

HE ANSWERED: When we left, signora Camilla had finished playing with the Abbot. I don't know what she did next.

He was asked who was with him yesterday at the home of Camilla, besides those aforementioned.

HE ANSWERED: There weren't any besides those I told you about, so far as I could see.

He was asked whether he knows a certain courtesan named Pasqua the Paduan.

HE ANSWERED: Signore, no, and I don't know where she lives. *Adding to a question of his Lordship*: Camilla might have mentioned this Pasqua, but it hasn't stuck in my mind.

Then the lord ordered him to be put back in his place [in jail] with the intent [of continuing] and ordered to be brought in:[6] **Camilla the Sienese**, *who swore and touched [the scriptures] and said as follows.*

She was asked whether she knows or presumes to know the cause of her present examination and detention.

SHE ANSWERED: Signore, no! Me, if anybody had told me this morning that I'd have to go to jail, if it had been a man, I'd have peeled off his beard and if it had been a woman, I'd have ruined her face.

She was asked to tell what she did and where she was on each day from last Thursday down to the present.

SHE ANSWERED: Thursday You're asking me about! I don't remember. Friday, I don't know, for the life of me! Saturday, I washed my hair. Then I rode off to signore Paolo Giordano, to his house, but I didn't find him there. His gentlemen took me where he was, in the house of Giuliano Cestini.[7] When we arrived, those gentlemen helped us dismount, me and Paola da Forlì.

And the lord said, let her tell if she entered the house of Giuliano Cestini and if she did anything when she was there.

SHE ANSWERED: I'll tell You. When we went into the house, I couldn't find signor Paolo and I went looking for him.[8] I found he was behind the bed with a woman in fur-trim whom I didn't recognize.

The signore came toward me and I began to say, 'Oh, what stinks? Oh, what stinks?' because the signore was wearing a garland of musk in his hat. At this point, that woman got up and I saw it was Pasqua the courtesan; I don't know where she's from.[9] She began to say, 'What do you mean, "stink!"? What do you mean, "stink!"?' The signore came over to put his arms around my neck and Pasqua began to call me a slut and wanted to throw a candlestick, but the signore held her back and gave her a big shove. Those gentlemen who had come with me had their spurs in their hands, and when they tried to intervene, so they've told me, they touched her a little in the face with their spurs and gave her a bit of a scratch. I wanted to leave. The signore didn't want me to. I sat down. Pasqua began again to say insulting words to me. I told her I didn't want a shouting match, nor did I care a bit what she said. And then the signore, who wanted nothing better than for us to have it out with our fists, seeing I didn't want to, said, 'Now you've satisfied me. Be off with you!' So Paola and I left.

Sunday, I went to mass at San Salvatore.[10] Not finding my lover there, I left at once. I found the servant of that lover of mine, named il Genovese. When the servant told me he was at St Peter's, I went there. *Adding on her own*: I would have gone anyway to see the little girls of Santo Spirito.[11] I went into the church of Santo Spirito, where I heard mass. Then I went back home, ate, and went to bed. Then I got up and I stayed at home, talking at the window. In the evening, I had supper and then I went to bed.

Yesterday, I never left the house except when, around five in the afternoon, I went with Paola to Marta's house. Marta wasn't there, so I came right back home and I haven't been out of the house again until this morning, when I came here to jail.

She was asked at what hour she had supper yesterday evening. Was she alone or in company, and with whom?

SHE ANSWERED: It must have been half past seven in the evening that I ate. Paola, Paolo di Grassi, Dario, alias the Abbot – that's what he's called because he's from the abbey of Farfa – and Chierico ate with me.[12] They usually eat in my house. And Gabriele, Paolo's servant, was there. *Adding to a question of his Lordship*: After supper we stayed chatting for a while, until nine in the evening. I played trionfetti[13] for a little while with the Abbot and then I went to sleep with Paolo di Grassi.

She was asked who of those she just named was the first to leave the house.

SHE ANSWERED: They all left at the same time, except Paolo, who stayed to sleep with me.

She was asked whether in the past days she sent out to buy anything from a spice merchant.[14]

SHE ANSWERED: Nothing. *Then she said*: Saturday, after I had washed my hair, I sent my servant woman to buy a baiocco's worth of dragante[15] to make curls.

She was asked what kind of light those others were carrying when they left her house.

SHE ANSWERED: They weren't carrying any light at all.

She was asked if last year the back door of her house was burned.

SHE ANSWERED: It was burned a bit on me.

She was asked if she knows that the door of Lucrezia the Greek was burned.

SHE ANSWERED: Signore, yes, it was burned on her.[16] She lives across from me.

She was asked if she knows who burned the door of Lucrezia's house.

SHE ANSWERED: Signore, I don't know, but she says that it was one Captain Tommaso the Genoese.

She was asked if she knows at whose instigation Lucrezia's door was burned.

SHE ANSWERED: Signore, no! I don't know. She was in love with him. She was really driven crazy about him. She even burned his shutters with candles.

She was asked if that Pasqua she was talking about had been for some time her friend who wished her well.

SHE ANSWERED: Signore, yes! She has been my friend and I still consider her my friend.

She was asked if she had ever confessed to any man or woman that it was at her command that Lucrezia's door was burned.

SHE ANSWERED: Signore, no! Upon my life! May God protect me, me and my mother! *Adding on her own*: Ask her about it, and messer

Marcantonio Borghese, because they know all about it.

She was asked what she would say if it were said to her face that she had said, 'The door of Lucrezia the Greek was burned. I was the one who had it burned.'

SHE ANSWERED: The first thing isn't so. I never said it to anybody. And if anyone wishes me ill, let him vent himself in some other way besides these shabby tricks.

She was asked where she acquired the big lantern which was found in her house.

SHE ANSWERED: In my house there are neither torches, nor big lanterns, nor lanterns. There is nothing but candlesticks.

She was asked who were those two who last evening came to her house around ten at night.

SHE ANSWERED: Since I went to bed last night, no one has been to my house except the police.

She was asked to remember well and was reminded of the penalty for telling lies. Let her say if she had confessed that it was at her instigation that the door of Lucrezia the Greek was burned.

SHE ANSWERED: I never said such a thing, may God content me! And if it isn't true, let him never let me prosper!

She was asked if she knows where Pasqua lives. And how far is it from her house?

SHE ANSWERED: She used to be at Monte Giordano.[17] I don't know if she's still there because it's been more than a year since I was there. *Adding on her own*: She is jealous of a lover of hers, who had no more to do with her than with this table.

She was asked if she had quarrelled with Pasqua. And for what reason? And where?

SHE ANSWERED: Never at any other time! *Adding on her own*: She is angry enough at me, but I have never been where she is since she became jealous about that lover of hers.

Then the lord ordered the arraigned to be put back in her place [in jail] with a mind to continue.

In the presence of lord Tommaso, substitute fiscale, and the aforesaid, etc.

17 May 1559
There was examined in the chamber of the magnificent lord Gaspare Arsillo and before me, the notary: **Chierico di Domenico**, *a Corsican, witness*[18] *for information of the court, who swore and touched [the scriptures] and said as follows.*

He was asked if he knows or presumes to know the cause of his present examination.

HE ANSWERED: All I know is that, yesterday evening, messer Paolo di Grassi told me that I had to be examined on account of Camilla.

And the lord asked why he thinks he is to be examined on account of Camilla the Sienese.

HE ANSWERED: As for me, I couldn't say or imagine why in any way at all.

He was asked where he was on Monday evening, from seven in the evening until morning.

HE ANSWERED: Monday afternoon I went in the company of messer Paolo to Camilla's house, where we stayed to talk for a while, until supper hour arrived. We ate a little after the Ave Maria.[19] After the meal, we stayed a bit to talk. Because Camilla was a bit miffed at messer Paolo, she set out to play *trionfetti* with the Abbot. They may have played together about an hour. When they got up from the game, I went to sleep at messer Paolo's house, leaving in Camilla's house messer Paolo and one Paola da Forlì.

He was asked what hour of the night it was when he left Camilla's house and went off to sleep at the house of messer Paolo.

HE ANSWERED: It could have been between nine and half past nine in the evening, round about.

And the lord asked if he left Camilla's house alone or in company. And with whom?

HE ANSWERED: I left with the Abbot, and no one else. The two of us were alone. And we went to sleep at messer Paolo's house.

He was asked if Gabriele, messer Paolo's servant, left Camilla's house with him and the Abbot.

HE ANSWERED, after he had thought for a while: I think so.

And the lord said that he should be careful to remember whether Gabriele left Camilla's house together with him and with the Abbot.

HE ANSWERED: I remember well that Gabriele left with us.

And the lord asked if the three of them were together the whole time they were going from Camilla's house to the house of messer Paolo.

HE ANSWERED: When we were at cardinal Pacheco's house we sent Gabriele ahead to have the door of the house opened so we wouldn't be held up. And when we arrived, Gabriele had fetched the light.

He was asked if, after Gabriele left them, they did not go straight to messer Paolo's, but went elsewhere. And where was it?

HE ANSWERED: We came down by way of the Via dei Chiavari and went over to the Piazza di San Luigi, where we found some youths who were singing and playing music.[20] We stopped there for a little while and then we went home.

He was asked if he had spoken with any of those young men who were singing.

HE ANSWERED: We spoke with one whom we knew, for he was a friend of that courtesan. We said, 'How's it going? What's up?' and things like that and then we went off. *Adding to a question of his Lordship*: I know the one we talked to by sight, and I don't know where he lives, or what his name is, or what work he does. I am pretty sure he's a soldier, even though nowadays he doesn't carry a sword, but from his speech he seems to me a Tuscan.

He was asked whether he knows if the Abbot knows that young man.

HE ANSWERED: I don't believe he knows him.

He was asked if he went anywhere else before he arrived at the house of messer Paolo.

HE ANSWERED: Signore, no, we did not go elsewhere.

He was asked if he knows a courtesan named Pasqua the Paduan.

HE ANSWERED: I know her in that I've seen her and heard her name, but I've never talked with her. She lives below Monte Giordano. It's about eight days since I saw her at the windows of that house.

He was asked if he knows that the door of Pasqua was burned. And when was it burned?

HE ANSWERED: I heard it said yesterday that her door was burned the night before. I heard it in Camilla's house from messer Paolo and from Camilla's servant women, after Camilla was put in jail.

He was asked who is thought to have burned that door.

HE ANSWERED: They said they didn't know.

He was asked to say how they came to be talking of the burned door.

HE ANSWERED: They came to talk of it because when messer Paolo went to signore Paolo Giordano's house, he saw Pasqua's door burned. When he came back to Camilla's house, he told the servant women.

He was asked if there had been any suspicion as to who had burned the door.

HE ANSWERED: Nothing was said.

He was asked if he himself knows anything about who burned the house.

HE ANSWERED: Not at all. And if I know anything about it, I can go up these stairs upside down and God can show miracles about it.

He was asked if, in the past days of the holiday, in conversation with others in the house, he had said anything about Pasqua.

HE ANSWERED: I heard Camilla and Paolo talking about the brawl that happened between Camilla and Pasqua in the house of Giuliano Cestini, where signore Paolo Giordano was, and she said someone came off the worse for it.

He was asked if he had heard Camilla threaten Pasqua.

HE ANSWERED: By God, I heard nothing!

He was asked if he was there when Camilla spoke with certain men about Pasqua. And what did they say?

HE ANSWERED: Signore, she did not speak in my presence with anyone else except us people of her house. And she said that Pasqua had come off the worse for it and that Pasqua was a gallant woman.

He was asked how long it took Gabriele to go back yesterday evening to Paolo's house.

HE ANSWERED: He didn't take half an hour, for it's a short trip.

Then he undertook the obligation to appear in court as often as called under a penalty of one hundred scudi. His Lordship released the suspect because he had obligated himself by an oath.

The same day
Arraigned in person before the court in the same place and before me, the notary: **Dario di Pietro of the Abbey of Farfa, alias the Abbot,** *who swore and touched [the scriptures] and said as follows.*

He was asked if he knows or presumes to know the cause of his present examination.

HE ANSWERED: All I know is that messer Paolo told me yesterday evening that your Lordship wanted to examine me and that You want me to think about the matter that I should be examined on.

He was asked where he was on Monday evening. And in whose company, and what did they do there?

HE ANSWERED: Monday evening, I was in the house of Camilla the Sienese together with messer Paolo, who stayed there to sleep.

He was asked at what hour he went to the house of Camilla.

HE ANSWERED: It could have been around six in the evening when I went to Camilla's house. *Adding to a question of his Lordship*: When I left, it might have been half past nine at night.

And the lord asked what he did in the time that he was in Camilla's house.

HE ANSWERED: We waited until supper was ready, we supped, and, having eaten, we stayed a while at table talking. And Camilla invited me to play cards and we played for about a quarter of an hour. Then messer Paolo got undressed to go to sleep, so we left.

And the lord asked if he had been alone or in company, and with whom he went and where he went when he left Camilla's house.

HE ANSWERED: I left in the company of Chierico.

And the lord asked if anyone else left Camilla's house with him and Chierico. Let him remember carefully.

HE ANSWERED: It seems to me that Gabriele came. I didn't see him in the street, for it was night-time, and when we arrived home, we found him at the house.

And the lord said that he should tell the route taken by himself and Chierico, when they went from Camilla's house to the house of messer Paolo.

HE ANSWERED: We went to [cardinal] Pacheco's and from Pacheco's to Piazza Madama and to San Luigi and from San Luigi to messer Paolo's house.[21]

And the lord asked if, on that trip, he ever stopped. And where did he do so?

HE ANSWERED: I don't remember that we stopped at all.

He was asked whether, on the trip, they came across any people who were singing. And where were they? And did they stop there for a while?

HE ANSWERED: Signore, no! We never found anyone who was singing. We did meet some who were walking along, talking in Venetian, down by San Luigi.[22] And I didn't talk to any of them and I didn't hear Chierico speak to anyone.

He was asked if, on that trip, he was always with Chierico.

HE ANSWERED: We always went along together and never left one another.

He was asked and warned to tell the truth. Had he on that trip met anyone singing and had he or Chierico spoken with them?

HE ANSWERED: I don't remember seeing anyone who was singing, nor that Chierico spoke to him.

And the lord said that it is not probable that in the short span of a single day he could have forgotten so much about the things he heard and did on that night. And let him answer precisely, yes or no, and not with the words, 'I don't remember.'

HE ANSWERED: Let me put it this way. If I had thought that I was going to be examined, I would have paid better attention, but I never gave it much of a thought and I don't remember.

He was asked if those persons whom he said he found speaking Venetian were standing still or walking. And did they have any musical instrument?

HE ANSWERED: They were walking along and chatting. I neither saw nor heard if they had a musical instrument.

And the lord asked where they encountered them.

HE ANSWERED: We found them between San Luigi and Piazza Madama and they were going along ahead of us eight or ten paces.

He was asked what he would say if it were said to his face by Chierico, his companion, that he had found some persons singing and that they stayed there a while and spoke with them.

HE ANSWERED: Maybe he remembers better than I do. I didn't pay much heed.

Then the lord ordered **Chierico** *summoned. And he was brought in and they made a mutual recognition of names and persons and he swore and touched [the scriptures] and in Dario's [the Abbot's] presence he was asked to say, to the face of Dario, who was it that he found when he was coming back from Camilla's house to the house of Paolo di Grassi.*

HE ANSWERED: This is what I say. That when Dario and I arrived between San Luigi and Piazza Madama we found certain young men who were going along talking in Venetian and playing a guitar. And I spoke to a young man, saying, 'Good evening.' And this Dario was always with me.

Dario was asked what he would say about these things.

HE ANSWERED: I say that we found them between Piazza Madama and San Luigi, and they were going along ahead of us eight or ten paces shouting in Venetian so loud you would have thought there were fifty of them.

Chierico was asked if the servant Gabriele was with him and Dario.

HE ANSWERED: Signore, yes! He was with us and he came with us as far as the piazza of Pacheco and then went ahead to have them open the house.

Dario was present and he said: I say that Gabriele didn't come with us, but that we found him in the house and he had the light in his hand.

Then the lord sent Chierico off, who had not given up what he had said, and, continuing the examination, he asked Dario if, during the recent holidays, he had been present at a conversation in which Camilla spoke of a brawl with Pasqua the Paduan in Giuliano Cestini's house?

HE ANSWERED: Signore, no, I was never there.

He was asked what he would he say if Camilla said in his face that she had talked to him about the brawl.

HE ANSWERED: I would say it is not true.

He was asked if he knows anything about Pasqua the courtesan.

HE ANSWERED: I don't know her, and I don't know her house, and I've never seen her, except yesterday.

The lord asked where he saw her yesterday. And whom was she with?

HE ANSWERED: I saw her yesterday in the house of the governor. She was talking with Jacopo the Neapolitan. I was alone.

He was asked if he knows that the door of her house was burned. And when?

HE ANSWERED: I heard it yesterday in the house of the governor.

He was asked if he heard it in Camilla's house.

HE ANSWERED: Yesterday, after Camilla was put in jail, they talked about it in Camilla's house. I forget who said it, but messer Paolo was there, and some other people I do not remember.

Then, at the end of the testimony, the suspect obligated himself to appear as often as he was summoned, under a penalty of one hundred scudi. Since he obligated himself, the lord dismissed him.

18 May 1559
There was arraigned in person before the court at Tor di Nona, before the magnificent lord Gasparo Arsillo and me, the notary, **Camilla the Sienese,** *a courtesan, who swore and touched [the scriptures] and said as follows.*

She was asked if she is ready to tell the truth about the questions that will be asked below.

SHE ANSWERED: I am resolved to tell the truth about everything that you are going to ask me.

She was asked what this truth is that she says she is willing to say.

SHE ANSWERED: The truth that I wish to say is about what you will ask me if I know about it.

She was asked if she knows that the door of Pasqua the courtesan, with whom she had a brawl last Saturday, was burned last night.

SHE ANSWERED: I know nothing about its being burned on her or not. And if I know anything about it, I can be killed by the hand of my husband, if he is alive.

She was asked whether it is true that on Sunday or Monday last, speaking with certain of her friends about one thing and another, they talked together about the brawl between herself and Pasqua.

SHE ANSWERED: I never talked about this with anyone. Except that, Saturday evening, when I came home, my mother asked me what had happened. I said that signor Paolo wanted me to have a fist fight with Pasqua.

She was asked and warned to tell the truth. Talking with what other persons about Pasqua, had she threatened Pasqua with words like, 'Be it in God's hands, I don't want two days to go by without your having news about this'?

SHE ANSWERED: Signore, no, you will never find that I said these words or others either. I thought no more of Pasqua than of things I never see.

She was asked what she would say if they said to her face that she had said such words or words like them.

SHE ANSWERED: Let these gentlemen come say that to me! Please, do let them come, for I'd love to hear a thing like that! And, likewise, anything else I might hear! *Adding on her own*: If Pasqua lodges a complaint against me on this point, let her come justify herself.

She was asked what Dario and Chierico came back for after they left her house last Monday night.

SHE ANSWERED: They didn't come back, may God guard my life!

She was asked what she intended to do with the quantity of pitch and turpentine that were found in the lower part of her house in a certain pot.

SHE ANSWERED: I don't believe you could have found such a thing in my house.

Then the lord ended the examination for now and ordered the suspect to be put back in her place [in jail] with the intention of continuing.

17 May 1559
There was examined in Rome in the office of me, the notary, before the magnificent lord Gasparo Arsillo, auditore, and me, the notary: **Antonio Peruzzi**, *alias* **Vecciano**, *of Parma, a witness for the information of the court, who touched [the scriptures] and said as follows.*

He was asked if he knows or presumes to know the cause of his present examination.

HE ANSWERED: I know nothing about it.

He was asked if he came on his own accord or if he was summoned.

HE ANSWERED: I was summoned, according to what the signore told me. I came at once to the office.

He was asked if he knows Pasqua the Paduan, a courtesan, and Camilla the Sienese, the Skinny, a courtesan.

HE ANSWERED: Signore, yes. I know them both.

He was asked how long it has been since he talked with either of them. And where was it?

HE ANSWERED: I think it was this past Easter day I talked with Camilla. I talked with her in her house. *Adding to a question of his Lordship:* I am certain I did talk with her, and I talked with her freely. And to Pasqua I spoke on Monday. I talked with her on Monday, which was the second day of Easter, and it was after the midday meal. She called me when I was walking by there.

And the lord said that he should tell what conversations he had with Camilla when he first spoke to her.

HE ANSWERED: I stayed in Camilla's house on Easter day for about a quarter of an hour. All we said to one another was, 'Signore, I kiss your hand, how are you?' And she would ask after other gentlemen; there were words like that.

And the lord asked if there were any conversation or any words about Pasqua.

HE ANSWERED: I did not hear Camilla talk about Pasqua or about other courtesans.

He was asked if he knows what happened between Camilla and Pasqua last Saturday in the house of Giuliano Cestini in the Banchi.[23]

HE ANSWERED: Pasqua herself told me, and I heard it from certain gentlemen who had heard it said by some gentlemen of signore Paolo Giordano.

He was asked if Camilla had complained to him about those things that happened that day between Pasqua and her in the house of Giuliano Cestini.

HE ANSWERED: Signore, no, to me she did not complain at all.

He was asked if, when she complained of Pasqua, Camilla used threatening words about her.

HE ANSWERED: I say that Camilla did not talk to me about Pasqua. How do You think she could have threatened her if she did not speak to me about her?

He was asked if he had heard from anyone that Camilla had threatened Pasqua.

HE ANSWERED: Signore, no! Certainly not ! *Adding on his own*: I am not on familiar terms with her, except for talking in public about things, but I had no words about Pasqua.

He was asked what Pasqua said when she called him.

HE ANSWERED: She told me the story of the fight she had in the house of messer Giuliano Cestini, telling me that, when she was in the house of messer Giuliano and signor Paolo Giordano was also there, Camilla came there too. And, because of certain words she used when the signore went toward her, they ended up pulling hair and that the mark that she had on her face was made by messer Jacobo Jacobacci.[24] I've not seen her since.

He was asked, and warned to tell the truth, whether Camilla had in his presence threatened Pasqua. Or does he know that Camilla threatened Pasqua?

HE ANSWERED: In truth, I cannot say. All I can say is that Camilla did not tell me either good or ill of Pasqua. Nor have I heard from anyone that Camilla had threatened her.

He was asked who was there on Easter day, when he was talking with Camilla.

HE ANSWERED: There were present messer Francesco Lucino, a merchant at the Pellegrino,[25] messer Aloigi Castellani, also a merchant, who lives in Via Giulia,[26] and a Cremonese with a doctorate who lives with Aloigi, and Paula da Forlì and messer Paolo di Grassi and the house servants. *Adding to a question of his Lordship*: The conversation wasn't of the sort that everyone could understand.

He was asked if Mario Tazzerino was there.

HE ANSWERED: When I was there, Mario wasn't there. *Adding on his own*: And I don't think he would have been because he is in his house taking a purge.

[He was sworn to] silence.

18 May 1559
*There was examined in the house of the most reverend father De Torres, in Piazza Navona: messer **Mario Tazzerino**, witness for the information of the court, who swore and touched [the scriptures] and said as follows.*

He was asked if he knew and knows a certain Camilla the Sienese, a courtesan, and what was the cause of his knowing her.

HE ANSWERED: I have known her for three years now. The first time I met her was in the house of messer Jacobo Jacobacci.[27] One evening she was there, and she stayed to sleep in that house where I was visiting.

He was asked how long it has been since he last saw Camilla. And does he know what her situation is now?

HE ANSWERED: I think it's been more than six months since last I saw her. Now I hear that she's in jail on suspicion that she had Pasqua's door burned, so I've heard. *Adding to a question of me, the notary:* I heard it from Pasqua and from a messer Gieremia da Volterra. *And to another question of me, the notary, he said:* Pasqua told me yesterday and so did Gieremia. But I have not heard that Camilla threatened to do any harm to Pasqua. I have indeed heard that Pasqua had a fight a few days earlier. That is all I know.

18 May 1559
*There was examined in the chamber of the magnificent lord Gasparo Arsillo, one of the auditori in criminal matters: madonna **Paola da Forlì**, a courtesan in Via dei Pontefici,[28] witness for the information of the court, who touched [the scriptures] and said as follows.*

She was asked whether she knows or presumes to know the cause of her present examination.

SHE ANSWERED: Signore, no! Not unless you tell me.

She was asked if she knows the courtesan, Camilla the Sienese, the Skinny.

SHE ANSWERED: Signore, yes! I know her. *Adding to a question of the lord:* It has been three or four days that I haven't seen her. I saw her in her house.

She was asked whether during Easter she was in Camilla's house, and for how many days.

SHE ANSWERED: I went there Saturday evening. I stayed there Sunday and Monday. Tuesday I went back to my house. I went there because she invited me because I am making a *traversa*[29] for her.

She was asked what conversations she and Camilla had together on Saturday.

SHE ANSWERED: First we talked about how she wanted to go find signore Paolo Giordano to write a letter to a beloved of hers. Then she came back. There were various discussions of lovers. With us, it seems that we don't talk about anything else except lovers.

She was asked whether she and Camilla said anything to one another about Pasqua the Paduan, a courtesan.

SHE ANSWERED: Signore, no, we didn't talk about her.

She was asked what happened between Camilla and Pasqua in the house of Giuliano Cestini. Let her tell the story in order.

SHE ANSWERED: This is what happened. Camilla went over to kiss the hand of signor Paolo and when she went into the room in messer Giuliano Cestini's house, she couldn't see signor Paolo because he had withdrawn with Pasqua behind the bed. And because there was a great smell of musk in the room, Camilla said, 'What stinks? Phew! Phew!' She was about to leave. Then the signore got up from behind the bed and embraced Camilla. Then Pasqua said, 'What does "Phew! Phew!" mean, you baggage?' Camilla answered, 'I am not saying it about you, signora. Rather, I am saying it about the signore, who stinks of musk.' Then, after those insults, Pasqua took a candlestick to throw it at her. Those gentlemen got in between them and they didn't come to grips. And even though the signore wanted Camilla and Pasqua to pull one another's hair, Camilla didn't want to, and we left.

She was asked whether, on Sunday and Monday, while they were staying together, they talked about the matter and Camilla complained of Pasqua.

SHE ANSWERED: We talked about various things, but never a word about the business of Pasqua. I am not aware that Camilla threatened her in any way. While I stayed with her I didn't once hear her mention Pasqua for good or for ill, neither the evening we left messer Giuliano's house nor in those two days I stayed with her.

[She was sworn to] silence.

THE SECOND TRIAL,
CONCERNING A NOCTURNAL BRAWL

[It is Vacant See, the papal interregnum, a time of civic disorder. Unknown assailants attack Paolo di Grassi, a Roman gentleman, after dark in his stables and wound one of his men. Paolo and his followers pursue the attackers into the street. As Gioanbattista Vittorio, a local magistrate, tries to calm him, Paolo utters seditious words that provoke his arrest. Two of his servants and Chierico, a henchman, end up in Tor di Nona jail, Paolo in Castel Sant'Angelo. Major officials hear the case, a sign that the matter is grave. For five days (21–25 November), Romolo di Valenti, the governor's chief deputy, questions Paolo, his men, and a Milanese swordsman who was present. To the end of the trial are appended five depositions, made the next April, to a notary of the court about Paolo's attacks on courtesans' houses.]

In the name of the Lord Amen.

In the 1559th year since the Nativity, in the second indiction,[30] on the twenty-first day of November, in the absence of a shepherd of the apostolic see because of the death of Pope Paul IV of happy memory.

21 November [1559]

Arraigned in person before the court at Tor di Nona before the magnificent lord Romolo di Valenti, lieutenant, and in the presence of me, the notary: **Agnolo**, *the son of the late Francesco Fachetti, a Florentine, who swore the oath to tell the truth and having sworn, touched [the scriptures] and was asked by the lord about the cause of his arrest.*

HE ANSWERED: I was arrested for nothing much. *Adding:* Because they took me with my master, who is messer Paolo di Grassi. As for him, I don't know why he's been arrested.

And the lord said that he should think a bit about the cause of his arrest. He might perhaps have some suspicion why.

HE ANSWERED: I believe that messer Paolo was arrested along with the rest of us on account of a certain quarrel that came up the other night. Because messer Paolo said that he had been attacked by a good sixteen men in his stables.

And the lord said that he should tell the story of that brawl, whatever he knows and how he knows it.

HE ANSWERED: Messer Paolo and the others of the house had a lively supper with the signora [Ottavia, Paolo's courtesan], and then we three servants sat down to eat with the serving lads of the storehouse. And the stable boy, who had also sat down with us, was suddenly called by messer Paolo and told to fetch the keys to the stable and to go with him to see the horse. And they went out of the house, armed with their usual swords. Think of it! If they had had a mind to go do wrong, it would have been a strange business to go like that without a cape, for nobody had a cape.

And the lord said that he should specify the kinds of arms they carried and their names.

HE ANSWERED: Everybody was carrying swords and daggers and mail jackets and sleeves except for Chierico, who carried a sword and a pointed halberd. They were messer Paolo, Chierico, Cecco who was wounded, Vincenzo, and Gioanbattista, the fencer. And while we were still eating, messer Paolo came back all worked up and told me and Bastiano the Frenchman, his servant, to take arms. He took a halberd and I took a pike and we ran downstairs. As we came out, we met the signora, because the fencer was bringing her back to the house. The Signora went into the house and, with messer Paolo, we went running back toward messer Paolo's stable, which stands by the stables of cardinal Crispo, next to the house of a master of the horse.[31] And messer Paolo, when he was in the piazza, outside his house, shouted I don't know how many times, 'To arms! To arms!' But nobody came running, and we arrived at the stables alone and found that the caporione had already come by that street that runs from the house of the cardinal De la Cueva, the one that goes up towards the Salvatore.[32] The caporione said, 'What is going on? What is going on?' And messer Paolo said, 'Messer Gioanbattista, it's me! I have been assassinated[33] by fifteen or sixteen of those men of the governor.' And right away up came the caporione of Ponte and the caporione of Santo Stefano,[34] over there near my master's stables. Messer Paolo went off talking a while with messer Gioanbattista.

His Lordship said that he should specify the words between Paolo and messer Gioanbattista Vittorio.[35]

HE ANSWERED: Messer Paolo was angry, and he said that he had been assassinated, as I said, and they went walking off. And I was all tangled up with the many other people who were there and didn't hear any more.

And the lord said several times that he should think carefully and tell the whole conversation, for if Paolo was burning with fury and anger, he must have said many things in a loud voice that could have easily been heard both by the witness and by many other people. In this matter, as in others, he should beware of any lies, so that the truth might be had from him in the ordinary way and it would not be necessary to have recourse to extraordinary remedies.[36]

HE ANSWERED: If I had heard, I would say it, just as I said the other things, and I will tell everything that I know. *And continuing his narration, he said*: After we met the caporione, he accompanied messer Paolo to his house, where messer Paolo gave an arquebus to the caporione, which messer Paolo had carried and given to a servant of the storehouse – I don't know if it was Antonio or Battista – when he came back to call the rest of us to take arms. He said he had taken it from one of those men of the governor in the first brawl. The caporione left on his usual rounds and we went back home. Messer Paolo undressed. And Cecco was wounded.

And the lord said that he should tell what was said and done by Paolo and the others after they came back home once the tumult had quieted down.

HE ANSWERED: All messer Paolo said was that he took it badly that Cecco had been wounded.

And the lord said that he should tell what Paolo said about the wounded man.

HE ANSWERED: Messer Paolo didn't say anything.

And the lord asked how the witness could know that Paolo took it ill that Cecco had been wounded. He must have said something if the witness could say such a thing.

HE ANSWERED: All he said – I didn't understand – messer Paolo was put out because the man had been wounded. Messer Paolo didn't shout. And he didn't rant. He said that it was the first time any of his men had ever been wounded and that this time the disgrace had fallen on him. I went to fetch the barber and didn't hear any more.[37]

He was asked if anyone came to messer Paolo's house after they returned home and talked to him.

HE ANSWERED: There came someone who wears a pair of hose of black velvet, trimmed with yellow velvet, who lives in the house of signore Domenico di Massimi.[38] I don't know what he's called. But I went twice for the barber and didn't hear them say anything.

He was asked how long he has been in the service of Paolo di Grassi, and at what salary.

HE ANSWERED: It has been exactly two months. And he has promised me a scudo a month. I go at his stirrup. I undress him, I dress him. I didn't go with him at night. I went with him in the daytime. In the night time I went with him when he went to sleep with the girl, that is, with Camilla the Sienese.[39] I couldn't keep count of the number of times he has slept with Camilla. He went to her house and she came to messer Paolo's house.

And the lord asked whether he had kept messer Paolo company when he went to that house of Camilla where she is now dwelling, near the most reverend Santa Fiora.[40]

HE ANSWERED: I have never accompanied him there, neither by day nor by night, except the day before he was arrested, when he went by there on horseback toward mid-day. *Adding to a question*: I don't know anything about a brawl that happened in the night where signora Camilla is now living.

And the lord said that he should think about that carefully.

HE ANSWERED: What can I tell You? I can't say anything, except what I know.

He was asked to tell how that woman called Ottavia was brought to Paolo's house. And by whom?

HE ANSWERED: I was in the house when the signora came, and all of them were with her. That is, messer Paolo and his other companions. I think that Chierico was there. It was three days before we were arrested, although I don't remember it all that well.

And the lord asked whether he had been with messer Paolo that day on the evening of which she was brought to his house.

HE ANSWERED: Signore, I fell down the stairs and broke my head. For fifteen days I couldn't go out with him.

He was asked whether messer Paolo had other light arquebuses in his house besides the one the police had found in his house.[41]

HE ANSWERED: I don't know of any light arquebuses besides the one the bargello took. I don't know if they loaded them or unloaded them there in the house, because he sent us about on errands. Nor do I know that, after the *bandi* [against arquebuses] came out, any of messer Paolo's men, or messer Paolo himself, carried light arquebuses.

He was asked whether he had been present at a certain quarrel between Paolo di Grassi, who was acting on behalf of the caporione one evening, and some soldiers assigned to the protection of the most reverend lord governor.

HE ANSWERED: I don't know anything about it. I wasn't there. It could be this quarrel happened after I broke my head falling down the stairs.

Then the lord dismissed him and ordered him put back in his place [in jail] with the intention of continuing.

The same day, 21 November 1559
*Arraigned in person before the court in Tor di Nona before the lord Romolo di Valenti, lieutenant in criminal matters of the most reverend lord governor, in the presence of me, the notary: **Bastiano Crepini** of Paris, a Frenchman, who swore the oath to tell the truth and having sworn, touched etc., was asked by the lord about the cause of his arrest.*

HE ANSWERED: I don't know why I was arrested. I know that I have not done any wrong here, nor have I done any anywhere else either. *And he cried while he said this.*

He was asked why he was crying.

HE ANSWERED: I am crying because the shame of being in jail hurts.[42] Because I have never been in any jail in the world.

He was asked how long it has been since he came to Rome, and how long he had resided there. And with whom did he live? And what did he do and what was his trade?

HE ANSWERED: I came with cardinal Bertrand.[43] I arrived in this land the same day he did. I left Turin and came to Rome to find a master and to be in service. I serve in the bedchamber. I don't know how to serve in the stables. I have not had any patron except the one I have now, who is called Paolo di Grassi. With him I have not made any pact about a salary. Another Frenchman, whom I do not know, got me the job here. He saw me one day and asked me if I wanted a master. When I said I did, he brought me to Paolo di Grassi. And I've been with him for eight days. I served him in the bedchamber and I went with him at his stirrup.

He was asked if it is his custom to keep his master company by day and by night.

HE ANSWERED: In the day-time I always went. In the night, messer Paolo didn't go out, except one evening when he had a fight, which was one or two days after I came to stay with him.

He was asked to tell what he knows about this quarrel.

HE ANSWERED: All I know is that they had a quarrel. I wasn't there because I had stayed in the house with that other servant, called Agnolo, to eat supper. And Paolo with some four other soldiers and with signora Ottavia went out to the stable. And then signora Ottavia came back. They hadn't yet given us any supper, and she said that there was a fight. And first messer Paolo came in and took from the house a spear – I don't know what it's called – and went running out. And none of the others came back with him. And I went out the door of the house to see what was happening, as far as the middle of the piazza, without carrying any arms at all, because there weren't any in the house, and because the stirrup servant, who had gone with messer Paolo the first time he went out, had taken my sword. In the middle of the piazza, I met Cecco, who was coming back wounded, and I went back into the house with him.

He was asked with what weapons were Paolo himself and the others armed the first time when they went out of the house with Ottavia. And let him name Paolo's associates.

HE ANSWERED: Messer Paolo was carrying a sword and a dagger and a mail jacket and sleeves. Chierico had a sword and a dagger and he was carrying the halberd. The one who was wounded was carrying a sword, a dagger, and a jacket. And Gioanbattista was carrying a sword, a buckler, and a jacket and sleeves of mail. There was another one, called Vincenzo, who likewise was armed with a sword, a dagger, a jacket, and sleeves. The signora had Paolo's velvet hat and cape.

He was asked what Paolo and the others said after they came back to the house.

HE ANSWERED: He was complaining and he was angry because

that man of his had been wounded. But I don't know who he was angry at because I don't know who the fight had been with, because I was in the bedchamber and I didn't even hear him say.

He was asked whether the others who came back in with Paolo and Paolo himself were carrying arms of any sort besides the aforesaid. And were these light arquebuses?

HE ANSWERED: At the time of the brawl nobody was carrying a light arquebus. And that light arquebus that the bargello found in the house had been carried in, I don't know by whom. I saw messer Paolo carrying it in his hand around Rome on foot the day before he was captured. And those soldiers were going with him. I only saw him carry it once. *Then he said*: The master was in the shop and he sent me upstairs to the bedroom to fetch the cape and the light arquebus. I brought it down to the shop and I put it on the counter along with the cape. He was about to go out, but at that point along came certain of his friends who kept him in the house for a while. I was upstairs. Then Paolo went out with those friends and soldiers. I think he was carrying the light arquebus, though I didn't see it, except in the evening, when they had come back and it was upstairs on the table.

He was asked whether on that evening on which the brawl happened he was carrying a spear.

HE ANSWERED: I wasn't carrying a spear, but when the master came back, I took the one that he had, because I didn't have any weapon at all when I went out.

And the lord asked what he would say if Agnolo gave deposition to his face that he had a spear the second time Paolo left the house and that, with Paolo and with Agnolo, he had run armed to the brawl.

HE ANSWERED: I didn't carry arms, except what I took from the master.

*Then the lord ordered **Agnolo** to be brought in, about whom see above, and when they had made mutual recognition, Agnolo, to a question of his Lordship, said*: When Paolo came back to the house, and we were eating supper, he made us take up arms. I took a pike and the Frenchman here took another pike and we went with our master as far as the stable.

BASTIANO THE FRENCHMAN ANSWERED: I didn't carry it. How can this be?

AND AGNOLO ANSWERED: Look, you carried it, like me. This doesn't make any difference to us. This has nothing to do with us.

BASTIANO ANSWERED: When messer Paolo and Agnolo ran off with the spears, I took one too and ran after them.

His Lordship asked why he had denied it at first.

HE ANSWERED: I didn't know what 'a spear' meant.

Then the lord dismissed Agnolo and had him put back in his place. At the same time, he sent [Bastiano] back to his place [in jail] with the intention of continuing.

On the same day, 21 November 1559
Arraigned in person before the court in Rome in Tor di Nona before the magnificent lord Romolo di Valenti, lieutenant, and in the presence of me, the notary: **Chierico**, *son of the late Domenico, a Corsican, who swore the oath to tell the truth and touched and was asked by the lord what his profession is.*

HE ANSWERED: My work, it's been some while ago now, was being a butcher. Then, because there was my mother, who lives near the palace where Coltello[44] has his house, and because it seemed to me I could always find a bit of bread in my house, and a glass of wine, but no more, and, as young men do, giving thought to my needs, I began to devote myself to arms. I went with Bindinello Sauli in the galleys. We made two voyages, one to the Levant and one to Barbary.[45] That took about eight months. Finally, arriving in Genoa as happy as could be for all the booty taken on that trip, I learned that here in Rome a little girl – my sister – had died. I took my leave and came to Rome. It was almost three years ago now. I set myself up with Cesare Muti, who had a company of soldiers. So I served him all this past war, in Rome, in Romagna, wherever we were needed. Then, when peace came, I kept myself as best I could, with my mother, and then with an uncle of mine in Civitavecchia who worked the land. Then I came back to Rome and moved in with a friend of mine called Dario, from the Abbey of Farfa, who was a friend of Paolo di Grassi, and he took me one morning to Paolo's house.

We fell to talking the way young men do. After that Paolo brought me I don't know how many times to eat at his house, so that we became friends. About a month before the pope died, I had gone off to be in his [Paolo's] company, and I ate and drank in his house. But he didn't give me so much as a quattrino's worth. In the middle of this, it came to pass, before the pope died, one evening around eight at night, I was arrested by the police on the pretext that I had been carrying a sword and had thrown it into a cellar, and that I had resisted the police. Finally, when no case could be made against me, messer Alfonso Villanuova, in whose house I have lived – You can ask him about me – had me set free, about twelve days after I was arrested and some seven days before the pope died. My poor mother paid six or seven scudi to set me free. I was let out and it was four or five days before I went back to the house of Paolo di Grassi. One day I met him around Rome. He asked me why I had been lying so low. 'It's been so long!' I got back together with him and began to go to his house again. Then the Vacant See came and I stayed there.

He was asked in what ways he served Paolo di Grassi.

HE ANSWERED: I went in his company with sword and dagger. I had no other arms. I accompanied him by day and by night if I happened to be in his house, for I didn't always sleep there. Of the eight nights of the week, I slept three or four in my mother's house.[46] I didn't go with Paolo every night, because he sometimes went to sleep with Camilla the Sienese and I didn't go there. Before Paolo had a fight on his hands, he used to go around Rome alone, but this Vacant See, Vincenzo the Sicilian stayed with him, as did that Cecco who was wounded.

He was asked if he knows the cause of the row or brawl, which had to do with Camilla and Paolo, which arose in the street before the house in which Camilla now lives, by the signori di Santa Fiora.

HE ANSWERED: I don't know anything about that fracas. Once, when I was escorting him, we found the count of Santa Fiora and signor Alessio in Camilla's house.[47] Paolo went in upstairs, and signor Alessio said to him, 'What are you doing, messer Paolo?' Paolo answered, 'I am here to serve Your Lordship. I came to see the signora.'

He was asked whether he knows that Paolo has a friendship with any other courtesan, and with whom.

HE ANSWERED: With Camilla he has had a long friendship. Then, six or seven days before we were arrested, he brought home a Spaniard called Ottavia. And, once, about a month before the pope died, I kept him company when he went to sleep with one who is called Beatrice. I don't know if, this Vacant See, he has slept with Beatrice, but I know that he has talked with her three or four times, down at the door and at a grilled window that is down below. Certainly, we have gone down that street at night. Paolo has had the habit of whistling and, when she heard it, she would come to the window and talk with him. Paolo told me that Beatrice was in love with him and that she had come many times to find him at home. There's no need to knock on the door at night; to talk with her all you need to do is whistle at Beatrice's windows. He has never used violence, so far as I know, and I was there. I call God to witness, who knows everything.

His Lordship asked if he knows the origin of the friendship between the Spanish courtesan and Paolo.

HE ANSWERED: We were going with Paolo, and when we were by Beatrice's house, which is in front of San Luigi, we met this Spanish woman whom Paolo didn't know.[48] I think that it was to spite Beatrice that Paolo went up to her and looked at her hard and said to her, 'Give me a kiss!' And the Spanish woman refused to give it to him. Paolo said it to her again, and the whore said, 'Not here in the middle of the street!' And Paolo said, 'Please, kiss me!' so much that she kissed him. He asked her where she lived, and she said, 'Go to your Camilla and to your Giulia the Neapolitan!' He said to her, 'I don't want either the one or the other any longer.'

Ottavia left and went into the Salvatore. Paolo waited for her, told her where he lived, and asked her if she wanted to come and sleep with him. She answered that she could not, for she had promised a friend of hers, a gentleman from Carpi. Paolo replied that he wanted her to go there [to his house]. Ottavia went off toward her house and Paolo stopped to talk with the parish friar in the piazza of San Luigi. And he said to me, 'Follow her a bit!' So I set to tailing her and behind me came Paolo with Vincenzo and Cecco and on the way I found another friend of his called Giacomo Romano. When they saw me turn toward the Column, they followed me that way, just a little back. So we found the house of the whore, which is before you reach the Column, after Piazza Capranica, just in front of that house where you turn to go to Montecitorio.[49]

When I learned where the house was, I turned back and met messer Paolo in Piazza Capranica. We went there and Paolo knocked and Ottavia's mother came to the window and said that she didn't want to open the door because certain gentlemen were there. He knocked again and Ottavia came to the window and said that she didn't want to open the door for him because there were two gentlemen. Paolo said, 'Open, please!' She replied that she didn't want to open for him because she could not. Paolo said, 'Open, I pray you! I'll go right out again.' Ottavia opened the door and we all went in, except Vincenzo, who waited at the door and then went off to do some errand or other in the Banchi.[50] Later, he came back and found us in the very same place, almost after dinner, toward seven or half past seven in the evening. Ottavia decided to come sleep with Paolo, who had begged her many times to come, but she had kept refusing. When those gentlemen left – the ones we found in her house, who had been paying a call on Ottavia's sister – Paolo said to Ottavia, 'Come, I pray you, come! I want you to come,' and other such words.

At this point, along came a certain captain who was a friend of the man Ottavia was waiting for. Paolo asked who he was. Ottavia said he was a friend of that gentlemen she was expecting. Paolo said to him, 'I pray you, if that gentleman Ottavia is waiting for comes, tell him I've taken her to my house, and, whenever it pleases him to do so, he can let me know and I will send her back home.' When the captain had promised him that he would do so, Paolo brought Ottavia to his house. Afterwards, when we were at Paolo's, that gentleman to whom Ottavia had promised the evening, named messer Costanzo – now I remember! – wrote a note to messer Paolo and sent it by a servant of his, praying Paolo to be so good as to send back Ottavia. Paolo answered the servant, 'Go tell your master that I thought he would have enough courtesy that he would not ask for her this evening. Tell him that I don't want to send her back, not this evening, nor tomorrow, but only when the spirit moves me.' The very same servant came back with the same request and with new pleas, but Paolo got mad and said to him, 'Don't come back here again, or I'll break your head! I don't want to send her back, except when I feel like it. If he wants anything from me, I know why and he knows where we can meet.'

The whore let it be known that she was happy to stay and told me that if messer Paolo wanted to cover her expenses and if she could buy clothes, she would stay with him if he gave her fifteen scudi a month.

He was asked if he took part in the brawl that arose a few nights ago near the stable of Paolo di Grassi. Could he tell it in order, as it happened, from the beginning to the end.

HE ANSWERED: Messer Paolo had eaten supper and so had we others with him, that is Vincenzo, Cecco, Gioanbattista, and I. After supper Paolo wanted to go see the horse. All of us went out with him, and with us came Ottavia. None of us were carrying spears, except for myself, who carried a halberd, and that Gioanbattista had a sword and a buckler. The others wore mail jackets and carried swords and daggers. The horse had arrived and while we were in front of the stable, Gioanbattista the fencer said, 'Here is a fine blow to parry this way.' And they began to fence there. At this point, down the street of Piazza Madama, from towards San Luigi, there came at us – for we saw them coming from that piazza – as it appeared to us, sixteen or twenty men.[51] They came from Piazza Madama. And when they saw and heard the noise we were making among ourselves with our fencing, they came running shouting, 'Who is there? Who is there?' And we answered back, 'Who is there? Who is there? We are friends!' Those coming from Piazza Madama, without any further ado, fired off two arquebus shots, one of which hit that Cecco who was wounded. After firing off the arquebuses, maybe because they thought there were more of us, they fled, for we had turned and gone after them. We followed them as far as the corner of the house of [cardinal] De la Cueva. When they were as far as Piazza Madama, the ones who had fired the arquebuses shouted, 'Governor! Governor!'

At that point, from over toward the governor's,[52] up came running two halberdiers, one of whom I know by sight, though not by name. And they said, 'To us! To us, the governor's men!' And I said to the one I knew, 'Ah! Ah! We belong to messer Paolo! We are neighbours here. Who are these others?' And the halberdier answered me, 'We don't know them.' And the ones who had shot at us fled away, some of them toward Piazza Navona and some toward the Via dei Chiavari, toward messer Pirro Tari.[53] Then we turned back to go back toward the stables, where Ottavia had stayed, to take her back to the house together with the wounded man. But then up came the governor's men, who had risen at the shout, 'Governor! Governor!' raised by those who had fired the arquebus shots.

Then there arrived the caporione himself, that is, messer Gioanbattista Vittorio. He met with messer Paolo and asked him what was the matter. We said that we had been assaulted by the governor's men, because we had heard those who had attacked us shouting, 'Governor! Governor!' And the governor's men answered that they had come out afterwards, like us. 'We are down here on your side!' And the caporione said, 'What's going on here, messer Paolo?' He answered, 'We have been assaulted and assassinated by these men of the governor's. They shouted, "Governor! Governor!" What sort of business is this? Do we have to put up with this? We are in our own house. We are Romans. In Vacant See, we are the masters. The Popolo is the master.[54] If it was the governor's men, it would be best we went to cut them all to pieces and burn them alive in their house. All we Romans have to help one another, and if it was them, burn them.'

And messer Gioanbattista Vittorio answered him, 'No, Paolo, Justice is the master.[55] Let it be understood; if it was the governor's men, the governor will punish them. Let's go back home!' So we went back from Piazza Navona with the caporione. And we went toward the Vicolo [alley] dei Cesarini, and came out toward Giulio Cesarini, and turned and went to the house of the caporione.[56] Then the caporione accompanied us home. There messer Paolo expressed his grief and anger, when he saw that wounded man. He said, 'Ohimè! How we have been assassinated! Us! This has happened to us in our own house! If it was the governor's men, as I believe it was, because we heard them shouting, "Governor! Governor!" then we Romans have to get together and go burn them out!' And he repeated everything he had said to the caporione with much anger.

And the lord asked if any words that tended to the prejudice of the honour of women were uttered by Paolo and what were they?

HE ANSWERED: In truth, I didn't hear anything said about women. *And he was made to say the oath and he touched [the scriptures] and he was asked to tell the truth as to whether Paolo said these words or some like them, that is*: 'They fuck us our wives and they fuck us our sisters.'[57]

HE ANSWERED: I didn't hear that, signore. If I had heard it, I would tell it as I have told the truth about the rest. *And continuing his narration of the facts, he said*: Messer Domenico di Massimi sent Ottaviano Lilio to Paolo's house to talk to him. He offered Paolo, on the part of Domenico, men and help. And, if need be, Domenico would come in person. Messer Paolo answered that he didn't need it and that, if he did, he would let him know. And he repeated once more the same words and threats, 'We Romans have to stick together and set the governor on fire!' And when we were back in the house, Lilio answered, 'First we have to find out who they were, and how many of them there were, and what sort they were.' He left. Messer Paolo undressed and the wounded man was treated. Nothing else happened.

He was asked where the arquebus came from and how it came to be in the hands of Paolo di Grassi on the very evening of the brawl, the one that was handed over to Gioanbattista Vittorio.

HE ANSWERED: After the two arquebus shots were fired and those who had fired them ran away, and more and more people had come running, among the others up came a fellow with a light arquebus. He went toward Paolo and Paolo turned on him and took the light arquebus from him. And he said, 'Ah, messer Paolo, we are here on Your side! Don't You recognize me? I am a kinsman of captain Ettore. Give me back the light arquebus!' And Paolo answered, 'No! I want to hand the light arquebus over to the caporione and he can do with it what he thinks best.' I believe messer Paolo carried that light arquebus when walking in the company of the caporione. Later on, when we were in Paolo's house, after the caporione had accompanied us, Paolo handed it over to him.

He was asked whether Paolo or any of the others he had named had carried the light arquebus through the city, by day or by night. And whose were the light arquebuses found in Paolo's house by the police?

HE ANSWERED: I never saw him carry the light arquebus. The one the police found in the house belonged to messer Orazio di Massimi, who brought it to us a day or two before we were arrested, as I said above. And when Dario showed it to messer Paolo, messer Paolo told him, 'Let's put it aside for a bit.' So he gave it to Paolo. When Dario brought it into the house, he carried it loaded.

Since it was late, the lord stopped the examination and ordered the arraigned person to be put back in his place [in jail] with the intention of continuing. In the presence of signor Alessandro Magno, substitute fiscale, who was here for the greater part of this examination but left for vespers [...].

23 November 1559
Arraigned in person in Rome in Castel Sant'Angelo[58] before the aforesaid magnificent lord Romolo di Valenti and the magnificent lord Sebastiano Atracino, procuratore fiscale, in the presence of me, the notary: messer

Paolo di Grassi, son of Virgilio di Grassi, Roman, and who swore and who was interrogated by his Lordship.

He was asked to tell the story of his capture and to say whether he presumes to know the cause of his present examination.

HE ANSWERED: I have no idea why I should be in prison, unless it is because of the fracas that happened the other evening near the palace of the governor. I had been wronged and I wanted to come talk and lodge a complaint with monsignore [governor]. And I had already talked about it with Cencio Capizucchi, with whom I wanted to come and do it.[59] But as things went on from day to day, I didn't come. Had I come, I would have shown his Lordship that, if anything had been said about me, it must have been the strangest opinion. Because, if I were to tell You the tale, You would have to hear that, the evening of the brawl, a whore named Ottavia was having supper in my house; she had come to my house two or three evenings earlier; I had never seen her before. And after I ate supper, I had an impulse to go out to the stall to see my horse. And the whore told me that she wanted to come too, so I gave her my cape and I went off. Just think that I didn't put on my mail gloves, but went as is my custom with my [mail] jacket and sleeves! And with me there came Chierico, Gioanbattista the fencer, Vincenzo the Sicilian, and Cecco, who got wounded with an arquebus shot, and the stable boy. And while we were in the stable, I said to Gioanbattista, who was carrying a sword and a buckler, 'If I had a sword and a dagger, as I do here, I wouldn't be scared of you.[60] How would you parry this blow?' And so we began to fence and at the noise up came running certain soldiers of the governor – in my estimation, there were ten or twelve, or maybe more – and they came up to where we were, saying, 'Who is there? Who is there?' I went forward and said, 'What business have you here?' And they fired two arquebus shots and then fled. I followed them as far as the corner of San Luigi. I didn't want to go further, thinking there might be more of them. I believed they had done it to do me a great affront and to take away my whore. Still, I turned back to lead the whore back to the house, and I fetched the pike. And I paid no attention to who came with me carrying pikes. And I returned toward the same street and I met with Storto, the *capo di strada* of the caporione of [the rione of] Colonna. When he asked me, I replied, 'We are assassinated in our house!' Just then, I saw people appear, down by the corner of the house of [cardinal] De la Cueva and I shouted, 'Follow me this way! Follow me this way.'[61] And Storto said to me, 'I cannot pass that way.'[62] And we were two or three *canne*[63] below the corner of San Luigi. Then it turned out that the people we had seen at the De la Cueva corner were messer Gioanbattista Vittorio and certain soldiers of the governor.[64] Messer Gioanbattista wanted to know what had happened at the brawl. I told him truly, just as I have told your Lordship. And the caporione said, 'Let's go!' and escorted me home. And because I had taken a light arquebus from one of the governor's people – I will show you who it was if I see him and I'll say to you, 'He's the one I took it from!' – and I was carrying a buckler that I had had all along, since the arquebus shots were fired at us, the caporione said to me, 'I would like you to do me a favour. Hand the light arquebus over to me.' I said to him, 'Here you are, but if its owner asks for it, could you give it to him.'

He was asked if he knows that those men by whom he says he was attacked were and are some of the soldiers deputized to the protection of the most reverend lord governor.

HE ANSWERED: I saw some whom I recognized in that company. I am not talking about the halberdiers. I am talking about the soldiers, and among them was that one who usually carries a two-handed sword. Even if I didn't recognize him, there certainly was a fellow there who was carrying a two-handed sword. The others were soldiers of the governor, though I couldn't say for sure, except that they shouted, 'Governor! Governor!' And if we hadn't heard this shout, we would have gone further forward. And it seems to me, to tell You the truth, that over in the house of a woman who lives near San Luigi was the canon of Palis, a man who loves me like a brother. And, I think, with the canon were those soldiers who often go about in his company. And I am all the more convinced of this because I know that back in the time of the other governor, there were some halberdiers – I don't know who – who escorted the nephew of the governor, who went there to that woman near San Luigi.[65] And I have seen the halberdiers around there. It is true that that night, because it was dark, I did not see them, nor any of the others, nor other soldiers whom I know, but I came to believe that they were the governor's men, because they shouted, 'Governor, Governor!'

He was asked to tell what brawl had happened several nights earlier between himself and some soldiers who guard the lord governor.

HE ANSWERED: I will tell you exactly as it happened. I was going one recent night to sleep with Camilla. I was accompanied by my soldiers, that is, by Cencio, Cecco, and Chierico. And when I was there, by the palace of the governor, certain soldiers confronted me. They were coming from Piazza Madama, but they weren't out of the palace yet, because the door was locked except for the little window up top. They said to me, 'Who goes there?' I answered, 'Who goes there to you?' And so there followed some words on this side and that, so that I was moved to take one of them by the shoulder and lay hand to my dagger, and to say to him, 'I've a mind to teach you to do your duty. It is the caporione's job to ask names in the night.'[66] At this, they unsheathed their swords and so did we, and they shouted, 'Out, soldiers! Out, soldiers!' Then out came the soldiers, and we retreated into the palace of De la Cueva. Then I went up to those soldiers and said, 'I am Paolo di Grassi. If anyone among you wants to get killed by me, come on over!' But someone among them, I don't know who, answered, 'Messer Paolo, we didn't recognize You!' and so we remained at peace. That was all there was to it.

He was asked with what weapons his soldiers were armed, the ones who were with him at the stable when the first brawl happened and when Cecco was wounded?

HE ANSWERED: No one was carrying arms except Chierico, who carried a pointed halberd. It is a miracle that I didn't carry a pike that evening, as was my custom on other evenings.

He was asked to say precisely what words passed between himself and Gioanbattista Vittorio when Gioanbattista was remonstrating with him after the arquebus shots.

HE ANSWERED: I was shouting at Gioanbattista Vittorio, saying that he hadn't wanted to do what I had told him to do, to dispose his patrols in the streets with an order not to let anyone pass in a company of more than two or three. And I told him that we were assassinated in our house and he asked me, 'By whom?' And then I was angry and I didn't want to tell him, but then, going down the street, I said that it was those men of the governor and that we were always letting ourselves be assassinated in our own house. What I meant was that if he had taken steps to assure that people could not go around at night in troops, that evening the disorder would not have happened.

His Lordship asked if he had used other words against the soldiers or against anyone else that evening.

HE ANSWERED: I don't remember that I said anything else.

And the lord asked if he had not said these words or something like them: 'If it is true that it was those men of the governor, we'll have to strike back by word and deed.'[67]

HE ANSWERED: I didn't say these words, and if I'd wanted to do a deed, I could have killed any one of them, for they were falling and fleeing like whores, but I didn't want to. *Adding:* When the caporione came toward me, Chierico came forward and, not recognizing him, hit him with a halberd, having seen that the servant of messer Gioanbattista had hit me twice in the chest with a halberd and I still have the marks of it. And I was angry. I don't remember anything. *Adding to a question of his Lordship:* It is true that Ottaviano Lilio came to my house that very evening to offer himself to me, thinking that I had been attacked, maybe by my enemies, and I told him that nothing was needed, and that it was certain men of the governor who had fired arquebuses at us, but I don't remember saying anything else to him.

Then the lord stopped the examination and ordered the witness to be put back into his place [in jail] with the intention of continuing.

25 November 1559
Arraigned in person before the court in Rome in the palace of the reverend lord governor in the chamber of the magnificent lord Romolo di Valenti, lieutenant, and in presence of me, the notary: **Gioanbattista di Giacobo Grippi**, *Milanese, who swore to tell the truth and touched [the scriptures] and was asked by the lord how long had he had dealings and acquaintanceship with Paolo di Grassi.*

HE ANSWERED: It has been three weeks that I have been keeping company with Paolo di Grassi. For I am skilled at weapon-play and captain Pompeo from Castello[68] passed me the assignment – for Paolo had a fight on his hands – to give him practice in fencing.

He was asked if he was at a certain brawl that came about a few days ago in Piazza San Luigi and near Paolo di Grassi's stables.

HE ANSWERED: I happened to be at supper that night in Paolo di Grassi's house. After supper Paolo said to a whore he had there named Ottavia the Spaniard, 'Let's all go for a bit to see my horse.' We decided to go there, and while we were at the stables, Paolo came out of the stables, having seen his horse, and he put his hand to his sword and began to play with me, for I was carrying my sword and my buckler. And he said to me, 'How would you parry this blow?' and I answered him, 'We've already had so many blows that I am hardly worth fencing with.' So we began to trade I know not how many blows, striking one sword with the other, and although there were only the two of us fencing, we were making a great racket. And while Paolo and I were going at it hand to hand, some people came and began to say, 'Hey there! Don't do it! Back off! Back off!' And Paolo said, 'Who's there?' They answered, 'Friends, friends! We came running to separate you. We came running with good intent. We thought you were fighting.'

At this point, Paolo said, 'What good intent? What good intent?' and began to lay into them with the sword he had in his hand. And they began to fight back, but finally they retreated and someone gave a shout, 'Come out! Come out! Caporione! Caporione!' At the noise, people came running and there were two arquebus shots. Cecco, who was with us, was wounded. And who it was who fired the arquebuses I cannot tell you. But they were fired after those people who had come to separate us had retreated. Meanwhile, the ruckus grew, and up came messer Gioanbattista Vittorio, and the caporione of Colonna, and the caporione of Ponte. And messer Paolo and we others who were with him went with our caporione, that is, with messer Gioanbattista Vittorio, who then escorted messer Paolo home. And when messer Paolo had come back in, I too went upstairs, but I stayed there scarcely at all, because I was going back to the house of Captain Pompeo to sleep.

He was asked if he could tell more clearly what words passed between Paolo di Grassi and those who came running to intervene.

HE ANSWERED: When they came running, they said, 'We are come with good intent, Paolo.' He answered, 'What good intent? What good intent?' and began to lay on with his sword.

He was asked whether, when the fight was going on, Paolo said any other words.

HE ANSWERED: I heard no other words.

He was asked, and sworn under pain of the penalty for perjury with which the lord threatened him, if anything was said about the lord governor and what, and by which party among the brawlers.

HE ANSWERED: I didn't hear anything said about the lord governor, and I didn't hear him named that evening, nor shouted about, nor did I hear anyone say, 'Governor, Governor,' because I, having a pain in my hand – the right one, because of a stab wound I suffered about a month and a half ago from a blunted fencing sword – I couldn't follow messer Paolo too closely and I couldn't hear whether he named the lord governor.

He was asked what Paolo said when he was remonstrating with the caporione.

HE ANSWERED: I couldn't hear because I was a little behind them.

He was asked if he at least heard what Paolo said and threatened when they were back home, and against whom he said it.

HE ANSWERED: I didn't hear anything.

He was asked if he had noticed that Paolo was angry.

HE ANSWERED: How could You think I could know a thing about it?

And the lord said that, by someone's words and his other actions, the witness can understand easily when a person is angry or calm. His Lordship wonders why the witness cannot say by such signs or others like them whether or not messer Paolo was turning livid.

HE ANSWERED: I don't know. I heard very well that he was talking with the caporione, who was scolding him for his going about at night, and Paolo was saying to him, 'I thank you. If you did not love me, you would not be saying such a thing to me.'

He was asked how and from whom Paolo took a light arquebus that he later returned to the caporione.

HE ANSWERED: Messer Paolo took the light arquebus from one of those people who came running toward our place, at the beginning, when they said, 'With good intent.' And it was one of the first ones, who knelt down on the ground, and I saw him, and besides the light arquebus he was carrying a buckler. I don't know whom he belonged to. And he was saying to messer Paolo, 'Spare my life, for the love of God!' and I heard these words. This fellow is a young man, almost just like me. And I've also seen him many times around Rome, and if I find him, I'll bring him here because I know him by sight.

Adding to a question of the lord: I don't believe he is one of the soldiers of the lord governor, or I would have seen him one of the many times I have passed by here.

He was asked if he knows any of those persons who came running up to separate them, and could he say how many of them there were.

HE ANSWERED: I didn't recognize any of them, because they ran away. The one with the small arquebus stayed with us, and so I could make him out, and besides I have seen him around Rome, but not in the house of anyone in particular. By my judgment, there could have been seven, or eight, if there were so many. And if I told you exactly, I would be telling you a lie.

At this point, the lord stopped the interrogation and dismissed the witness.

Thursday, 25 April 1560[69]
There was examined in Rome in the chamber of the magnificent lord Michelangelo Forolongo, lieutenant in criminal matters of the most reverend lord governor, by me, the notary: messer **Niccolo Giardino**, *a Frenchman from Rouen, a servant of the magnificent lord Sebastiano di Gradi of Genoa, a witness for the information of the court, who swore and touched [the scriptures] and answered the questions of me, the notary, as follows.*

Yesterday evening around eleven at night I was going to the house of signora Camilla, and I was at the door of the signora, about to go in. There passed before that door messer Paolo di Grassi, a Roman, with three companions, all of them with swords and daggers. I saw them and recognized them. There was messer Paolo, because I know who he is, and I've known him a fair while. As for the companions, I don't know who they are, except by sight. I can tell you I saw them because I had a lit torch in my hand. When the door was opened to me, I went up. I found three Spaniards up where signora Camilla was. The signora said they were singers from the house of cardinal Pacheco. I didn't know them. And there was a signora Laura, a courtesan, who lives across from that house. I was there for the space of an 'Our Father' and we heard a knocking at signora Camilla's door. Without anyone of the house's having answered, or opened it, in no time up came messer Paolo and his companions. Messer Paolo had opened the door with his dagger, for he is used to being in the house, as I have heard from signora Camilla. When they came in, they found in the doorway a young lad of the signora's called Cicco who had gone to close the door. Because he began to complain that they had come in without the door's having been opened, messer Paolo gave him a slap in the cheek.[70] And, when, as I said, they came upstairs, messer Paolo began to berate and to threaten signora Camilla, saying, 'Whore! slut! You talk to the cops and don't want to see gentlemen. I'll cut your face. And I'll give you a spanking.' All the while, he kept his hand on his dagger.

The signora answered that she didn't care what he did. He should go about his affairs and leave her in peace, and other mild words. Then messer Paolo raised his hand to hit her. Because I was right there, I took him by the arm so he wouldn't strike. He turned toward me to hit me, but I pulled back. Nothing else happened and all four of them left.

He was asked why the witness believes Paolo made this assault and insult to Camilla.

HE ANSWERED: I heard from signora Camilla that Paolo did this above all because he was angry at her. *Then he said*: It was one of the companions of messer Paolo who said to the signora while Paolo was yelling at her, 'If I get hold of you, I'll throw you out the window.'

He was asked about the name and the description of that companion of messer Paolo.

HE ANSWERED: I don't know any of them except by sight. If I saw him, I would know him.

He was asked about the circumstances and the life of Paolo, and if it was his habit to do bad things like that with other courtesans.

HE ANSWERED: I have been told that this is the third time he has given signora Camilla a dressing down, as you will hear from her women. I can't tell you about his good or bad behaviour because I don't know much about him.

[He was sworn to] silence.

*Then there was examined in the same place by me, the same notary: **Gioanna**, the daughter of the late maestro Antonio, a Paduan woman, servant of signora Camilla, who swore and touched [the scriptures] and said as follows.*

She was asked for what reason she had come to the present examination.

SHE ANSWERED: Because, yesterday evening, around nine at night,

I was in the courtyard of the house of signora Camilla the Sienese to wash some clothes. When I heard a knock on the door, I went to the window of the kitchen to see who was there. Then I saw messer Scipione di Mazatosto, a Roman, who had opened the locked door with his dagger. I went downstairs and when I was at the door, I begged messer Scipione not to go upstairs because the signora was busy and she had company. And he said 'Be quiet! Be quiet!' and began to whistle, and then Paolo di Grassi came into the house with some other men. I asked them please not to go upstairs. They answered, 'Be quiet! Be quiet!' And they started to go up. On the way, they ran into the servant of the signora called Cicco. When he complained that they had come in without the door's having been opened for them, Paolo gave him a slap on the cheek and they went up. I stayed down below. After a bit, they came down. When they were at the door to go outside, messer Paolo stopped because he wanted to go back up, saying he wanted to go back up to give ten cudgel blows to the signora, but one of the companions – I do not know his name, but he had on a pair of yellow hose – opposed him and would not let him go back. So they left.

She was asked what she had heard Paolo had done against signora Camilla upstairs.

SHE ANSWERED: I heard from those who were upstairs that messer Paolo threatened and shouted at signora Camilla a lot but that he didn't do her any harm.

[She was sworn to] silence.

Then, in the same chamber, there was arraigned before the court the aforesaid: signora **Camilla the Sienese**, *a courtesan, before me and she swore and touched [the scriptures] and said as follows.*

[The day before] yesterday, around nine at night, he [Paolo] was riding by the door of my house. Because he saw three cops come out of my house – they were there on an affair of mine – he began shouting at me (I was at the window). 'Hey, you cowardly slut, you keep cops in the house and hold audience for them and, as for gentlemen, you don't want to see them.' I answered him, 'Maybe, for the reason that they came to my house, now they might come for you, too!' At that, he left.

Then, yesterday morning, Paolo came by with Orazio da Camerino.

He knocked on the door and, when my servant came, he said, 'Look! There's no company here to sleep with the signora!' Then, in the evening – that was yesterday evening around nine in the evening – I was tired after supper and was listening to the singing of three Spaniards from the house of cardinal Pacheco, without the least expecting it, I saw coming into the room Orazio da Camerino and, after him, Paolo di Grassi, Scipione Mazatosto, and Mutio Moscha. And when they were in the room, Paolo came up, laid a hand on my belt, and began to say 'cheap slut' and other such insults, 'I want to give you a thrashing and I want to cut up your mug!' But I answered him, 'All of you be my witnesses that these men come yelling at me in my house.' Then Orazio da Camerino said, 'You cheap woman, if I lay hands on you, I'll throw you out the window!'

At this point, Scipione stepped in with soothing words and cooled the others off and they left. I really believe that if it hadn't been for my good luck that I had the company of those Spaniards and of a servant of messer Sebastiano di Gradi, my friend, and of a neighbour called Laura the Roman and my mother, they would have hit me, if not done me worse harm.

And to a question of me the notary she said: I was told that my door was locked and that they opened it with their daggers. This Orazio is in the habit of opening the door that way. And besides I have heard that after they were at the door to go out, if it weren't for his companions, Paolo wanted to turn back, saying he wanted to cut my face. *Then she added*: When Paolo began to yell at me in the room, I said to him, 'Watch out, Paolo! It's not Vacant See any longer!' And he was swearing, 'By the blood of the Madonna, I'll make Vacant See come myself!' *Then she added*: Many times Paolo has pestered me and, among other things, shortly after the death of the pope, when it was Vacant See, several times he beat me, hitting me in the face with his mailed gloves.[71] But these things I forgave him. All I want is that he leave me in peace.

[She is sworn to] silence.

30 April 1560
There was examined in my office by me, the notary: **Sebastiano di Gradi**,[72] *a witness, who swore and touched [the scriptures] and answered as follows to the relevant questions of the notary.*

Last night I slept with Camilla the Sienese and toward dawn I heard a noise at the windows of the house. And going to the window, I saw that one of Camilla's shutters had been taken off, on the outside of the ground floor, and I saw six or eight men who ran off, some one way, some another.

He was asked if he knew any of those who were running away.

HE ANSWERED: No, because when I opened the window they all ran away.

And to a question of me: the notary, he said: One Agnola who lives in the house next door to Camilla's said that she knows that the one who tore down the shutter was Paolo di Grassi, and that he had a pike with a broad blade; she recognized this Paolo very well and the others who were with him. *Adding on his own*: It can't have been anyone but Paolo because he has said at Camilla's door that she offers a screw to nobody but tavern-keepers and cops and last night he stuck on this note. *Showing a note that went like this*:

Camilla the Sienese the thin
Has a dive for cops, for pub-keepers,
For louts to sleep in.[73]

And this was attached to the door. *Adding on his own*: Last night they broke the shutters at the house of Giulia the Neapolitan and of Hortensietta the Roman who lives in the Ortaccio.[74]

Then he was dismissed with an oath to silence.

1 May, 1560
There was examined in the office of me, the notary: madonna **Hortensia Falcona**,[75] *a Roman, a courtesan living in the place called the Ortaccio, a witness for the court brought under summons for the information of the court, who [...] and touched [the scriptures] and said as follows.*

She was asked for what reason she had been summoned to come inform the court.

SHE ANSWERED: I have no idea of the reason unless that it was because I went in a coach, for which Monsignor Governor gave me a scolding.[76]

She was asked if she was in a wagon or a coach. And how many times and with whom, after the ban of the most reverend governor came out?

SHE ANSWERED: I certainly do not know that there is a ban by this governor that one cannot go in coaches. But if I did go, I had permission from the past governor.

And I, the notary, replied that she should answer the question.

SHE ANSWERED: In the past eight days I went two or three times. And [once] I really was forced to go. The other time was the other evening, when I went with cardinal Del Monte[77] and with another friend of mine called Fausto Ventura, the Sienese.

She was asked if she has any quarrel and enmity with anyone. And who is it, and for what the reason?

SHE ANSWERED: I have no enmity or quarrel at all.

She was asked if she has suffered any annoyance or insult in the past month. And from whom, and for what reason?

SHE ANSWERED: I have not suffered injury from anyone, so far as I can remember, except that last Thursday, in the night, my door was burned. The following Saturday, it was fouled. I mean smeared with shit, if Your Reverence would forgive me. And the following Monday my shutters were ripped off and dropped on the ground. I expect that tonight some other harm will be done to me, because they do it one night and not the next.

She was asked from what person or persons she suffered this harassment.

SHE ANSWERED: I don't know, for I do not have a quarrel with anyone. *And to a question of me, the notary, she said*: I put the blame on Paolo di Grassi and Orazio da Camerino, his companion, because it's their habit to perform such courtesies. And I believe all the more that they're the ones, because Monday night, in just the same way, the shutters of Camilla the Sienese and of Giulia the Neapolitan were pulled down to the ground. Because Paolo and Orazio used to be friends with them [too]. *To another question of me, the notary, she said*: I think it was Paolo and Orazio who did this to me, because they sent word [?] that they wanted to carry me off and they wanted to whip me with stirrup thongs,[78] because I did not want their friendship. And the same night that the door was burned, Orazio slept with me. And because Paolo knew about it, I believe it was with his assent that he [Orazio] did this thing [the burning] to me. But, indeed, I do not know it for sure and I would not want to blame a person who didn't do it.

She was asked if she had any other harm or annoyance from Paolo and Orazio besides the one she just told about.

SHE ANSWERED: Nothing. So far as I know, I have not suffered any other injury, and I do not know for sure that the one I mentioned came from them, except that [...] I can imagine that it was for the reasons that I told You.

She was asked if she had heard that Paolo had been annoying any other courtesan. And whom?

SHE ANSWERED: I don't know anything.

[She was sworn to] silence with an oath.

THE COMMENTARY

These two trials are now stitched together in a larger codex. More than old binding string joins them, for, although they record separate judicial proceedings, they share at once a cast of characters and a recurrent theme: the struggle for honour. Their two most central figures are the chief defendants. One is Paolo di Grassi, who counts himself a Roman and, emphatically, a gentleman, though, with his shop and storehouse, he runs a business. Unmarried but hardly unattached, he is surrounded by dependents, friends, and allies of both sexes. Paolo is boisterous, aggressive, outspoken, vituperative, and sometimes cruel; in all these traits he can stand for many men of his age and station. The second major figure is Camilla the Skinny, a courtesan. She first appears as Paolo's friend and sexual partner and, later, having broken with him, as the butt of his anger. Unlike Paolo, she is not Roman, but Sienese, and, unlike him, she may have married, though her husband has died or vanished. Still, like Paolo, she has many friends and allies in the city. And like him too, she is boisterous, aggressive, outspoken, and vituperative, although perhaps less often cruel. In all this, she too may stand for many women of her status and profession. Like Paolo, Camilla cares for honour; like him she is swift and rough in its defence. Camilla's reputation is the weaker of the two, for the prostitute's perch is far more slippery. Yet, both need the steady nerves, gall, and nimble improvisation that suit the daily politics of Roman honour.

Most of the minor characters in these stories belong to the entourage of the gentleman or the courtesan. There are friends, allies, clients, servants, guests, lovers, some of whom, such as the erstwhile butcher, Chierico, speak here with lively voices of their own. In the second trial, there is yet one other central player, the government itself, which locks horns with Paolo both in the court and in the midnight streets in a struggle to assert its authority despite the Vacant See. In the affair of the fray at Paolo's stable, the prestige and the power of the Papal State vie with the honour and the liberties of a Roman gentleman.

Five distinct stories thread their way through these two trials. Paolo is central to four of them and Camilla to three. The first of the five relates the brawl between Camilla and another courtesan, Pasqua the Paduan. Camilla tells it with flair and humour. On a Saturday in mid-May, she and her colleague, Paola da Forlì, seek out a gentleman friend and find him behind a bed with Pasqua. At the smell of the musk in the band around the man's hat, Camilla cries out, 'What stinks? What stinks?' Insulted, the other courtesan rises in fury and rushes at Camilla, hurling epithets and a candlestick. In the ensuing scuffle to keep the women apart, a male friend of Camilla's scratches Pasqua's face with a spur. At the end, the host dismisses Camilla, disappointed that the women have not grappled and pulled each other's hair. The story is saucy enough to have made the rounds as gossip. The court can thus extract three more versions of it, one from Camilla's friend, Paola da Forlì, another from a guest of Camilla's, and a third from a henchman of Paolo's. Seeing no crime in this fray, the court does not push for the truth about it. Thus, since all four accounts come through Camilla or her friends, one cannot say how Pasqua would have told the tale. That is too bad, for, as the court knows, the fight may have served as a cause for war between Pasqua and Camilla. The next story will concern Camilla's suspected retaliation. Yet the Sienese courtesan, who wants to deny any such deed, may wish to play down any affront she suffered. Thus, in her account, while she remains placatory and unruffled, it is Pasqua who suffers the first, unintended insult, who rages, and then comes out of the tussle shamed by a disfiguring scratch to the face.

Then, two nights later, on Monday evening, someone sets fire to Pasqua's door. A ritual insult, such an attack, scars honour as well as property. The court next morning arrests Camilla and three men of Paolo di Grassi. One of these, Gabriele, is a servant. Two others, Chierico and the Abbot, are soldiers in Paolo's entourage. They have been with their master at Camilla's until almost ten at night and then gone off homewards. The court suspects that Paolo's men have made a detour and, at their master's behest, have avenged his courtesan's honour by scorching Pasqua's door. Other clues point at Camilla's instigation. For one, the police have found a pot of pitch and turpentine in her cellar. For another, undisclosed informants have tattled on her, saying that in her own house she has made boastful threats against Pasqua. The court pursues two main lines of questioning: first, how did Paolo's men go home, whom did they see, how long did they take; and second, has anyone heard Camilla utter threats? In both inquiries, the magistrates find their witnesses less than frank. While no one betrays the courtesan's words, the bumbling inconsistencies of Paolo's men, who, for instance, cannot tell if they have seen Florentines or Venetians, suggest the presence of a guilty secret.

A circuitous homeward route may also implicate the men. There is guesswork here, for it is not altogether sure where Camilla lodges; the courtesan's dwelling place appears only in the second trial, from the fall of 1559. Then she lives by the Santa Fiora palace, near Santa Lucia della Chiavica, a church in the street of the Banchi, well west and a bit south of Paolo's dwellings at the Dogana. From Santa Lucia, Pasqua's lodgings at Monte Giordano are an easy walk of three blocks northwards. The homeward route the henchmen describe is consistent with such a raid. They have made a detour, for it is very clear from landmarks that they have descended on Paolo's house from the north, rather than come up, as they might more readily have done, from the south. Old maps of the city suggest that, having walked north to set their fire, they have crossed homewards along the long, straight Via dei Coronari, cutting southwards to Paolo's house only after passing cardinal Pacheco's house, north of Piazza Navona. The court has good reason to suspect them.

This fire, if Camilla's, is not her first. Two years earlier, she has almost certainly instigated a similar attack against the house of another courtesan, Lucrezia the Greek. Both times, she has attacked an enemy indirectly, targeting her house as a surrogate for her person. Though other Romans, both men and, more rarely, women, sometimes use such tactics, prostitutes are very often the butt or instigator. With both these fires, Camilla has waged war, in male style, in a contest turning on the honour of two rival prostitutes.

This courtesan's honour is as ambiguous as her social place. While respectable women derive honour from the chastity guarded by the men with whom they shelter, the prostitute, by contrast, having foresworn both chastity and its wardens, is by definition a creature tarred with shame. By her nature, she thus pollutes. But, liberated by that very shame from some of the female modesty and self-abasement enjoined by honour, a woman like Camilla enjoys the luxury of a kind of shamelessness that allows her both forward ribaldry and a pugnacity audible in her tongue, visible in her fights with rivals, and palpable to sight and smell and touch in her scorching of their doors. Camilla and her peers need the franchise to behave like men, for the insecurity of a life without a steady male protector requires a resourceful combativeness akin to Paolo's.

Between the first events, in May 1559, and the next two tales, which take place in November, pope Paul IV dies. The demise of a pope always turns the life of Rome on its head. *Sedevacante*, Vacant See, when the pope's empty throne awaits a successor, cancels most of the operations of the Papal State. A monarchy without a dynasty, the State of the Church, since it lacks an heir apparent, lapses during an interregnum into a kind of suspended animation. The old institutions of the commune of Rome step in to fill the vacuum, reasserting ancient liberties otherwise lost a century before. Vacant See thus offers sixteenth-century Romans a nostalgic holiday from autocracy. Some of the liberties they celebrate are collective and communal, others personal. Thus, for instance, in an affirmation of both communal and individual freedom, the jails are opened. Then the prisoners ceremoniously parade the rope of torture through the streets and make their former jailors ransom it back. Like many public celebrations in pre-modern Europe, Vacant See is a festival of inversion and misrule, a reprieve from the normal order and constraint. Like other such events, it is often rude and dangerous. Vacant See is always a time for the settlement of old accounts and for new brawls, assaults, insults, and abductions. But the Vacant See of Paul IV stands out as do few others for the violence that attends it, for seldom has a pope been so loathed by his subjects as is this meddlesome and puritanical autocrat who has harassed them with his beloved Inquisition. The great riots that celebrate his demise on 18 August set the tone for the ensuing four popeless months.

Although Vacant See sets the lawless stage for the third tale, it does not much shape the action. The story recounts peremptory, devious seduction of another man's courtesan. Our sole source is Chierico, the Corsican ex-butcher, now a soldier, who has attached himself to Paolo di Grassi and who recently has taken to sleeping in his house the better to protect him from some quarrel and from Vacant See. Paolo, it turns out, is a man of many women, all of them courtesans. He sleeps most often with Camilla, but he flirts with others, among them one Beatrice, who is in love with him and who comes to the window when he whistles for her. One day he espies a Spanish woman, Ottavia, in the street outside the house of Beatrice and, to spite Beatrice, successfully begs a kiss from the Spaniard. When she leaves, Paolo has his men trail the new woman home and then stands at her door wheedling entry. Once inside, he convinces Ottavia to break her commitment to await another gentleman and come home with him instead. He promises a friend of the jilted guest that he, Paolo, if asked, will send Ottavia back at once. Nevertheless, once safely home with the girl, Paolo breaks his word and twice rebuffs a servant sent for her, first with cavalier preachments on courtesy and then with the threat of a beating to the messenger and a challenge to his master. When Paolo says, 'If he wants anything from me, I know why and he knows where we can meet,' he is daring the man to fight him for the girl.

Sometimes, the more historians can see, the clearer are the limits to their understanding. Here is rich detail that raises hard questions about the witness, Ottavia, and Paolo himself. Chierico's narration itself is problematic. For, as in his testimony in May, the man is a client who seems careless of his patron's good. When, in November, he tells about Ottavia, Chierico is in jail for taking part with Paolo in the brawls of our fourth story. Although sometimes reticent, his testimony is far less assiduous than most to protect di Grassi. Thus, here, in answer to a simple question about how Paolo knew Ottavia, he offers the court a long account that paints his patron as rude, spiteful, and faithless. Chierico may just have a wagging tongue that delights in telling of his patron's clever coup. Perhaps, also, he hopes to give good grounds for Paolo's edginess at the nocturnal fights soon to follow. Certainly, the two incidents seem connected; having stolen the girl from her gentleman, Paolo, fearing reprisals, has taken lessons from a fencing master and drawn his soldiers tighter around him. There are questions about Ottavia, too. What sways her to come with Paolo? Is it the prospect of steady money and a steady partner that induces her to leave a household of her own, which she governs in concert with her sister and her mother? As one man's woman, she will have fewer clients and thus, perhaps, fewer allies in the city. Though in Paolo's house she is still a prostitute, not his concubine, for the relationship is temporary and she earns a monthly fee. Her status in the new household evokes ambivalence. To the servants she is their master's 'signora,' while to Paolo and his associates she is just his 'whore.' Paolo himself also offers puzzles. His faithless promise to Ottavia's gentleman could be calculated or impulsive; it is his way to remake his rules as he goes along. If Paolo is in fact inconsistent because headstrong, does he in this whim of iron represent the culture of men of his sort?

Paolo is again pivotal to the fourth story, where Vacant See is central. About a week after he brought Ottavia home, Paolo, on another impulse, leads his men from the supper table out to the stable to see the horse. Taking Ottavia with them, they sally forth bearing a fair arsenal – one pike plus swords, daggers, mailed sleeves, and shirts all around – for Vacant See is dangerous. At the stable, Paolo suddenly challenges Gioanbattista, his Milanese fencing master, to a bit of skirmishing. At the clangor of sword on sword, a crowd of armed men comes running to break up the fight. There is a muddled fray in the deep pre-modern dark, in the midst of which two shots ring out, one hitting Cecco, Paolo's man. Still, Paolo and his remaining bravos rout the others and chase them up the street. Many details of this fracas are obscure, because the unconcerted testimonies vary so. To believe Paolo and his men, they are the victims of aggression by perpetrators who, perhaps deceitfully, invoke the name of the governor, whose palace is nearby. Gioanbattista the fencer, who is neither in jail nor a client of Paolo's, tells a sharply different tale. According to him, it was Paolo who dealt the first blow to men who came in the belief that they were making peace. Rather than firing a hasty shot in the dark, those who came running first skirmished hand to hand. Nor, according to Gioanbattista, did any of the first combatants, in the clash by the stable, call out the name of the governor. His testimony elaborates and subverts Paolo's coyly skimpy version of the event.

There is also contradictory testimony about the next stage of the fight. Once the first band has fled, other men come rushing up, these too shouting, 'Governor! Governor!' This cry is politically important, for, normally, the governor's police are supposed to suspend operations during Vacant See, ceding their authority to officials of the rioni, who belong not to the pope, but to the commune. At the same moment as this cry, there arrive three communal officials, Gioanbattista Vittorio, the caporione of Paolo's own district of

Sant'Eustachio, and his colleagues from two neighbouring districts. It is not easy to quell the brawl. Paolo seems to have forced one of the second party to his knees and to have seized his gun. Even the caporione suffers a jab to the chest from Chierico's halberd. Eventually, blows cede to words, but they too are violent, for Paolo is beside himself with fury. He rages at the governor, shouting, 'What sort of business is this? ... We are in our own house. We are Romans! In Vacant See, we are the masters. The Popolo is the master [*Il Popolo è il padrone*]. If it was the governor's men, it would be best we went to cut them all to pieces and burn them alive in their house.' Paolo's call for an attack by all Romans on the governor's palace is truly incendiary in a city that has recently seen riots and burnings. Paolo, of course, is angry because one of his men is wounded and because he feels assaulted in his own 'house,' a seat of his honour. But his ire is not only on behalf of his own person; he claims to champion the collective honour of his class. Paolo, in his rage, voices the political beliefs of the old Roman families. They see in Vacant See the shadows of their cherished communal liberties, which had once guaranteed self-rule to the *Popolo Romano*, that is, to the 'people' as a sovereign collectivity. The caporione is thus a potential ally, a municipal official assigned to watch the streets, to keep the peace, and to supplant the pope's authority at a time when, properly, the governor should shut down his court and keep his police locked up in his palace. But the caporione fails to take up Paolo's cause. His answer, '*No, Paolo, il padrone è la Giustizia!*' rebuts his call head-on. It is not the People that is master, even in Vacant See, but 'Justice.'

There are two possible readings to the caporione's rejoinder, one abstract and lofty, and the other concrete and pragmatic. He may mean that 'justice' rules, rather than Paolo's wrath. But, much more likely, he means that the forces of the state, as embodied in its police and its magistrates, are the true and proper masters of the city, even in Vacant See. Certainly, Italians then called the forces of order, collectively, '*la giustizia.*' That second reading gives the second trial a clear context, for the governor's police and court have not ceased to function. We are still 'in the absence of a shepherd of the apostolic see,' as the introductory lines to the second trial take note; there is still no new pope on 21 November, when Paolo's henchmen appear in Tor di Nona prison to explain themselves, nor on 23 November, when Paolo has to answer for himself, even more ominously, in the pope's prison fortress of Castel Sant'Angelo. Paolo's defence takes two tactics, first to deny any compromising words and actions and, second, to drop the name of a Roman of weight and reputation, Cencio Capizucchi, as if he were an ally. The prisoners know that the state is far less interested in Paolo's deeds than in his scornful words, which fly in the face of its dogged attempts to assert its honour and authority, even in the midst of Vacant See. Paolo and the others have reason to fear the state, for they are in its hands, and thus have good cause to hide his inflammatory speech. Even Gioanbattista the fencer, who is neither Paolo's client nor a prisoner, sees fit to have heard nothing at all. Typically, and somewhat puzzlingly, it is again Chierico who tells too much for Paolo's comfort.

Paolo escapes punishment. The log book of the prison, a separate register, records a formal promise, guaranteed by Cencio Capizucchi and by Alessandro Colonna, another Roman notable, that Paolo, 'as is proper in a man of honour,' will for the rest of Vacant See behave 'peacefully and modestly, both by day and by night, according to the custom of the other Roman gentlemen, and would not even take actions on the behalf of the forces of the law.'[79] As often, a trial here ends in an extrajudicial settlement. Legal proceedings, indeed, are designed to encourage just such solutions. Unpunished, Paolo is yet neutralized, at least for the moment.

Nevertheless, it is hard to keep a bad man down. The fifth tale, which dates from April of the next year, finds Paolo again making war, this time on Camilla. Since 26 December, there has been a new pope and a new regime; the noble sponsors' November pledge is stale and void. Thus the quarrel with Camilla is some months old, for as long ago as Vacant See, she says, he had beaten her, hitting her face with a mailed glove. At some point, enmity has usurped their friendship. Paolo, clearly, has been a pest to Camilla. On 23 April, she calls the police into her house. Paolo, seeing them leaving, shouts out, 'Hey, you cowardly slut, you keep cops in the house and hold audience for them and, as for gentlemen, you don't want to see them.' Camilla replies that, maybe, in the same affair, he will soon see the police at his house, too. Paolo thus acts as if, in having the reviled police in her house in place of him, Camilla has affronted his honour. The next morning, he throws open her door to shout insulting questions about who is sleeping with her. The same evening he returns with a body of his bravos. They force the lock with a dagger, rush up the stairs, slap the serving boy on the cheek, and, before her guests, lay hands on Camilla and threaten to shame her with cuts to the face and a spanking. One of them volunteers to heave her out the window. For all this bluster, no blows fall. Paolo storms off, only to return five days later. Then, in the middle of the night, he and his men rip down a shutter and afix to the door a defamatory note accusing Camilla of keeping a rooming house for cops, pub-keepers, and louts. That same night, probably by coincidence, someone tears down the shutters of two other prostitutes, one of them Giulia the Neapolitan, who has also been a friend of Paolo's.

Although this whole last incident is on file because it tells the court yet more about Paolo's habit of committing what the law called 'excesses,' it interests us as well for the questions it raises about more general patterns of violent behaviour. For Renaissance acts of scorn very often take ritual forms. Whether intended or instinctive, such gestures invite a symbolic interpretation that lays out at once the actors' strategies and the habits of their culture. In this last tale recur, as throughout these trials, the themes of faces and houses. Both are seats of honour and both, therefore, come under attack in vengeful exchanges where honour is concerned.

Let us look first at the visages. When first arrested in the matter of Pasqua's burnt door, Camilla claims that she would have peeled the beard from any man, or laid waste the face of any woman, who would have said she would come to jail. These are drastic actions one can swear by. Notice how Pasqua is scratched in the cheek, how Paolo di Grassi gives a cheek-slap [*sguanciata*] to the servant boy as he storms up Camilla's stairs, how in Vacant See he has hit Camilla in the face. According to Niccolo Giardino, when Paolo came upstairs, he said to Camilla, 'Whore! Slut! You talk to the cops and you don't want to see gentlemen. I'll cut your face. And I'll give you a spanking!' Here is a speech that performs a double inversion. It starts down low, abasing Camilla by reviling her as a low prostitute. It then asserts that she sees lowly *sbirri*, not elevated gentlemen like Paolo; thus, rhetorically, the speech scales the social ladder. Paolo's tirade then turns to the hierarchic body, taking Camilla by the top, the face, and threatening to mutilate and degrade her there. He then up-ends Camilla, swooping down to her shameful anti-face, her bottom, and threatening to spank it. If Paolo said such words as these, he must have blurted them in a rage. Their spatial logic, therefore, is not so much his as that of the culture that dictated the forms of impulsive action and the structures of memory and of storytelling.

The same kind of symbolic reading holds good for houses. Just as honour resides in faces, so too it dwells in the facades of houses, and in their interiors. Both faces and facades could well be besmirched and mutilated in rituals of scorn. Note how often doors and windows, and their shutters, appear in these five stories. Windows are everywhere: Camilla gossips through one; Beatrice comes to hers when Paolo whistles; Paolo courts Ottavia through hers and spites Beatrice by kissing another woman under hers. And on the very night Paolo attacks Camilla's shutter, the same fate befalls two other houses. Like windows, doors are often the objects of assault. Camilla's, Lucrezia's, and Pasqua's all are burned. Paolo attacks Camilla's, sullying it with a nasty note and making his men break through it by picking the lock with their daggers. Indeed, much of the final drama between Paolo and Camilla turns on the subject of her door, which she wants to close to him and to open to others: the police, her guests, her lovers. Could one go so far as to say that, metaphorically, Camilla's door and her vagina were symbols easily interchanged? Certainly, Paolo, who acts the jilted lover, twice forces his way in. But the symbolic meaning of houses is not always sexual. Notice how, to Paolo, the street before his stable is 'his house.' Attacked there, he threatens to pay back the affront by attacking the governor. Where? In his house, of course.

Though, in all these contests, honour is at stake, it is better not to isolate and concretize this measure of prestige. Paolo's honour and Camilla's are not only ends in themselves, but also means to power, advantage, and security. Thus, the uncertainty that both suffer must render concern for honour even more acute. Paolo's bachelorhood and his position somewhere on the lower edge of the elite of Roman families that constitute the true *popolo* may both have given grounds for vigilance. Camilla as a prostitute was far more at risk than he. For both of them, aspirations and fears combine to politicize daily life.

The register of sentences of the governor's court offers a postscript that proves that Paolo would remain true to type, for, on 29 June 1560, he and two companions, with a 'little prostitute' in tow, picked a quarrel in the street with a *scalco*, a serving man, of two cousins of cardinal Gaddi. The gentlemen and the *scalco*, though unarmed, tried 'with placid words' to calm things down 'as upright men should do.' Paolo's fuse was as short as ever. 'But, without an answer, [the defendents] drew their swords and rushed upon them, with the wish and the deliberate intention of killing them. They pursued messer Cosimo and messer Pietro, wounding them in the arm and the shoulder blade, respectively. Messer Bartolomeo fell to the ground in flight. They hit him with diverse lethal blows in various parts of his body and left him all but dead.'[80] This time, no noble sponsors extricated Paolo; the court condemned the aggressors to confiscation of all their goods.

CHAPTER THREE

Ottavia and Her Music Teacher

THE TRIAL

[In late January 1559, the music teacher, Bernardino Pedroso, helps his adolescent pupil, Ottavia, to escape from Rome dressed as a man. The pair head for the Neapolitan frontier but are arrested south of Rome. Brought back to the city, the two are confined in the bargello's house, where, on 24 and 25 January, Ottavia testifies. On 7 February, two other witnesses report an incriminating conversation with Bernardino. Moved to the Corte Savelli jail, Bernardino in early March undergoes torture. The court treats the incident as a case of abduction, aggravated by carnal knowledge.]

24 January 1559
Arraigned before the court in the house of captain Ventura, bargello of Rome,[1] *before the magnificent lord Francesco Salamonio, auditore of the Rota:* **Ottavia,** *daughter of Camilla Rosignoli and of the late Constantino di Rosignoli, who swore and said as follows.*

She was asked if she knows or presumes to know the reason for her present examination.

SHE ANSWERED: I think it is on account of this thing that I did.

She was asked what it was she had done. Let her tell the whole matter from beginning to end and say why she thinks she is being examined. And she was warned to refrain from lying.

SHE ANSWERED: For the past two years there visited in our house a man named Bernardino Pedroso, a Spaniard. For a cousin of mine had married a Spaniard named Martino Garzia. When this cousin of mine became affianced to Martino, the other young man came to play the clavicembalo.[2] One Sunday, after the mid-day meal, I went to see my cousin and found this Bernardino playing. Then Bernardino came to my house with that cousin's husband, Martino, my cousin-in-law, and promised my mother to teach me to play the clavicembolo. All Bernardino had to do was to come sometimes to the house with Martino, my brother-in-law. He began to teach me. But I don't remember when it first was that he began to teach me, or whether it was in my cousin's house or in mine. So Bernardino taught me how to play, with my mother's permission, and he kept teaching me for almost a year.

And I said to him, 'Signor Pedroso, please do me a favour and find a way of sending me away, of sending me out of here.' I began to say this to him a whole year ago. And he promised to do it. He loved me and I loved him, because I had fallen in love with him because of the playing, and he promised to carry me away but never got around to doing it. And he touched my hand, and once he kissed me while he was with me in the house. And so, finally, last Saturday we agreed to settle the matter. He said he had hesitated to carry me off, because, he said, 'My people will call me a traitor.'[3]

Finally, we decided that on Saturday evening I would go find him in his house and that I should go there at half past seven in the evening. So, at half past seven, when my mother was by the fire with two of my sisters, I made a show of going up to my room. I stayed there a little while, and then I came down and slowly, slowly I opened the door and went outside.

She was warned again and again to tell the truth and to avoid lies.

SHE ANSWERED: Signore, I want to tell the truth, forgive me! The arrangement that Bernardino and I had was this: that on Saturday evening at half past seven, he would come to our house and wait there, out front, that I would come out of the house and then we would go away. For, on Friday morning, Bernardino said to me, 'Well, I believe we will go away tomorrow evening!' And again on Saturday morning he told me that on Saturday evening at that hour he would come for me. So Bernardino came. So I left the house, pretending to go upstairs, and I came down slowly, slowly. And all I had was a fine striped cloth and a shawl and those clothes I have on now. I opened the door slowly, slowly and I went out. Bernardino was there, outside, and he took me to the Inn of the Chain, where the mulateers who go to Gaeta stay.[4] We slept there together, dressed, until six in the morning, and he had sexual intercourse with me. Then we got up at six and went away through the Porta San Sebastiano,[5] I riding on a horse and he on a mule. I had wrapped up this women's clothing and tied it to the saddle. We arrived for the mid-day meal at Velletri and from Velletri went to Cisterna.[6] Then Bernardino went to bed and I did too, because I felt a little sick. We heard someone knock at the door; it was the watch and the castellan of Cisterna. Bernardino was put in prison and they made me go to the house of a woman of the neighbourhood. Bernardino's idea was to take me to Naples, according to what he told me, and to take me as his wife. But I never said anything about his marrying me. About marrying me, he spoke to me many times. In my house he wanted to bind me to a vow that I would not take another husband than him and he would swear to take none other than me. I told him that I didn't want to swear because I did not know how things would turn out, for, maybe, I would not have wanted to have him.

She was asked if Bernardino told her for what purpose he took her to Naples.

SHE ANSWERED: He said that he had a plan to make things go well for me, but he didn't say anything else about why he was taking me to Naples. And he told me nothing else about what he intended to do with me.

She was asked if Bernardino had any helpers and abettors in the abduction.

SHE ANSWERED: I don't know that he had anyone help him when I left home. He was there alone and I know of no go-between, for Bernardino came visiting here in the house every day. Except that, for the last few days, he didn't come here so often. While he was teaching me, we used to talk together.

She was asked whether, before she went off with Bernardino and was led away by him, she had been known by him carnally.

SHE ANSWERED: Signore, no!

She was asked how many times and where she had been known carnally by him.

SHE ANSWERED: Bernardino had dealings with me only once, at the Inn of the Chain.

She was asked what moved her to flee with the said Bernardino and to subject herself to him, committing such an impropriety toward herself and her house and her family.

SHE ANSWERED: Thanks to my mother, who made me do it. She drove me to desperation with the nasty words she said to me. Whatever I did, she scolded me without cause.

She was asked how many brothers and sisters she has and what their names are.

SHE ANSWERED: I have a brother called Silvio and two older sisters, one called Fulvia and the other Dianira.

She was asked where Bernardino acquired the men's clothes with which he clothed her.

SHE ANSWERED: I believe he bought them. He took my measure for the stockings and the doublet and I wore his cape and a rough shirt[7] that he had bought.

She was asked if Bernardino has a wife.

SHE ANSWERED: He said he has a wife in Spain. She is sick with consumption.

She was asked if Bernardino is well-to-do.

SHE ANSWERED: I understood that he has a house and a vineyard. Here he lived by teaching music.

The court asked if any property had been transferred to him.

SHE ANSWERED: Signore, no, except when I made him some handkerchiefs and collars. But this was known to my mother, because he took nothing from her for his teaching music; this seemed cheap to my mother and she made me give him a pair of handkerchiefs.

Then, because the hour was late, the court suspended the interrogation and left the witness in the house of captain [Ventura, the bargello].

25 January 1559
Arraigned in the same place as above,[8] before the aforesaid lord Francesco Salamonio: **Bernardino Pedroso** *from Logroño, in the diocese of Calahorra, a Spaniard, aged, as he affirmed, 29 or 30, who took the oath and touched [the holy scriptures].*

The court asked what was the cause of his arrest and of his present examination.

HE ANSWERED: I am here on account of a young woman named Ottavia, because she led me off.

He was asked who this young woman is and what family she comes from.

HE ANSWERED: This young woman is a Roman, daughter of one Camilla – I do not know her surname – who lives in Via Giulia.

He was warned to tell the whole story from beginning to end without any digressions.

HE ANSWERED: I know this house and the people of this young woman through Martino, a Spanish used-goods merchant, who is married to a cousin of Ottavia's, the daughter of a sister of her mother, who is married to a saddler. This May it will have been two years I have been coming to her house on account of music. She knows how to play and I am a music master. I teach whoever pays me. It must be two years ago that I began to give lessons to this young woman, on the clavicembalo. When I couldn't go in the daytime, I went in the evening to give her the lesson. And because we came to know one another, Ottavia told me all about her affairs. Among other things (as her sister Fulvia knows), because she has not a quattrino of dowry, she kept on importuning me, with all the insistence in the world, to content her, because she could not stand what her mother did. And she was determined to leave, and she wanted me to accompany her because she wanted to go away from Rome, if I could find a carrier. I promised her. Fulvia told me to make her the promise because, in effect, Ottavia was right, because her mother really has a devilish disposition so that one cannot bear her.

I kept telling her I could not see my way clear to do it in any way 'because of your honour and the great danger.' And Ottavia said, "I want to do it. I haven't a quattrino of dowry and all my mother wants is for me to get out of her way, and every day she scolds me for nothing and she says to me all the bad in the world.' And this situation went on for almost a year, up till now. I have always talked to her, counselling her not to do it and saying that in no way should I do it. Recently, talking to me [at a proper distance] face to face – because there was no place where she could say to me what she wanted to, and lest either her mother or anyone else become suspicious if she were seen talking in my ear – she gave me a letter. And in that letter she begged me to accompany her to a place she would name to me when we were out of her house. I gave this letter to someone to save, to send it to me from Rome when I was [in Naples (?)], telling him to keep this letter for me because my safety hangs on it. In the letter, in substance, she confessed to me to have done with a man what he wished, and that he had promised to take her to wife. This letter is in the hand of Ottavia. And when I saw the letter, since I knew that signor Alfonso Sanguini, a Neapolitan, told me that he was in love with Ottavia, and the mother of Ottavia told me this too, and the sisters too – and if it had not been for a reason I do not know about, Alfonso would have married her. As I have heard, sometimes he slept in Ottavia's mother's house and he was almost master of the house, because Silvio, Ottavia's brother, had been pardoned in some way for a homicide through this Alfonso's intercession. And Ottavia also told me in that letter that her mother wanted to give her to someone who would give her a dowry. Also, the mother told me this, standing by the fire. I suspected that Alfonso was this person, because Ottavia told me that she had promised to marry him. When I saw this, I decided – when I saw how much she was begging me to take upon myself the trouble of keeping her company – because she told me that leaving Rome was an enormous benefit to her and a useful thing and a service to God and that, if she had stayed in Rome, she would have been the cause of a great wrong. She asked me to find some way that she could leave. Otherwise, I would be doing her the greatest possible harm in the world.

Seeing how she begged me, I went off to talk to a mulateer, at her advice, to go to the Kingdom [of Naples], where I know this signor Alfonso is. When I saw that she wanted to go to the Kingdom, I suspected that this affair of messer Alfonso was what she had in mind. I spoke with the mulateer and made an agreement to go with him as far as Gaeta. Then, last Saturday, she had arranged that I should come in the street by her house and make a signal and she would come out. And I didn't want to do it, thinking that she would soon get over this crazy idea.

And I stayed put in Monte Giordano.[9] Ottavia came there, begging me, as she has begged me all along, to accompany her. And in Monte Giordano, in my room, I gave her a tongue-lashing: why had she come out of her house? She told me that I knew well why and that I knew well the sense behind her reasons and that she had decided that she would sooner throw herself in the river than ever go back to her house. When I saw this, we went together to the house of the mulateer at the Inn of the Chain, where she undressed and put on men's clothing. And I settled with her for the clothing, for she had given me ten scudi. All this was on her advice.

So, when I went to harness the animals, she was sick. For she has a sickness, a pain of the body that comes to her often. She lay down on the bed dressed as a man. I lay down, dressed, on the bed where she was, because I was so tired that I couldn't do any more, for I had already arranged all the things. And she was crying out. Then [...] I went to the mulateer and told him to harness the horses, the animals. So we rode off and departed. She was still sick and she said to me, 'I have such pleasure at leaving my house that I don't feel my pain.'

We came to Velletri. We ate there. I had almost to force her to eat. We arrived at Cisterna. It was three in the afternoon. She said that she felt ill and she wanted to go to bed, and I didn't want her to go any further. She kept saying in the street that she wanted to go to bed and that I should go to bed with her. Then, when we got there, because of a little suspicion about her, I was put in prison. They asked me what woman that was. I don't remember what I told them, so that they let me go to the inn right away. I had dinner prepared. She told me that ever since the day of Christmas she had been fasting and that she hadn't felt well, and that her period had come. She dined on a pigeon and went at once to bed.

And if I had suspected any trouble, I could have gone away freely. I didn't suspect anything, because I had gone very slowly with the mulateer by way of the street. And when she was in bed, I warmed the sheets for her. She begged me to get into bed. I undressed, and because I have a bit of mange that I can show you, I began to scratch, for it had been two days that I had not taken off my hose. She scolded me as heatedly as could be, saying, 'Don't scratch yourself any more. Come to bed.'[10] I had asked the innkeeper to give me another bed. The innkeeper did not have another bed. I went to bed. She was off by herself complaining. I was off by myself because I wanted to sleep, without wanting for the world to touch her carnally in any possible way. At this point the police and her brother arrived. I got up to open the door. They made me dress and they took me to prison. I say that the mulateer is not guilty at all because I told him that it was a prostitute, so he would not suspect anything. And this is the truth and on it I will die.

Then, occupied with other business, the lord ordered the witness put back in his place [in jail] with an intention of continuing.

Saturday, 4 February 1559
Arraigned in person before the court in Corte Savelli and in the usual place of examination before the magnificent lord Francesco Salamonio, surrogate auditore, in presence of me, the notary: **Ottavia**, *daughter of madonna Camilla of Rome, who swore to tell the truth and touched [the scriptures] and said as below, viz.*

She was asked whether what she has said in her other examination was true. And will she confirm that it was true in substance in the face of Bernardino the Spaniard?

SHE ANSWERED: Signore, yes, it is true and I will say it to Bernardino's face, because I spoke the truth.

She was asked if she had given Bernardino a sum of money for buying male clothing, the better to go off with him.

SHE ANSWERED: Signore, no. But I believe he bought them for me himself with his money.

She was asked if she was known carnally by another man before she was known carnally by Bernardino.

SHE ANSWERED: No one else has had to do with me [sexually] except when I was a little, little girl. So I don't remember when it was. He forced me and he hurt me – I don't remember if he broke me or not – so that I hurt for I don't know how many days. But I was a really little girl, maybe seven years old.

She was asked if it is true that Bernardino came to her house on the evening he abducted her, as above.

SHE ANSWERED: I told him to come to my house. He didn't want to agree to it, but I asked him so much that he came, so we left. And the time that I begged him was before we had arranged to go away. But that evening he came there, in the street before my house. So when I came out, I found him walking near there, waiting for me.

Then the lord ordered **Bernardino** *brought face to face with the arraigned woman. When he was brought and both swore to tell the truth and both touched [the scriptures] and when a mutual recognition of names and persons was made, Ottavia was asked to tell in the presence of Bernardino here* *how the abduction from the house of her mother Camilla took place, and how much arrangement and negotiation between them had been made, at least in substance.*

SHE ANSWERED: When my cousin Lavinia married Martino Garzia, a Spaniard, messer Bernardino here went one day to play music in my cousin's house. My mother took me there one holiday. It was there we began to know one another. That was when I first began to get to know my brother-in-law. And my brother-in-law came to see me at my house together with messer Bernardino here. When he was there, we began to play music together, and he said he would teach me because my brother had asked him if he wanted to teach me a little. And he kept on teaching me until two or three months ago now. For he didn't continue. And already, a year ago, driven to distraction by my mother, I told Bernardino here to take me away. He answered that he didn't want to take me. Then several days went by without our discussing it further. And I was in love with him, and I believe that he was in love with me. Finally, I said again that he should take me away, and he didn't want to take me, because he said that he did not want the danger to the soul that comes from carrying off a virgin. And I begged him so much that I even got down on my knees before him, asking him to take me away. And he didn't want to take me. I begged him so much that we agreed that he would take me away. We arranged to leave Saturday in the evening. We had these conversations between us upstairs when we were playing. He told me that if that wife of his were to die, he would take me to wife. And he also said it to my mother, that his wife [were she dead (?)], he wanted to marry me, but he didn't tell my mother that he wanted to take me away. When it was arranged Saturday evening, I said to him to come to my house, that I would come down slowly, slowly and we would go away. He told me that he would lead me off dressed as a man. His idea was to go to Naples, but he didn't tell me precisely where he was going to take me.

So Saturday evening, around eight in the evening, I pretended to go upstairs and I went down out the door, which I opened slowly, slowly, and I found Bernardino there in the street. Then he took me to the Inn of the Chain dressed as a woman and we went into an upstairs room. We stayed there until the hour of the evening meal. He dressed me as a man. He gave me a pair of knee-pants and a pair of hose, and a doublet and a rough shirt of cloth. With me dressed as a man, we ate the evening meal, he and I and one other who I think was from Gaeta. After eating we went to the room and sat for a while on the bed. I said to him, 'What will my people be saying and doing?' Then we lay down on the bed dressed, and then we began to sleep. But first he had intercourse with me one time.[11] So we stayed like that in the bed. He fell asleep, but I didn't sleep. And after a bit, we both got up and went off by horseback. I rode a horse and he rode a female mule or a male one. And that man from Gaeta who had been eating with him in the evening came with him on foot. We arrived at Velletri at breakfast time. Then we went to Cisterna. It must have been around four in the afternoon that we arrived. I dismounted and went to rest. And, then, when Bernardino arrived, he was arrested because a priest noticed me and, so I have been told, told the castellan of the place, as I believe, that he was taking me off. He was arrested and they came to ask me who I was. I told them I was a woman and, thinking I could save myself from going to jail, that I was a courtesan. So they let me be and they asked me if I had relatives or anyone. I told them that all I had was an aunt. The castellan asked me, 'Being who you are, how could you go off alone, even so?' The castellan didn't ask me anything else, but he put me in a woman's house. I spent the night there and the next morning, until the hour of the midday meal. But, first, when messer Bernardino here was set free, we ate the evening meal together. And after we had eaten, I went to bed, and he got a little way into the same bed, and then got up to arrange the [bed]-clothes.[12] At that moment, the police came and arrested messer Bernardino. And the castellan then made me stay with that woman. I stayed there until the hour of the midday meal and then my [brother][13] took me away. And those are the facts of the case, just as I have told you.

Bernardino was asked how he would respond to the deposition to his face by Ottavia, here present.

HE ANSWERED: I told Your Lordships. I refer back to what I said in my other examination. And where she says I have had sexual dealings with her, she is lying through the throat. It is not true that I had intercourse with her.[14] And I could have done it other times when I had the opportunity. For, when I went to sleep in her house in the same room where they were in bed, and I was sleeping alone, don't you remember Ottavia, you [tu] came into bed with me and lay down and stayed about an hour and I didn't touch you?

OTTAVIA ANSWERED: It is true that I came into your [tuo] bed and you didn't do anything to me.[15] At that time, I was content to be there next to him. But it is really true that You [voi] did it to me in the inn. And I went into the bed then in my house because I loved you [ti volevo bene]. I am here to confess the truth.

BERNARDINO ANSWERED: If I had wanted to, I would have done what I wanted when she came into my bed that time.

OTTAVIA ANSWERED: I have told the truth, and what I said is true but You [voi] are not telling the truth.

BERNARDINO ANSWERED: She is lying through the throat six hundred thousand times. And as to her saying that I had intercourse with her in the inn, if it were true I would say so, because it is no great matter that you could not remedy with money, for she hasn't a quattrino of dowry, and I'd give that much to her right away in order not to be mixed up in all of this. But because it isn't the truth, I'd rather die. And I say that the Saturday that she is talking about, it is indeed true that we had agreed that she had told me to go in front of her house because she would come out of the house. But I didn't want to go off. Rather, I wanted to persuade her not to do secret things. It's been a year that I've been keeping her company.[16] And Fulvia, her sister, knows it well, because she said that Ottavia was right to leave, but I have always advised her, saying that March, when it will be warm, will be a better time to leave. She said that she could not wait and that if I did not accompany her out of Rome within fifteen days she would go off to do wrong, be it with the bishop or with the bishop's son.[17]

She gave me a letter, the one I have referred to. One night in the house, when we were talking, I said that the brother of the rosary-maker wanted to keep me in his house and that some Spaniards wanted to give me one and a half scudi a month for playing. When she heard me say these things, she took a light and went upstairs and began to cry, because I didn't want to do what she desired. I exhorted her not to do the wrong thing, that it would not befit her honour, for, although she was poor, God would help her. And, turning toward the lord auditore, he said: Your Lordship asked me some days ago if I had given anything to her, or she to me. Once she gave me a pair of handkerchiefs and in recompense I gave her what I mentioned in my examination. And when I talked with Ottavia while I was teaching her how to play, she told me all about this accursed going away. And she said that she was doing it because of her great need and because she couldn't stand her mother. And because her mother wanted nothing better in all the world than to be rid of her. And Ottavia told me that when she was in some house or other, a man came to her bed and stayed in bed with her, because he would give her a dowry. And I have believed all along that she is not a virgin. From what she said, not because I've tried her. And what I did for her, to keep her company, I would have done for any sister of mine, because when a person makes me a part of her affairs, she obligates me to put my life on the line. And I once made her go to the school of the nuns where I play, and out of regard for me, they were as nice to her as they could be. And then, informed of her infamy, the nuns almost threw her down the stairs. And then I talked with those nuns about having her sister made a nun and they would have nothing of it, because of the infamy they have. And I also spoke with the nuns of the [Tiber] Island, but they didn't want her either because of her infamy.[18] She said that she had a skin disease. I want her to say if it is true or not that she has had a skin disease.

OTTAVIA ANSWERED: This is not true, nor is it true what you [*tu*] say about my infamy. The nuns said that we were good virgins. Nor is it true what he says about that man who had to do with me sexually. I did tell him that, but it was about those things that I mentioned above, when I was a little girl, and all that I said before is well said and it is the truth.

Ottavia was asked whether she gave Bernardino any sum of money for buying male clothing that she could wear for leaving the city and for the abduction.

SHE ANSWERED: Signore, no! I don't even have so much as a Christmas-Eve-penny to give him.

BERNARDINO ANSWERED: But You told the castellan they were yours, and he gave them to you.

OTTAVIA ANSWERED: It's true, that is what I told the castellan, but the money wasn't mine, because I have never given You any money.

She was asked if she had ever given any letters to Bernardino before leaving.

SHE ANSWERED: I never wrote him a letter, except that, one Sunday, I wrote him a letter in case we were taken on the road. That's to say, in it I begged him to take me away and to keep me company. This letter was made as a pledge that he was not forcing me and that

I was asking him to take me away, in case he was arrested on the road.[19]

BERNARDINO ANSWERED: I say that in this matter of the letter, I refer the court to what the letter says and I confirm whatever it contains, that this pardons me. It was written by her because she is poor and has no dowry and she thinks that I could get her a dowry. And after I told her in her house that my wife was dead, she stormed all the more for me to take her away. I refer you to what I said in my confession, which is the truth.

Then the lord ordered Ottavia to be taken back to the place where she was being detained. And he ordered the said Bernardino to be put in the public part of the jail and gave him a term of five days for preparing his defence and he ordered a copy of the whole trial to be made.

4 February 1559
On the orders of the lord the aforesaid **Ottavia** *was seen and diligently inspected in the usual fashion. She was seen by Cressida and Francesca, midwives in the city, as they assert. They made their declarations and were subsequently examined. Their depositions are in the first book of the Investigations, folio 84, under the date of 4 February 1559.*[20]

7 February 1559
There was examined in Rome in the office before the magnificent lord Francisco Salamonio, surrogate auditore: messer **Gioann' Battista,** *son of Simone Fossaro of rione Arenula in the parish of Santa Caterina in Via Giulia, aged 26 or 27 or thereabout, as he asserted, who swore and touched and said as follows.*

He was asked if he knows or has known Bernardino Pedroso, a Spaniard, and since when.

HE ANSWERED: I have known Bernardino for about a year and a half.

He was asked if he knows or has heard that he is held in prison, and why.

HE ANSWERED: I have heard that he was in jail and I have heard that he was in jail because of a virgin he led away.

He was asked about the name and the family of the said girl. Has he had or does he have any information about her?

HE ANSWERED: The girl is called Ottavia, daughter of messer

Constantino de Rosignoli, now dead, who used to be a dry-goods merchant. And the mother is named Camilla.

He was asked if the said Spaniard, before he abducted Ottavia, had ever spoken with the witness to the effect that he was pondering the abduction of any girl and had asked him, if he did it, what punishment would be imposed on him.

HE ANSWERED: Some ten or fifteen days before Ottavia was carried off, I happened to be at the door of San Salvatore in Lauro,[21] for they were saying vespers. This Bernardino Pedroso chanced to pass through the piazza and called me over. I approached him and asked him what he was up to. He answered me, 'There is something I want to know. What if I led a virgin astray and carried her off and took her virginity. What punishment goes with that?' And he said, 'I would like to inform myself about this.' I answered him, 'I do not know about this, but I would think that if you did it you would go either to the gallows or to the galleys, unless you took her to wife and gave her a dowry. But I don't really know about this, for I haven't studied law.' At that point, while Pedroso was asking me, a messer Curzio, happened by. I don't remember his family name. According to him, the punishment was just as I had said to the Spaniard who was planning to carry off a virgin. Curzio heard our conversation, except for the beginning, when he wasn't there. And the Spaniard asked him the same thing he had asked me. I said to him, 'Well, signore Pedroso, why are you asking me about this?' I forget what answer he gave me and then he added in reply, 'I know a prisoner who has done this crime, whom I would like to help, but I want to help him according to what I have seen.' And that was just what he turned out to have done, as we found out afterwards.

He was asked about the morals and the reputation of Camilla and of Ottavia and Camilla's other daughters.

HE ANSWERED: I have been their neighbour for fifteen or twenty years, and I have always known them as women of good repute and I have seen them keep the company of honourable women. And they are known and reputed as women of good life and nothing has ever been said about them, except about this thing that happened with Ottavia, who was led away by this Pedroso. And I have seen them going to communion in our parish, which gives me a sign that they are women of good life.

Then the lord sent the witness off with an injunction to silence.

The same day
Examined in the same place by the said lord Francesco: **Curzio**, *son of Brizio*
of Monte Gambaro of the diocese of Rieti, age 27 or so, witness for the in-
formation of the court, who after swearing and touching [the scriptures],
said as follows about the aforesaid questions.[22]

HE SAID: I have known messer Bernardino Pedroso since last summer, for I went with him to have fun one evening, because he delights in playing music. And I invited him to my house to play for a
couple of weddings. I don't know that Pedroso is in prison nor for
what cause. I have no knowledge of Ottavia nor of her mother nor of
her sisters. I have never heard anything bad said about those women.
And as for Pedroso, some days past, it could be about a month,
coming from the Borgo, there in the piazza of San Salvatore in Lauro
– I was going to see if there were letters – I found Pedroso in the
square. He was talking with a big young fellow. I don't know his
name. Pedroso asked what the punishment was if you led astray a
young girl or virgin and carried her off and took her virginity. And
we said the punishment would be the gallows or the galleys, de-
pending on the quality of the person, or to make her a dowry or to
take her to wife. He said too that he had already led one astray in
Spain on behalf of a captain of his who had commissioned it. That is
all I know.

Then the lord dismissed the witness.

11 March 1559
Arraigned in person in Rome, in the presence of the magnificent lord
Francesco Salamonio, auditore, and of me, the notary: **Bernardino Pedroso**,
about whom see above, who swore to tell the truth and said as follows.

He was asked whether he was resolved, after so many digressions and tricks,
to tell the whole truth of the matter. Where did he get the money with which
he bought male clothing and passage toward Naples?

HE ANSWERED: I have told your Lordship that I have no idea where
the money was found. She gave it to me. And when I was arrested at
Cisterna, as soon as I was in jail the captain demanded that I give
him ten scudi for himself, and so the cops[23] demanded ten scudi and
got them.

He was asked what were these ten scudi that he refers to for. And were they the very ones he had from Ottavia?

HE ANSWERED: They were the ten scudi Ottavia gave me.

He was asked what sum of money he had spent in buying the male garments, and how long before the abduction did he buy them.

HE ANSWERED: I've told you I do not remember. I believe I bought them the very same day. I don't remember very well. I refer you to what I said before.

He was asked if he is a close friend of Ottavia's brother. And how did he come to be a regular visitor in the house of Ottavia and her mother?

HE ANSWERED: I was a friend of Ottavia's brother. He showed me what a friend he was by arranging to betray me this way. I ate there and drank there, because the mother asked me to stay and eat, and the brother also stayed to eat and asked me to sleep there. And he forced me to do it. And the mother, too, sometimes made me stay there.

He was asked if it was not true that he was often in that house because he was Ottavia's teacher.

HE ANSWERED: At the beginning I went to teach her how to play an instrument, but in the end I taught her to sing. But I wasted my time doing this because they didn't give me my wages. In Rome, I'm paid a scudo per month when I go to the houses of those who are studying.

He was asked with what intention he was on familiar terms [with her], the whole time that he frequented the home of Ottavia and her father and mother. And was he on familiar terms with the mother?

HE ANSWERED: I went there as a teacher. I went there. I was always there as a teacher and my intention was to pass the time and to talk with all those ladies, sometimes of love and sometimes of Orlando, because they took great enjoyment from these things.[24] And I enjoyed it those days when I paid attention to Ottavia and chatted with one and another of them.

And the lord said that the witness should say more expressly what things he talked about with the inhabitants of the house.

HE ANSWERED: I would set out to tell stories about love matters with Ottavia and her mother and Fulvia and Dianira, who said that she [Fulvia?] was in love with Giovanni Battista Ioso. Fulvia told me she [Dianira?] had gone with one Francesco Cafosco who gave her money to do it to her.[25] And he came to me when I was in jail to tell me that Ottavia had been in the bed of someone else, who told the man who came to talk to me, but he [Francesco] didn't want to tell me his [the lover's] name. And I can point out a person I know by sight who saw Ottavia, when signor Alfonso the Neapolitan was a guest in the mother's house. He was beside the bed, and Alfonso was leaning his head on Ottavia's knees and he was singing. And this past summer, Giovanni Battista Ioso brought to the house a man named Domenico Guardino. The mother told me that she wanted to give her [Ottavia] as a friend to this man. When he was at the house and I went there, I had to go away. One night, when Domenico Guardino was eating supper there, I went to the door. At other times, when they heard me whistle, they used to come and open it for me. But when Domenico Guardino was eating supper there, the mother answered, saying that her son Silvio was not in the house. Then I said, 'Why are you telling me this? I am not looking for Silvio.' And the mother told me that Domenico Guardino was in the house and that I could not come in. I got angry. I was on a walk with another friend of mine. I went on. Then I found Silvio in the piazza of Sant'Angelo[26] and I quarrelled with him. I asked why he was treating me this way and said that I was a man who could enter their house even if the king were there if I was doing no wrong.

Then I went there again this past summer to give lessons to Ottavia. They invited me to come teach Ottavia, so I went back there and went into her house. Then they made more than ten times as much fuss over me as they had the first time, when I first went there, especially because I said that my wife was dead. Domenico Guardino used to take Ottavia to his house and they stayed there the whole day long, and he also went to their house and ate there.

He was asked if he had communicated to anyone what he intended to do, before he abducted Ottavia, especially to the innkeeper who took him and her in on the evening of the intended seizure and abduction.

HE ANSWERED: I didn't tell a person in the world, not even that innkeeper. She begged me not to say a thing to anyone.

He was asked what he told Ottavia he was going to do with her in Naples as he was leading her there.

HE ANSWERED: I told her that I had won favour with the cardinal

De la Cueva and the viceroy and that signor Alfonso Gelito[27] would take her to wife if she [Gelito's present wife] died, as he had told me. And signor Alfonso had had her; she told me so. Me, I never had sexual dealings with Ottavia. I couldn't leave this room if I've ever touched her carnally.

And the lord asked how could it be that, as he says, he never knew Ottavia carnally when he slept with Ottavia alone twice in the same bed after he abducted her from the house of her mother and brother, and when Ottavia herself had affirmed to his face that she had been known carnally and forcibly deflowered by him.

HE ANSWERED: I say that she is lying.

He was asked if he had had any accomplice in this deed, and how, and what sort, and what was his name, his family name and his home town.

HE ANSWERED: I did not have counsel or aid from anyone else.

He was asked what he was going to do in Naples.

HE ANSWERED: I wanted to go to Naples and, when the galleys left, to go to Spain, unless the women of the castellan of the castle of Naples made a good try [to stop me(?)].

He was asked what he would do with Ottavia in Naples. Was it his intention to take her to Spain?

HE ANSWERED: I didn't want to bring her with me. I wanted to leave her there with her husband.

And he was warned by the lord to tell the more complete truth, and to reveal whether he told the innkeeper who offered him room and board, as he had said, the facts, that is that he wanted to abduct Ottavia. He should stop giving evasive answers. Otherwise, by remedies of law and deed, he could be compelled by torture to say it.

HE ANSWERED: I can say nothing except what I have said. I didn't tell the innkeeper.

He was asked again and warned not to persist obstinately in not revealing the whole truth of the matter. He should reveal his accomplices, if such he had. [He should tell (?)] those things that he has not yet confessed. Otherwise he would be put to torture to have the whole truth, if it could not be had any other way.

HE ANSWERED: I have told your Lordship the truth, and I refer to what I have said.

Then the lord, on account of the evidence, the presumptions and conjectures, and the confession made by Ottavia and because of other evidence against him that could be found throughout the trial without a confession [...] to arrive at the whole truth, which could be arrived at by no other way than torture, he ordered him to be brought to the place of torture and stripped and bound and, if it should be necessary, to be raised on the cord and tortured. And he was brought and, while he was being stripped, he was urged by the lord to tell the truth and to reveal whether he had communicated to any other person what he was going to do before he abducted Ottavia from the home of her mother and brother.

HE ANSWERED: I told your Lordship that I communicated with no one, and I protest to your Lordship, and as for the rest I do not know the cause of this.[28]

And again, bound, before he was raised, he was urged to tell the whole truth and to reveal the accomplices in the abduction, if such he had.

HE ANSWERED: I have told the truth and the facts as they are. *Then the lord ordered him to be raised up, and when he was raised, he said*: Help me, Lord! Oh, Virgin Mary! Oh, My Lord! Oh, most holy Virgin! Oh, most holy Virgin! Oh, Lord! I always told the truth. *Oimè*! Help me, most holy Virgin! *Oimè*! Oh, most holy Virgin, help me! I always told the truth and this is the charity they do me, doing me this wrong. I protest to your Lordship! Oh most holy Virgin! Oh, Lord! *Many, many times he said*: Oh, Virgin, help me! Do me justice, signore![29] I have told the truth. Oh, Lord Jesus Christ, I didn't do this deed. Help me, Lord God, help me! *And he was urged by the lord again and again to tell the whole truth of the facts as they happened and to reveal if he had any accomplices in the above deeds.*

HE ANSWERED: I have told the truth and I refer to it. Oh glorious Virgin! *He exclaimed, saying*: Let me down a little. I have told the truth. Oh cruelty! Oh, Lord! Oh, God! *Oimè*! Have compassion on me, for the love of Christ! Oh, Lord God, have compassion on me! *He said again and again*: They made me come as a witness, and I had no other dealings with her. I told the truth and I communicated with no one and I told the truth. Oh, what great travail. *Exclaiming in a loud voice:* Oh, oh great travail, oh great torments! And she asked me to keep her company and I did it to do good and to be nice to her and not for any bad. I am having this for other sins of mine! Oh, Lord, how long do I have to stay like this? Listen to me for once! I know nothing else. Lord, help me! Let my soul not be safe, if anyone in the world does know. Have compassion on me! I would say if there was anyone else. Oh let me down a little and I will tell the truth! *And the lord asked if he would tell the whole truth.* Let me down and I will tell you.

Then in the midst of this the lord ordered him to be let down gently, when he had been raised for a quarter of an hour. And when he had been let down and urged to tell the whole truth, he answered: I told it already. Those women are really bad characters and, me, I am dying!

And he was gently urged to tell the whole truth and to reveal his accomplices, if he had any.

HE ANSWERED: I'll tell Your Lordship, may God save my soul [if he ever knows anything about them (?)] [...] and it will cost me dear to say it. The rest of the truth is what I said.[30]

And at this point at the lord's command he was raised up again and he said: They do me wrong because I would say, 'Look, was it a big deal that I screwed her?' Oh, Lord Jesus Christ! Help me, Lord! I am in the hands of the law and they do me wrong because they don't make the others come here and take torture too. Oh, Lord! Holy Mary! Oh, what great torments! *He said many times*: Oh, Signor Francesco! Oh, Lord Jesus Christ! I merit this because of other sins of mine. I didn't tell anyone. May God save my soul! May the devil carry off my soul if I told anyone, and I would have told your Lordship if I had done so. I am suffering this, and I have told the truth in the name of God, and I have not communicated this fact, and I would say so without this torture. I have never had any torture besides this one. Your Lordship is wrong. I am in agony. You are going to kill me making me suffer these tortures. Oh, Lord, ayee! I am telling the truth. If you want me to tell lies, put me down and I will tell you as many lies as you want. Oh, Jesus Christ, I have never had such torments! I give you permission to hang me. I have nothing to say but what I said already. It would not cost me anything to say it. I don't have anything to say. I don't know anything else. I have already said it. It wouldn't cost me a thing to say it. There is nothing to do but to say nothing at all. To the neck with this cord! Oh, signore Francesco Salamonio, let me get down for a little while. Give me a little water. I haven't done anything. Why are you torturing me? I didn't do anything.

And the lord asked if he would tell the truth.

HE ANSWERED: Let me down and I will tell the truth. Let me down and I will tell the truth, by God, whom I adore!

And the lord reminded him again and again that he could be let down. And he was asked if he would really tell the truth if he were let down.

HE ANSWERED: I will tell the truth. Put me down on the ground and I will tell the whole story. She came to me at Monte Giordano, to the inn. We had supper and I didn't screw her. *Then he added*: It is true that I got into bed with her. She tormented me, embracing me, kissing me, and I put my member between her thighs, but I didn't put it inside, and she told me I had got her shirt all wet and I didn't tell your Lordship, the first day, that I put it between her thighs because I didn't consider that to be intercourse.

Then he was put down because he had been hoisted up for two-thirds of an hour. When he was down, he was urged to tell the truth and he said: Signore, the truth of the matter is that, on the evening when I took her to the inn, she kissed me and embraced me and I put my member between her thighs and I corrupted myself between her [buttocks?] and she told me that I had gotten her shirt all wet and this happened only one time, at the Inn of the Chain.

The lord asked whether he had gone to the house of Ottavia in order to abduct her from her brother's and her mother's house as he had said above.

HE ANSWERED: I want to tell the truth because it was my idea to want to go away; that's not quite the truth. The truth is that we arranged together, Ottavia and I, that I would go that evening to her house and that I would give a signal by making a sound with the thing we Spaniards call a castañet and that she would be at the window on watch. So I went at eight at night. When I was close to the house, I sounded the castañets and she closed the window, which she had opened, because she was at the window waiting for me. I left her house and went to another little street to wait for her to come out, according to the arrangment we had made between us. She came running with her slippers in her hand. We went to the inn and she put on man's clothing, using those clothes I had bought. Then we ate supper. Then she went to bed dressed as a man. I stayed up a while to arrange the [bed]-clothes. She was complaining that she was sick and told me to get into the bed to sleep. I lay down wearing my jacket and she began to kiss me and caress me, and it came into my mind to have intercourse with her and so, because that was how I felt, I took off my hose [...] I put it between her thighs and so I corrupted myself between her thighs and she said that I had got her shirt all wet.

He was asked with what intention he had abducted Ottavia from the house of her father and mother to go to Naples and was warned to avoid digressions and lies.

HE ANSWERED: She asked me, as I have said, to take her away, because her mother wanted to send her away to an old man to serve him [as his mistress (?)] and also I intended to marry her myself when [...], [for I could have, if I could find her a dowry (?)]. She told me to take her where I wanted, and I answered that I would take her to Naples, and I would find a position that would earn four giulii a month and that we would live from that. She desired that I keep her as a whore and in whatever way I wanted.

He was asked with whose money he had bought the men's clothes that he prepared for abducting Ottavia toward Naples.

HE ANSWERED: It was my money. In truth, Ottavia did not give any money.

He was asked about the letter that he mentioned in his previous examination, written in the [name] of the aforesaid Ottavia.

HE ANSWERED: The truth is like this. I told Ottavia that, in case we were arrested, she could save me if we had a letter that said that it was she who asked me to keep her company, as I said. She wrote it for me in case we were captured. She was very much in love with me and I loved her, but not as much as she loved me.

He was asked to tell without obfuscation and to profess honestly whether in fact he knew Ottavia carnally.

HE ANSWERED: I put a little of my member inside and she said, 'Aiee!' and so she moved. I couldn't put it all in, and so I corrupted myself between her thighs and so I got her wet and this is the truth.

He was asked why he had so pertinaciously denied that before.

HE ANSWERED: I denied it in order not to be obligated to marry her because I had done her this injury.

He was asked whether [...] he communicated to anyone else his plan for abducting Ottavia.

HE ANSWERED: No, signore, to no one, and no one ever knew about it. I had no companions in doing this.

He was asked for how long, before he took Ottavia away, he had planned to do so.

HE ANSWERED: For a year before I took her away, and she was the first to say that she wanted to go away and, if I had thought she was a virgin, I never would have done this and now I am aware of the bad I have done and I have had this torture.

He was asked whether everything he had said since he was let down from torture was said as the truth.

HE ANSWERED: This is the pure truth and I will say it many times.

Then the lord ordered the witness to be put back in his place [in jail].

Sunday, 12 March 1559
Arraigned in person before the court in Rome in Corte Savelli in the exami-nation chamber beyond the torture chamber, before the aforesaid magnifi-cent lord Francesco Salamonio of Fara, auditore, and in the presence of lord Metello Armasillo, substitute procuratore fiscale, and in the presence of me, the notary, etc.: **Bernardino Pedroso,** *the Spaniard, about whom see above, and when he was given the oath about telling the truth and he swore and touched [the scriptures] and he spoke and made deposition as follows, viz. He was asked whether he had anything to say or profess beyond what he had said and confessed in his earlier examination when finally he was let down from torture.*

HE ANSWERED: Signore, I have nothing to say, other than what I said.

He was asked whether what he said he had said as the truth. And is he willing to confirm it as the truth? And is there anything he wishes in any way to add to it or take away from it?

HE ANSWERED: I spoke, and I refer to what I said, and I confirm it, because I spoke the truth. I have nothing to add. And what I did, I did as I told it, asked by her. She threw herself down on her knees before me, as even she has told you.

He was asked again whether all those things that he confessed the last time, when he was let down from torture, were and are true, and said as the truth. And does he confirm and ratify and approve them as true, about the abduction of Ottavia and the carnal conjunction with her on the evening of the abduction in the Inn of the Chain?

HE ANSWERED: The fact is as I said it that evening when your Lordship finally had me let down from the rope, and I confirm the fact because it is true.

Then the lord ordered him to be put in the public part of the jail and set a term of three days for preparing his defence.

Accepted in all its parts in the presence of the aforesaid lord Metello, substitute procuratore fiscale.

THE COMMENTARY

A key to this poignant and sometimes baffling story of love, seduction, flight, and disguise is Ottavia's missing dowry. Her restlessness at home and her despondency about her prospects, her courtship of Bernardino and her reckless willingness to gamble her name and her future in his company, though universal in their adolescent impulsiveness, yet are also particular to the constraints of time, place, class, and gender. For, in Ottavia's world, dowry is central to a girl's chances in the marriage market. Its lack, undercutting at once her bargaining position and her self-esteem, may force her to risk awkward expediencies. Thus, the rules of the marriage market help make at least some sense of Ottavia. But the dowry key is not enough to open all the secrets of the tale; Bernardino is a harder lock to pick. Honour, affection, lust, and inertia vie, in his case, as explanations for a line of conduct that makes little overt sense. Part of the evocative charm of this story is its imperviousness to tidy cultural logic.

It is worth reviewing the outlines of what happens. On an evening in January 1559, Bernardino Pedroso, a music teacher from Spain, is arrested at an inn in Cisterna, a small town a day's journey south of Rome. As he answers the knock at the door, behind him, in the bed, lies Ottavia, the teenaged daughter of a Roman dry-goods merchant no longer living. Clad as a boy, Ottavia has fled Rome with her music master. The pair have headed for the Kingdom of Naples, but are still many miles short of the border when the authorities and Ottavia's brother, Silvio, track them down and seize them.

The fugitives are hustled back to Rome, where Bernardino is tried for abducting the nubile girl. In its proceedings on this charge, the court wants to determine, in detail, how the flight has come about. Whose idea was it to run away? Had the other party agreed and, if so, under what circumstances? Who had supplied the money and arranged transportation? Had anyone other than the girl and the music teacher known of or abetted the plan? The magistrates also seek to learn if there has been sexual intercourse, whether forcible or willing.

Behind these inquiries lies the court's obligation to establish that a crime has occurred and to determine who is, in what degree, responsible. Particularly in the case of a mature man's relationship with a young girl, the law presumes male responsibility. Both age and gender, it holds, have given him the power to sway the weaker youngster to his will and should also have furnished the moral judgment to counsel restraint. Thus, when Bernardino and Ottavia are discovered in compromising circumstances far from the girl's home, the court is inclined by habits of mind and practice to label the situation as a criminal abduction of the victim, Ottavia, by the perpetrator, Bernardino. Similarly, if sexual intercourse has occurred, responsibility lies with Bernardino, for Renaissance coitus is, in theory, a lopsided bargain; while both may take their pleasure, only she gives up her honour. The seducer is thus perforce a debtor constrained to recompense. Law and custom ordain that a man who carries off and deflowers a virgin must marry her himself or at least provide funds so she can either espouse another or take the veil.

Ottavia, however, does not fit the usual legal and social formulae, for she is neither passive nor a virgin. Thus, the magistrates, while presuming male responsibility, are keen to know her part in the events, for her attitudes, her behaviour, and her sexual condition bear on the measure of Bernardino's guilt. If she has initiated and encouraged any of his misdeeds, if she has embraced the proposals willingly, even enthusiastically, and has not resisted her seducer or abductor, his blame is less. Furthermore, if she is not sexually pure, as she herself concedes, there is less harm to family and thus less crime to prosecute.

As in many trials, the magistrates here strive to fit the complexities of life into neat legal categories. Their interrogations circle around two possible interpretations of the crime, neither of which quite fits the facts. The law offers two felonies, which one could prosecute singly or together: *stuprum* and *abductio*. To sixteenth-century law, *stuprum* denotes illicit defloration, be it real or statutory rape. Although the rape of non-virgins seldom preoccupies Roman courts, and Ottavia herself is no virgin, the court still takes seriously Bernardino's breach of her chastity. Thus, despite anomalies, this case has elements of a conventional *stuprum* trial. *Abductio*, the carrying off of a minor, is also a grave matter, for it robs a parent of the control of offspring and undercuts, among other things, the right to make marriages. By legal theory, even in elopement, an abductor leads a woman off. But Bernardino has dragged his feet. The oddity of this case, then, is that, though the judges here confront the unwilling escort of a girl no longer pure, their doctrines and proceedings treat him as the instigator and her as the passive virgin.

In the face of uncooperative witnesses, in the end, the court resorts to torture to fit the facts of life to the categories of the law. Ottavia has been only partly helpful for, though alleging sexual intercourse, she still admits that it was she who inspired the elopement. Bernardino, on the other hand, like many males in such cases, obdurately denies sexual contact. The magistrates grind hard on Bernardino's denial. The recourse to torture always amplifies both questions and answers, for the urgency of the exchange rules out trivia, both for the victim and for his tormentors. Hoisting Bernardino aloft, the court asks about only two matters: accomplices and sexual intercourse. Because there has been an *abductio*, the court presumes there must have been conspirators to find and punish. Since the crime also resembles *stuprum*, the court insists on knowing just how far Bernardino's penis went. In body-matters, the sixteenth century was blunter and less squeamish than the twentieth. This line of questioning thus bears witness not to prurience, but to legal nicety. The organ that goes in crosses a threshold; as in moral theology, so in law, penetration deepens guilt and debt.

Such are the concerns of the governor's officials; their reading of the issues and their decisions will shape the fates not only of the fugitives, but also of others of Ottavia's family, without whose initiative the trial would never have happened. If the brother, Silvio, had not hastened to intercept them, Ottavia and Bernardino might well have slipped over the border, beyond the grasp of the authorities of the Papal State, and gone on to whatever, never very clear, fortune they hoped to find in Naples. But Silvio, probably acting in concert with the mother, has intervened, has had the pair arrested, and presumably, by a formal denunciation, has initiated the trial against Bernardino. What does the girl's family seek? How do they think the courts might help them?

As a girl of marriageable age, Ottavia has posed a problem for her family. Convention decrees that a family must provide their grown daughter with a social niche suitable to their wealth and honour. In other words, normally, they must secure a husband for her or, failing that, place her in a convent. Outside prostitution, there is little room in Italy for unattached, unmastered young women. So, parents labour to dispose and secure the futures of adolescent girls; historians speak of families as pursuing 'strategies' as they go about the business of choosing for their child a spouse whose alliance would preserve or even enhance their resources and assets. For marriage involves the linkage and transfer not only of persons, but also of valuable economic and political assets – land and money, skills and social connections. Most prominent among these nuptial exchanges is the dowry, a substantial material contribution that the girl brings to her new family. Ideally, it should include cash or promissory notes. For the duration of the marriage the dowry remains in the husband's hands and forms part of the couple's capital, but if the man dies, his widow is supposed to receive back an equivalent to the dotal gift, to serve for her continuing support. The dowry system produces endless headaches. Accumulating the capital, paying it over, extracting it, reclaiming it, all can occasion worry, conflict, and litigation. For a family like Ottavia's, where social pretentions outstrip means, the need to supply fitting dowries provokes gnawing anxiety.

This is the riddle for the Rosignoli family. While seemingly not in dire straits, Ottavia, Fulvia, and Dianira are in the awkward state of being *senza dote*, without a dowry. Various causes might account for this predicament. With their flood and dearth and warfare, the middle years of the 1550s were cruel to Roman trade. While Ottavia's father was a merchant and thus perhaps a man of some substance, at his death he may have been either unable or unwilling to bequeath enough to dower the three sisters. For whatever reason, by the time Ottavia begins studying music with Bernardino, the family cannot come up with what is needed.

Like the family's economic situation, their social position also seems precarious. To lack a mature male head is for the household itself a weakness. In addition, the son, Silvio, who has had to step too early into his father's shoes, has succumbed to the excesses of youth; he has killed a man, brushed with the law, and required the services of a patron, Signor Alfonso, to extricate him. The tantalizing notion that this Alfonso might also be induced to aid the family by taking Ottavia off their hands surfaces intermittently in Bernardino's testimony. The mother, though she likely suffers the typical social disabilities of a widow, might at least have supplied the wisdom of maturity that notably eluded Silvio. But she, it seems, is not the level-headed sort who can keep a family on course. Instead, in Bernardino's and Ottavia's eyes, she is a lover of romantic gossip, an intemperate scold, and a transparent schemer. The mother has another liability in her difficult economic, social, and personal portfolio in another dowerless daughter, Fulvia, who, it seems, foments her sister's rebellion. There are hints of social aspirations: the music lessons, the desire to pay for them as a salve to pride, the attempt to place the girls in a nunnery. At the same time, dowries are out of reach. Thus, in sum, here is a family that would maintain the respectability to which the father's occupation had entitled it, but which, under the hardships due to the patriarch's disappearance, can perhaps secure the daughters' honour only by gambling with it.

Ottavia's is a case in point; the family must seek a husband who will accept her without a dowry. To compensate for the missing money, the mother hazards that other asset – honour, and especially Ottavia's sexual reputation. The family welcome various male guests, including the music teacher, in their home, entertain them, bed them and the girl in a common room, and allow them considerable freedom with her. What do the Rosignoli hope to gain? Will someone fall so in love with Ottavia that his heart will overawe the head's normal yen for gain? Will some man compromise her sexually and then by shame or litigation be forced to marry her? Bernardino, spiteful, depicts the mother as cultivating him, once she thinks his wife is dead. There might be a conscious strategy at work here – a deliberate gamble to achieve an end – or this may be just a loose-living household, intent upon present pleasures with little thought for the morrow.

Though a strategy may lie here, it is not easy to identify the strategists. In part, of course, individuals – the mother, the brother, the sisters – take steps on their own, sometimes in concert and sometimes at odds. It is hard to explain manoeuvres in a situation such as this, where impulses, passions, habits, and calculations cross, tangle, and coalesce. Thus, Fulvia encourages Ottavia to flee their unbearable mother, but Silvio gallops off to bring her back. But the collective family, obligated to its honour, has a role of its own in these events. It is an obscure actor rendered even dimmer by time's oblivion and by the blurred vision of court documents. But act the family does.

Consider the abduction itself. While Bernardino is undeniably legally responsible, at least in some measure, for carrying Ottavia away, he may have been at the same time the victim of a more or less conscious scheme to entrap a husband for her. The solitary music lessons, the belated gift of gloves, the invitations to dinner, the offer of a shared bedroom all suggest that the family have courted him. Though they assuredly neither promote or welcome the elopement, certainly their tolerance of Ottavia's friendliness with various male visitors risks inviting such a plan. And in whose interest is it to pursue the fugitives? It might be easier to let Ottavia fend for herself in Naples. Easier, perhaps, but far costlier; however taxed or tattered the family's honour may be, seemingly the damage to what remains of it is too great if she is seen to flee into concubinage or prostitution. The family, more than Silvio or the mother or any of them individually, needs to haul the pair back to Rome and to try, by judicial process, to extract a dowry in order to sew up some shreds of honour.

Although there is a familial strategy, Ottavia is only in part its creature. Unlike the rest of the Rosignoli, whom we can see only through the testimony of others, she speaks for herself. Subject to the authority of her mother and brother and dependent on them for her livelihood, she must be under pressure to play out a role that they have prescribed for her, that of the misguided victim of the seducer Bernardino. His condemnation might extort the dowry on which her future hangs. Familial prompting may thus have shaped Ottavia's testimony before the court. Nevertheless, she does not docilely recite the assigned lines, for at many points she volunteers to the magistrates information about intentions and actions that do not suit the abused innocent. There is, for example, the letter that she admits she wrote to exonerate Bernardino of the very charges under which he is being tried. Unlike most young women who complain in court of sexual wrongs, Ottavia never alleges Bernardino forced himself upon her. Other details of her account put her family in a bad light or undermine its case. She criticizes her mother, acknowledges having claimed in public to be a courtesan, and admits to having persisted in the plan to flee in the face of the music teacher's qualms.

Ottavia's words and behaviour stem not only from interest but also from emotions. She certainly has been in love with Bernardino. It is not clear what that feeling means for her. She disclaims expecting or even designing ever to marry him – she could not with his wife still alive, but she has been adamant in refusing to marry others whom she fears her family might force upon her. Has that threat prompted her haste to leave right away and not delay till March, as Bernardino suggests? Certainly, much youthful rebellion reverberates through her words to the court. Ottavia's testimony raises many questions about her motives and goals, which may have shifted over time; whatever her real intentions, she clearly acts and speaks as if she has a wish to make her own destiny, a desire at odds with her family's program.

Even more puzzling is Bernardino. Under torture he finally confesses to arranging practical details of the escape and to sexual dealings with Ottavia, if not quite full intercourse. His avowal is enough to content the court, for it clinches his guilt. Nevertheless, none of his confession explains persuasively why he became involved in the first place. He has known the risks – in the courts both of law and of honour.

Bernardino, perhaps because he a Spaniard, is the one who dons the rhetoric of honour, at least in retrospect. Thus, as if to impress the court, he tells of trying to dissuade Ottavia from her wild schemes by reminding her of the threat to her reputation. But there is no denying his presence in a bedroom with the girl, many miles from Rome. In his own defence, Bernardino abandons honourable loyalty, for his safety lies in casting opprobrium and responsibility on Ottavia. Bernardino cites her bad skin, her worse reputation, her loose behaviour, and her lost virginity. And he alleges all initiative, all funds, and all benefit to be hers. Bernardino thus tries the classic ploy of accused seducers; claiming for himself generous and honourable intentions and disavowing sexual contact, he blames and sullies the girl. The cruelty with which he strives to protect himself blends oddly with remnants of tender solicitude.

Bernardino's testimony leaves his motives much in doubt. Neither love nor lust explains his actions fully. One can dismiss mere lust, for, as he protests, he could have satisfied it without carrying the girl away and, if caught, at worst he would only have had to pay up for a dowry. (That he does not try to appease the family with such an offer suggests that perhaps he is short of cash.) There are signs of love; the elopement argues that he is kind, or infatuated, or at least ensnared by the girl's pathos, subtlety, guile, and tenacity. Few other motives than love make much sense of the whole escape. But though perhaps he loves her, he apparently intends to give her away in Naples. And, if once fond, still he is cruel to her in court. His feelings seem muddled. Perhaps, in the end, Bernardino is the innocent who pays the highest price. But the sentence is lost, the penalty unknown; despite the threat of the 'galleys or the gallows' uttered by the men-in-the-street, he does not appear in the catalogue of those put to death. Nor should he have, for customarily the cost of such indiscretion was less dire.

To gauge who, finally, is responsible, and how much, takes a very careful reading of the testimonies. One must sort out the several possible strategies of the numerous participants in the drama, those who speak directly in court and those spoken for. It is necessary to keep track of not only who does what, but also who says who does what and to whom he or she speaks and to what end. In Ottavia and Bernardino, whom we hear directly, we must distinguish their original intentions, perceptions, and feelings from their memory of them and from what shows in their calculated or coerced accounts in court. Here, as often, history seems an indeterminate science; different readers, however subtle and painstaking, will emerge with different views about what happened and about who was more right or less wronged. In its incompleteness and muddled contradictions, this tale is as baffling, as insoluble as life, and almost as poignant.

piggioni saluatici

CHAPTER FOUR

Agostino Bonamore and the Secret Pigeon

※

THE TRIAL

[Agostino Bonamore suffers a near-fatal assault, engineered, he suspects, by his in-laws. In mid-July, convalescent, he testifies against them in the house of a court notary. The same day, two servants from the in-laws' house give supporting evidence. Six weeks later, on 30 August, he testifies again, this time as a prisoner in the court of the Campidoglio; the in-laws have struck back, accusing Agostino of having suborned one of his witnesses.]

Contra Ferdiano from Lucca[1] *and Agostino Bonamore*

14 July 1558
Examined in Rome in the house of Claudio della Valle by me, the notary:
messer **Agostino Bonamore,** *a Roman, who touched the scriptures, etc.,*
and said as follows.

He was asked if he knows or presumes to know the cause of his present examination.

HE ANSWERED: I believe that, this Friday, it will have been eight weeks ago that, in the evening, around nine at night, I was in the shop, at a desk, dispensing a rhubarb medicine.[2] When I had dispensed it, I fell asleep on the desk-top. At that point, along came a boy all wrapped in his cape. He said, 'Where is messer Agostino?' Virgilio, my serving boy, answered, 'And so what do You want?' The lad replied that messer Agostino Paloni and madonna Giulia wanted me to come to them right away. Then Virgilio called me, saying, 'Messer! Messer Agostino has sent for You. He wants You there right now!' I said, 'Messer Agostino who?' He answered, 'Agostino Paloni and madonna Giulia.'

I was wearing my doublet because, at the time, I intended to go to dinner. I fetched my cape and left for messer Agostino's. When I got to the corner of the Santa Croce palace, by the shop of Cecco Fracasso, the goldsmith, I saw someone at the corner all bundled up, with a naked sword under his clothes.[3] I steered clear because I hadn't arms of any sort, and the fellow there with the naked sword asked, 'Bonamore Agostino?' I said yes and went on, walking fast because I saw him stir. And as I went toward messer Agostino's, at his house there was someone leaning, with a naked sword. When I got there, he lunged at my thighs with his right hand. I parried with my [medicine] box and jumped into the middle of the street. At that point, the one who had called to me back at the Santa Croce house caught up, and another one too, who came right from the alley of messer Agostino Paloni. The one who came from the alley gave me a blow in this left leg and lopped the bone short, as you can see. All the while they were laying into me, they were shouting, 'To the ground! To the ground!' I pulled myself over to the druggist's on the corner of Via dei Catinari, and out came an employee of the pharmacy with a pike and they went off saying, 'He won't make it another four hours.' One of them said, 'He can't hold out any longer. Let's get away!'

I believe they thought I had armour on because they hit me only on the legs and on the head. And there is a son of Tarquinio, the stocking-maker, who lives behind Santa Maria dell'Anima, who says that, when one of them was hitting me, he said to another, 'Hit him in the legs. Bring him to the ground.' And this boy saw when they were hitting me, and when they ran away, and everything.

He was asked to say if he knew any of those who attacked and wounded him.

HE ANSWERED: I didn't recognize any of the three who wounded me, but the one who struck the first blow was big. But you couldn't make them out because it was dark.

He was asked if he had had any enmity. With whom, and about what?

HE ANSWERED: I had no enmity or quarrel, except the one with my father-in-law, who is called Ferdiano from Lucca,[4] and with his brother, who came to Rome one month earlier or, really, two. The cause of the enmity was that, when he gave me his daughter as a wife, I married her and I slept with her and she didn't leave a sign the way other virgins do. I couldn't see her, for, because of this matter, I shrugged her off.[5] I told her father, messer Ferdiano. He answered me that the girl was good and pretty.

Then there came to Rome this messer Francesco, his brother, who said he wanted to know why I didn't go see my wife. I said because they hadn't given me the dowry they had promised me. I didn't want to tell him why it really was. Francesco said I would have to deal with him, himself, and not with his brother, and that he wanted me to tell him why I wouldn't go see my wife. In the end, I told him and Francesco then changed his tune and said, 'It doesn't matter. I want us to go have fun in Lucca. You will carry one hundred scudi, I will carry one hundred, and we will put them into some commercial venture. We will stay there enjoying ourselves. You won't spend a thing. That way this whim of yours will pass.' I answered him, in no way would I leave Rome, for I was afraid he would do me harm.

Then madonna Bartholomea, who lived in Ferdiano's house, told me several times not to go out at night, but she didn't tell me the reason why she didn't want me to go. But after I was wounded, this madonna Bartholomea told me that his daughter[6] also knows that Ferdiano, talking one day with his brother Francesco, told him, 'Since Agostino is doing this to us, we have to have him killed or lamed.' And his brother answered, 'We'll have to pay eight or ten pair of scudi.' And listen to this! The evening I was wounded, messer Ferdiano said at table, 'It won't be another two hours before Agostino is going to get hit on the head, and as for the wife, I want to make her eat with the dogs.' And Francesco was present, and a nephew of his, whose name I don't remember, and the daughter of messer Ferdiano, whose name is Caterina. And she went in tears into the kitchen to my mother[7] and told her, 'My father wants to have him killed! My father wants to have messer Agostino killed.' My mother wanted to come warn me. But by then I was wounded.

I heard this too from a servant of his named Vincenzo (I don't know his father's name), who, the morning after I was wounded, told my mother that he, too, had heard that messer Ferdiano wanted to have me hit over the head. He told her this in the house of madonna Bernardina, daughter of Piccino, the butcher.

I, the notary, asked what had come of this servant Vincenzo.

HE ANSWERED: They have sent him to Lucca. I've looked for him, to have him examined, but they have sent him away. *Adding to a question*: Messer Francesco, Ferdiano's brother, has also gone off to Lucca, but I don't know when it was that he fled. But they have brought all their kinfolk to Rome, and they escort messer Ferdiano, and he makes all the servants carry arms.

While I was kept to my bed, a nephew of messer Ferdiano, whose name I don't know, came and offered me money. Then he said to me, 'If the man who hit you came and asked your pardon and repaid your expenses, what would you do?'[8] I said, 'I would want to know why he had hit me. I don't conduct my affairs this way.' I got angry and he didn't say anything more. *To a question, he said*: When we had these words, it was between him and me. He didn't speak to me when there were people around. *To another question, he said*: Before I was wounded, messer Ferdiano used to come visit me every day. Since I've been wounded, I have never seen him.

The witness was sworn to silence.

The same day
Examined by me in Rome in the office of me, the notary: **Giulio di Stefano** *from Nice, cutler, a witness, who swore and said as follows.*

He was asked if he knows the reason why he was called to be examined.

HE ANSWERED: Messer Agostino asked me if I knew who wounded him. As for me, I don't know.

I, the notary, asked if he had at least heard it said by whom Agostino was wounded.

HE ANSWERED: I have not heard, nor do I know who it might have been.

He was asked if he had ever been in the service of Ferdiano from Lucca. And how long has it been since he left his employ?

HE ANSWERED: I served messer Ferdiano from Lucca eight or nine months. I served him around the house and he gave nine giulii a month. I think it's been about two months now that I have no longer been with messer Ferdiano.

He was asked whether he knows that messer Ferdiano is joined by blood or kinship with Agostino Bonamore.

HE ANSWERED: I know that messer Agostino is married to a daughter of messer Ferdiano called Margarita. *Adding to a question*: Messer Ferdiano complained that messer Agostino didn't come to see Margarita, his wife.

He was asked to recount precisely the words messer Ferdiano used when he complained of messer Agostino, who did not come to visit Margarita, his wife.

HE ANSWERED: Messer Ferdiano said that messer Agostino was not doing right, leaving his wife, and that if messer Francesco came, he would give Agostino his dowry or rather he would use the dowry to oblige him to stay.[9]

He was asked if he ever heard messer Ferdiano threaten to do Agostino Bonamore harm or have harm done to him. Let him say where, and in the presence of what persons.

HE ANSWERED: This I have heard: that if his brother came, he wanted Agostino to come to an agreement.

He was asked if he knows that, later, messer Francesco, the brother of messer Ferdiano, came to Rome. And does he know anything about him?

HE ANSWERED: Messer Francesco came to Rome and stayed in Rome a little while. Then he left for Lucca. *Adding to a question of me, the notary*: I left messer Ferdiano a month before messer Agostino was wounded.

He was asked to tell the truth. Had he ever heard messer Ferdiano threaten in any way to have his brother Francesco kill Agostino Bonamore?

HE ANSWERED: I heard nothing, save that if his brother came, he would have him punished.[10]

[He was sworn to] silence with an oath.

The same day
There was examined in the house of messer Hortensio di Riccardi in the rione of Pigna near the piazza of Santa Maria sopra Minerva: madonna **Bartholomea**, *wife of Pasquino, drinking-glass merchant, a Florentine, a witness, who swore and said as follows to the questions of me, the notary.*

SHE ANSWERED: I was in the service of messer Ferdiano from Lucca for about two months. The first day of Lent, I left, just as soon as messer Agostino Bonamore had taken his wife. I was in charge of the daughters of messer Ferdiano.[11] I left with the willing permission of messer Ferdiano.[12]

She was asked if in the time when she was in the service of messer Ferdiano she ever heard him complain of messer Agostino Bonamore, and if, in such complaints, he threatened to have him killed.

SHE ANSWERED: He was always complaining about messer Agostino because he would have liked messer Agostino to come to his house more often. And messer Agostino didn't come because they were all at odds, for messer Agostino wanted the dowry and messer Ferdiano said he didn't have it. And when he complained of messer Agostino, he said, 'I wish he'd get killed.' And I answered him sometimes, because I was a member of the family,[13] 'If messer Agostino has no quarrel, who wants to kill him?' Messer Ferdiano said that a pair of scudi would do everything and that he had done bigger things and that he had had things to do and had them done, but I didn't too much lend an ear. He said such ill of messer Agostino that one couldn't say more if one tried. *And to a question she said*: Many times I heard messer Ferdiano say, 'If Francesco, my brother, came, things would come to a finish.'

She was asked if she knows that messer Francesco then did come to Rome and how long he stayed.

SHE ANSWERED: Messer Francesco came to Rome, but he came after I left messer Ferdiano's house. I can't tell you how long he stayed in Rome because he went off to Lucca afterwards.

She was asked whether, at the time messer Agostino was wounded, messer Francesco was in the city.

SHE ANSWERED: Messer, yes! Messer Francesco was in Rome when messer Agostino was wounded. *Adding to a question*: I have never spoken with this messer Francesco. *To another question, she said*: When messer Agostino was wounded, I had left the service of messer Ferdiano.

And I, the notary, asked if she had ever heard messer Ferdiano quarreling with messer Agostino. Let her say what he said and who was present.

SHE ANSWERED: I have never in my life heard messer Ferdiano speak well of messer Agostino, and he yelled at him, as I said.

She was asked what sort of person she thinks messer Ferdiano is, and does she think he caused messer Agostino to be wounded?

SHE ANSWERED: I think the worst because messer Ferdiano is a man who governs himself by his own will.

[She was sworn to] silence, etc.

30 August 1558[14]
Arraigned in person in the court of the Campidoglio before me, the notary, in the presence of lord Francesco Salamonio, substitute fiscale: messer **Agostino Bonamore**, *who swore and touched [the scriptures] and said as follows.*

He was asked about the cause of his arrest and of his present examination.

HE ANSWERED: I have heard it said that when messer Ferdiano was in jail they brought a witness to some judge or other of the governor's who said I had had a false witness examined. They say this is why they got the warrant against me.

He was asked what witnesses he had had examined, for whose subornation he was accused and put in prison.

HE ANSWERED: The witnesses I had had examined were a servant of messer Ferdiano, whose name I do not remember, and a madonna Bartholomea, who used to live in the house of messer Ferdiano.

He was asked why he arranged to have those witnesses examined.

HE ANSWERED: I will tell you, signore. I was sent for around nine o'clock in the evening on behalf of messer Agostino Paloni. They said to me, 'Messer Agostino says that you should come to him right away.' And the boy who came to call me said to Virgilio, my servant, that he should wake me up, because it was something important. It was Virgilio who brought the message on behalf of that boy, so I never saw the boy.

So, in my doublet, without arms, I set off for messer Agostino's. As I was going along, not far from the house of messer Agostino, at the corner of the house of Cecco Fracasso, I heard the sound of someone clearing his throat. I was scared of what might happen to me, because the man who cleared his throat had a naked sword in his hand; I could see the gleam of the weapon. I went on my way briskly toward the house of messer Agostino. The man who had cleared his throat followed me. When I had gone some fifteen paces, someone who was at the door of a shop, hidden so you couldn't see him, struck out at me with his right arm. I threw myself into the street and he gave me another blow down near the ground, and another man who had been a bit further off came at me and gave me this wound that I still have on my leg. I was shouting all the while, 'Assassins! Robbers!' The one who had given the first blow thrust at me with a lance and hit a door, and the other one who had struck me said, 'Let's get out of here! I've got him to the ground.'

They went off by the street that runs before the door of messer Agostino's house. Because I was so wounded, I was carried home in a chair. Then my kinfolk came, and my mother, and they said, 'Who could it have been?' I was out of my head, and I know this only because they tell me. I went seven or eight days without knowing what was what. While I was in bed, a nephew of messer Ferdiano came to visit me. He offered me, if I needed them, twenty-five or thirty scudi, so that I would lack nothing, and would return to the house of messer Ferdiano. He would arrange for me to get medical care. My mother said, 'I don't want that man coming here, because messer Ferdiano is the one who had Agostino hit.'

So my mother told me the story, about how the evening before I was wounded, messer Ferdiano and messer Francesco Strolagho,[15] his brother, were talking together in their house, and my mother was there in messer Ferdiano's house, and my mother heard that they were saying, 'Before long, he will be getting his!' And she heard that messer Ferdiano and messer Francesco, the very evening that I was wounded, said at table, 'It won't be tomorrow night that Agostino will have a wound in the head, so he won't even be able to say "Help me!"' The very same evening that they said those words, I was wounded.

When I learned this from my mother, after I got better – I was forty-one days in bed – I went to the governor and told him the whole story. He told me, 'If you had a witness who would say that Ferdiano had said these words, I would punish him.' Well, I had also Caterina, my wife's sister, who that very evening told my mother that she should warn me because her father wanted to have me hit on the head. And my mother had asked Vincenzo, a servant of messer Ferdiano, if he had been present at table that evening and if he had heard those words they said about me that evening. Vincenzo had answered that he didn't want to get mixed up in these matters and that he prayed God that I would get better and that the whole affair would be settled.

I went looking for this Vincenzo because he had confessed to my mother that messer Francesco and messer Ferdiano had said those words that evening at table, but I was never able to find him. When I couldn't find Vincenzo, I did find, in rione Ponte, another servant of messer Ferdiano, who had been in the service of messer Ferdiano before I was wounded. I told him, 'Giulio,' – That's his name! Now I remember! – 'madonna Bartholomea has told me that You know who hit me. If you wish to, come willingly to be examined. If you don't want to, I will have you brought in under subpoena.' He answered, 'I don't know if I will be useful to one side or the other. I have eaten the bread of messer Ferdiano. I wouldn't want to do him harm, nor be useful to You. I wouldn't like to get mixed up in this.'

So I said to him, 'If you want to come, come! If you don't want to come, I know where to find you,' because he worked in a shop and sold knives. When I said these words to Giulio, I had with me one Francesco, the fishmonger, a Roman, who lives by Marforio.[16] He said to Giulio, 'Don't get fancy ideas.[17] Even if it had been your brother, you should take neither one side nor the other. Tell what you know and what you heard with your ears.'

So we went to the governor and I said to messer Claudio [della Valle[18]], 'Look! Here's the witness! Examine him!' So they went into the room and examined him.

He was asked whether Giulio, before he was led to the office, told him what he heard Francesco and Ferdiano say.

HE ANSWERED: Signore, no! He didn't say anything to me. Except that, in the street, as we were coming, he kept saying, 'I don't want to be examined! You are all kinfolk and friends. I don't want to get mixed up in this!'

He was asked if he had asked Giulio what he knew about the wounds he had suffered, who had wounded him, and who had arranged and ordered the preparation of the crime.

HE ANSWERED: All I said was, 'Madonna Bartholomea said that you know who hit me.' And he answered, 'I was in the house and I heard certain words. Let's go! I'll go be examined.'

He was asked whether Giulio uttered the words he had heard said in the house of messer Ferdiano.

HE ANSWERED: He didn't tell me any more, nor did I ask.

He was asked if it is really true that madonna Bartholomea said to him that Giulio was well informed about the facts of the crime.

HE ANSWERED: Signore, yes. She told me, and these were the words: 'Have Giulio examined. He will tell you everything.'

The lord asked where, when and in whose presence Bartholomea said to him, 'Have Giulio examined!'

HE ANSWERED: I went to find Bartholomea in her house to talk with her. She had learned that messer Ferdiano had spoken about having me attacked. She said to me, 'Have Giulio, messer Ferdiano's ex-servant, found, because he told me that he knows who had You attacked and everything.' Three old women were present at this conversation, but I don't know their names.

He was asked whether Bartholomea told him that she had heard threats against him by Ferdiano and Francesco.

HE ANSWERED: She told me that she could tell me little, 'But, if I know anything, I will tell the judge for you.'

He was asked whether Bartholomea specified what she knew about this thing she would tell about.

HE ANSWERED: She told me, 'Have Giulio examined, because he knows everything, because he told me such and such. It is true I have heard certain words, but I don't think they will help you at all. Giulio knows everything.' And she didn't tell me what those words were that she had heard.

He was asked whether he insisted[19] *to Bartholomea that she speak and reveal what she knew or had heard said.*

HE ANSWERED: I didn't insist at all that she tell me what she knew about this affair. She is alive and well and dwells in Rome.

He was asked why, if he didn't insist, he then went to Bartholomea's house.

HE ANSWERED: I went there to ask after that Vincenzo who had heard those words. And I also went to ask about a big fellow who went every day to messer Ferdiano's house to see if she knew who that big fellow was and where he lived. Bartholomea told me that she didn't know anything and told me, 'Speak to Giulio. He knows it all. He told me so.'

He was asked whether Bartholomea had told what Giulio said to her.

HE ANSWERED: She didn't tell me. *Adding to a similar question*: It is true that I asked Bartholomea what Giulio had told her. She said to me, 'He told me that he knows everything. Have him put in jail and have him examined and he will tell You everything.'

He was asked whether he had Bartholomea examined.

HE ANSWERED: Signore, yes. I had her examined that very day that I had Giulio examined, or the day after.

He was asked how many times he spoke with Bartholomea about the crime before he had her brought as a witness and had her examined.

HE ANSWERED: I spoke with Bartholomea twice.

He was ordered to relate the several conversations between himself and Bartholomea.

HE ANSWERED: The first time, I was going toward my house and I met Bartholomea just past the house of messer Ludovico Matthei, in front of a tree at the dyers', and she said to me, 'How are you, messer Agostino?'[20] I said, 'Well, a bit better now. There's nothing wrong except that I have two fingers gone to sleep; I don't feel anything in them.' She said to me, 'God knows, it went badly with you.' I asked her if she knew anything about what had happened. She said, 'Find Giulio, because I've talked to him and he says he knows who attacked you.' I asked where I could find Giulio and she said she had met him around Rome and told me the place, but I don't remember where, and said, 'Let me take care of it. When I encounter him, I'll get people to show me where he lives and everything.' She went off and there were no other words between us. Then I went back home. I told my mother about this. She begged me to let the matter drop, because God had given me my life. About two or three evenings later, one Saturday evening, I went toward Piazza Montanara.[21] There I ran into some men dressed like sailors, in ambush for me in some corners. I went to madonna Bartholomea, saying to myself, 'They're going to have me attacked again.' I asked her if she was willing to be examined. She said, 'In the examination, have the notary come here.' So I said, 'I'll look into it. I'll have him come.' And at that time we did not say any other words.

I went to the piazza of the Minerva[22] and I sent word to her, telling her that, if she was willing to go to the house of messer Hortensio di Riccardi, I would have the notary go there. So she came and was examined.

He was asked if he had sent anyone to speak to madonna Bartholomea about this matter of examining her.

HE ANSWERED: Signore, no! I never sent anyone to speak to her on account of this matter, except the one who went to call her to come be examined.

He was asked what he gave or promised to Bartholomea for her examination.

HE ANSWERED: Nothing, signore. If your Lordship finds that I gave or promised her anything, You should have me hanged by the neck.

He was asked, likewise, how many times he spoke with Giulio before he had him examined. Let him say where, and in whose presence and in what words. Let him recount it in order.

HE ANSWERED: I never spoke with Giulio, except that one time when I brought him to the governor. I found him in the shop, because they told me he sold knives down by the Castello corner.[23] I went there and didn't find him and, turning back toward rione Ponte, I found him in a shop. I said to him, 'Giulio, I've been out looking for you for three or four days. I've never found you.' He asked me how I was getting over the wound. I told him I wanted him to be examined. If not, I would have him sent to jail. He said to me, 'What do You want me to know about these things? I don't want to get in the middle between You. You are all kinsmen and friends and you will wish me ill.' I said to him, 'I don't want you to say anything except what you told madonna Bartholomea, and the truth.' So we went towards the house of the governor, and there were no further words between us. He came along, conversing with that young man who came with him, whose name is Francesco.

He was asked about the words between Giulio and Francesco as they went along.

HE ANSWERED: Giulio said, 'I am certain that messer Ferdiano will be angry that I am being examined.' So we walked on and Francesco said, 'Don't kid yourself!' and told him to tell the truth, and that he would always be considered a worthy man. There were no other words. So I took him to messer Claudio and he was examined.

He was asked whether he gave or promised anything to Giulio for being examined in this matter.

HE ANSWERED: Signore, no! That Francesco was there. Your Lordship can find out from him if I gave or promised anything, or if we talked about anything, for you could hear us because we weren't talking secretly. And if your Lordship finds that I have given or promised anything, You should punish me.

He was asked whether he told Giulio and Bartholomea what he wanted them to testify against messer Ferdiano.

HE ANSWERED: Signore, no! I told them only to say what they knew, and I told Giulio to say what he told Bartholomea, if it was true.

He was asked if he inquired of Giulio what he had said to Bartholomea.

HE ANSWERED: I didn't ask him anything else.

He was asked what might have moved Ferdiano to order him wounded or killed, if he really did, since he was his father-in-law, and in loco patris *to him.*

HE ANSWERED: With him, I have never had ugly words, except with Francesco, his brother, over matters of kinship; he said I didn't deserve the daughter of messer Ferdiano.

He was asked if he, at the time this crime was being perpetrated, would visit the home of messer Ferdiano, and go see his wife, since they were a married couple.

HE ANSWERED: I went to eat and drink in the house of messer Ferdiano and to sleep with my wife. It is true that sometimes I didn't go there, since I was tied up because I had to dispense some medicine.

He was asked if, before the crime was perpetrated, he had had a violent fight or in some way quarrelled with Francesco and Ferdiano.

HE ANSWERED: Perhaps eight or nine days before I was wounded, I had words with messer Francesco. He said that I did not deserve to be their kinsman, and that there was no one in my kin who was equal to his. I said that you judged things by their effects, and I said about Margarita what I told in my other examination, that I knew all about that business. They wanted to trick me. I talked to her father about it, because I myself saw the pigeon that they had brought to cut its throat in the bed. Bartholomea brought it in the sack. Because of this, they didn't trust me, and they didn't want Margarita to come to my house because her father had told her that I would kill her. Messer Francesco wanted to take me to Lucca to show me a good time. In spite of these things, I continued to go to the house of messer Ferdiano and I slept with my wife some twenty-five times, and I was nice to my wife, and she was even more so to me.

Your Lordship, think of it, they had such a grudge against me that, one day, when I went to the house of messer Ferdiano to see my wife, I lay down on the bed and I fell asleep. Messer Ferdiano was in the house, and my wife, who had to go to Santa Cecilia with my mother and my sister, came to the bed and woke me up, saying that I should not stay in the house but should go with them.[24] When I asked why, she said to me, 'Come, come! I don't want you to stay in the house!' I think, if she were examined, she would tell the whole story the way it is. I believe, too, that if you examined the sister, she would tell the truth about the words they said the evening I was wounded and everything. And she told me that Vincenzo went away with messer Francesco, and messer Ferdiano gave him money to go away and not be examined. When I went to talk to my wife, she told me repeatedly that she would go to the duke and the countess and tell them the whole story, just how it happened.[25]

He was asked where Giulio and Bartholomea live.

HE ANSWERED: Giulio was in a shop next to the Strozzi and Bartholomea lives next to Santo Stefano del Cacco in the little piazza.[26]

He was asked how long before the crime was done to his person did Giulio withdraw from the service of messer Ferdiano.

HE ANSWERED: About fifteen days. *Adding to a question*: I think messer Ferdiano punched him,[27] but he stayed serving him some days thereafter.

He was asked how he knows that Giulio, down on his knees before the judge of the most reverend governor, revoked what he had said.

HE ANSWERED: My mother told me, too, that Ferdiano had brought Giulio before a judge of the governor and that he said he had been forced to say what he said, and then Giulio went away.

He was asked whether he had used any kind of force, be it by words or by deeds, against Giulio to make him testify those things he said in this examination.

HE ANSWERED: Signore, no! If your Lordship makes that fishmonger Cecco,[28] the one who happened to be with me, come to prison,

You will see that all I said was good words. If You find otherwise, I am in prison.

Then he was put back in his place [in jail] with the intention of continuing. In the presence of the aforesaid magnificent lord Francesco Salamonio, substitute fiscale, accepting [the testimony in] part and parts, etc.[29]

THE COMMENTARY

This trial tells a one-sided story for cautious eyes. The teller, Agostino, really does fall victim to an assault by strangers in the nocturnal streets. So much, at least, is beyond doubt. Agostino's explanation, however, a tale of dark familial intrigue, is another matter. In the transcript, one meets only Agostino's version, corroborated by one friendly witness and by another, more reluctant, but summoned at his behest. Though the record is lost, the accused in-laws must have had their day in court. A sentence of the court, absolving Francesco, proves that the magistrates would not swallow all of Agostino's story. Then, nine months after this trial ends, just a year after the initial attack, Agostino will be hit again. This time the assailant, a mounted stranger in peasant dress, on the pretence of delivering letters, will call Agostino to the door of his shop and shoot him in the chest and shoulder. Once more, the apothecary and his wife will point accusing fingers at his father-in-law. In the ensuing trial, not published here, the court will examine Ferdiano at length about the earlier assault on Agostino. His testimony, though laden with special pleading and disingenuous remarks, will help solve some of the puzzles in this earlier trial. In the second trial, much that Ferdiano and the seventeen other witnesses and defendants will say will undermine Agostino's explanation of the first assault.

This trial, then, tells a vivid story that may well be full of lies. As often, the reader must try to sort true from false. Success is not assured; some of the true facts may be out of reach. Still, even when dubious, a persuasive tale is full of lessons about the teller, about the audience, and about the world described. For, as always, a persuasive falsehood must be couched in general truths.

One sixteenth-century truth that the story illustrates is the tension between two modes of settling differences, what anthropologists call 'self-help' on the one hand, and recourse to the courts on the other. Self-help, informal jockeying for position without recourse to institutions, was common practice in pre-modern Europe. Though they also use the courts, Ferdiano and his brother sometimes choose self-help; they try to settle matters on their own, through threats and violence. Agostino, by contrast, portrays himself as always sheltering in the law. At the outset, two matters are at stake: Margarita's missing hymen and the slow payment of her dowry. Once Agostino is wounded, other issues arise. Agostino, still interested in the dowry, wants also to protect himself from further blows and, if possible, to get even. Both in and out of court, his in-laws try to parry his moves. This male conflict draws in various women of the two families, who have agendas of their own.

To assess Agostino's version of the events, his jumbled narrative and his witnesses' remarks need sorting out. When reassembled, the purported facts in the first trial fall into place as a drama in five acts. Act One takes place in the house of Ferdiano di Ricchi, who tries to marry off a daughter, Margarita, as a refurbished virgin. To everyone's discomfiture, on the wedding day the groom discovers, he says, the instrument of fraud, the sacrificial pigeon whose blood was to have passed for hers. None the less, he takes Margarita to wife. But, months later, in May, the bride dwells in her father's house. In his deposition, Agostino at one point suggests the father is loath to let her go, fearing for her life at her husband's hand. Probably, in fact, Agostino, to extract the unpaid dowry, has brought her back. Whatever the cause, the daughter's staying in her father's house must have stirred gossip. Certainly, as Agostino agitates for his money, the scene grows ever tenser. Ferdiano, Agostino avers, then calls down from Lucca his brother Francesco, who is made of sterner stuff. Francesco tries in vain to draw Agostino out of town, promising fun and profit in Tuscany, but Agostino, fearing violence, he says, demurs. Finally, Agostino, stung by Francesco's insults to his lineage, oversteps a boundary by saying out loud to his in-laws what they surely already know he knows about his imperfect bride.

In the second, brief, and violent act of the drama, according to Agostino, to cow him, Ferdiano and his brother contract for an assault. The apothecary falls half-dead in the street. In Act Three, Agostino slowly recovers first his consciousness and then his health and seeks retribution, not by violence, but by recourse to the courts. He gathers evidence and rounds up witnesses to the conspiracy. His campaign culminates in the first appearances before the magistrates, in mid-July of 1558, when he, Bartholomea, and Giulio all testify. In the fourth act, although Ferdiano is in prison, the Di Ricchi regroup and launch a counter-suit. Sending the most incriminated members of the household out of town, indeed, out of the Papal State, according to the apothecary, they suborn one of his witnesses, their former servant Giulio, who recants. They then charge Agostino with priming Giulio and have him jailed. Thus, in a fifth and final act, Agostino is back before the magistrates, this time himself a defendant who protests the rectitude of his dealings with his witnesses. There ends the record, inconclusive and portending an uncertain future for the imprisoned Agostino, with his imperfect bride, his missing money, and, perhaps, his sanguinary in-laws.

A more precise chronology helps make sense of the story. Several fixed points help place other events. The first is Ash Wednesday, 23 February, when Bartholomea departs from Ferdiano's service. A month before the assault, Giulio also leaves the service of the Di Ricchi. Thus, the wedding of Agostino and Margarita must have taken place in mid-winter, within the two months of Bartholomea's employment, for she was available to smuggle in the pigeon. The second fixed point is 14 July, when Agostino and his two witnesses appear before the magistrates. Thus, the nocturnal assault takes place around 20 May, for Agostino tells the magistrate in mid-July that eight weeks have since passed. Since he is seven or eight days in coma or delirium and, in all, forty-one days in bed, all his rounding up of witnesses has been in the first two weeks of July. As for Francesco, although the servant Giulio says that Ferdiano's fierce brother, is in Rome for 'a short time,' we do not know how short, but only that he arrives after Bartholomea has quit, is there at the time of the crime, and leaves before the end of August. The third fixed point is 30 August, when Agostino is again before a court. We cannot put dates to Ferdiano's imprisonment and the purported Di Ricchi counter-plot, save to note that they take place in the last six weeks of summer.

The timing of Agostino's supposed remark about the secret pigeon is crucial to his story. Because the apothecary contradicts himself and no one else mentions it, it is hard to date his announcement. Agostino at one point says he protested soon after the wedding. That, by implication, is why his father-in-law kept the bride at home, fearing the outraged groom would kill her. But Agostino tells the court that it is a mere seven or eight days before his wounding that he broaches with Ferdiano his awareness of the pigeon. If so, then all the threats and wrangling of the past five months have indeed spoken only of the unpaid dowry. Note that neither Bartholomea nor Giulio mentions altercations about the imperfection of the bride. The husband may, however, mean that in mid-May, in Francesco's presence, he speaks openly about what everyone has known tacitly all along. If so, Agostino, by blurting out the unseemly truth, by asserting the dishonour of the Di Ricchi, might have forced their hands and brought on the plot to assault him. That, at least, is the sense which chronology gives his story.

There are some reasons to trust Agostino, for he has one strong witness and one weak one on his side. Furthermore, he is quick to name names of several others, such as Ferdiano's daughters, his mother, and Francesco the fish monger, who comes to court with Giulio, who all might corroborate his tale. It might be hard to direct so many players to stage a lie. Also, it is tempting to lay Giulio's recantation to justified fear of the Di Ricchi, who may just have shown their worst.

At the same time, there are grounds for caution. The second trial will show that all the next year Agostino keeps his bride at home with him and continues to do business with Ferdiano, hardly the behaviour of a young man disgusted with his wife and afraid for his skin. Likewise, Ferdiano's hand in Agostino's affairs does not seem the mark of a man badly stung by a real charge of attempted homicide. Witnesses in the second trial, while themselves prone to tell a slanted story, will counter Agostino's plea with other renderings of deeds and motives. In particular, Ferdiano will display skill at spinning tales, whose truth is hard to judge, but which jostle the credibility of his son-in-law.

Ferdiano, in the second trial, will paint Agostino as a man who does indeed abuse the courts. He will suggest first that Agostino's witnesses had reason to wish harm to their employer. Di Ricchi claims that Bartholomea was paying him back because he had jailed her for stealing handkerchiefs and Giulio was smarting from the master's punch to his face. Furthermore, the father-in-law will say that it was not he, but Camilla the Skinny who instigated the first attack on Agostino. Agostino had been owed money by the same combative prostitute who quarrels with Paolo di Grassi. Camilla had threatened her creditor, warning Agostino not to try to extract the money. Agostino countered with a fraudulent warrant, which, backfiring, sent him to jail. To bail his son-in-law out, Ferdiano spent, he claims, fifty scudi. These he deducted from Margarita's unpaid dowry. This rescue had, he will say, thus provoked the domestic quarrel of the year before. Plausibly, Ferdiano will tell the court that it was at this point that, to extract the dowry, Agostino had returned his wife to her father's house. But Camilla was not yet finished with Agostino, Ferdiano will recount. She next incites her lover, one Gradi, to orchestrate mayhem against the apothecary. He, surely, is Sebastiano di Gradi, who, in chapter 2, testifies on Camilla's behalf against Paolo di Grassi. Clearly, Camilla's rough ways are notorious enough to sound plausible in court. Still, as told, the story will sound flimsy. Here, Ferdiano, too, may be playing with the courts. Nevertheless, his version provokes the speculation that Agostino's accusation in 1558 may be a mere legal ploy that exploits his wounds to undercut his in-laws, rough play to shake loose the dowry.

However much it may misrepresent some facts, Agostino's tale very faithfully illustrates Roman culture. In particular, it shows how honour offers a repertoire of words, gestures, and transactions that shape the politics of family life and social exchange.

For instance, as Agostino pictures it, match-making here had to reckon much with honour. Like any father of a nubile daughter, Ferdiano has hoped to barter his daughter's assets – her youth, her looks, her social graces, her dowry, her family's power and honour – in exchange for a groom who offers wealth and status and whose own family would be a useful ally. But Ferdiano has had to trade in an adverse market, for Margarita, without her hymen, is a piece of damaged goods. Her dishonour is costly. To make good such a deficit, a father must either raise the dowry or lower his sights and aim for either an inexpensive nunnery, in which to shelve the girl for life, or, more likely, a husband below her station. Ferdiano seems to have adopted this latter course. Thus, he needs as a son-in-law a man he scorns.

There are many signs that the Di Ricchi do make such an unequal marriage. They seem indeed to outrank Agostino. The second trial will show Ferdiano to be a man of some position, a recent commissary of the papal grain office. He has much business in the Roman courts, and knows the ins and outs of government. The behaviour of the Di Ricchi, as portrayed, signals their higher rank. For one thing, Francesco scorns Agostino's kin to his face. Also, the transparent fraud at the marriage bed is a lie of the sort that the honour code permits against inferiors. Renaissance Italian honour lets a man lie to his male underlings, as he can seduce their women, with some impunity, for a challenge from below is beneath respect. Agostino's initial acceptance of the bride also suggests his inferiority on the scale of honour. But, finally, says the testimony, Agostino 'gives the lie' to Ferdiano and Francesco, daring to say to their faces what the Di Ricchi know he knows. When he rebels against humiliating pretences, he makes a claim for equality of honour. According to his story, he nearly dies for it. In all these details, the story makes good cultural sense.

Despite his moment of rebellion, however, Agostino, as he portrays himself, is usually slower than the Di Ricchi to invoke the code of honour. Nowhere, not even in his sickbed story about refusing the attempt to buy him off, does he cite it. True, he has some of honour's reflexes; Margarita's lack of virginity appears to offend his reputation more than it does his inner feelings. It is shameful to be at once duped in bed and cheated of his money. But there is no sign that Agostino would do her violence to avenge his honour. Not only does he claim to like her and to appreciate her protecting him in her father's house, but he is also content to keep her. A year later, at the shooting, Margarita will be living in his house. Nor does it seem that the Di Ricchi need arm their servants against his retribution. Not that Agostino is a lamb; the later trial will show him stab his brother-in-law in a quarrel over debts. Still, this time, rather than strike an honour-laden pose of self-sufficiency, the apothecary prefers to use the courts, both to attack the Di Ricchi and to shelter from the threats he claims they brandish. In August 1558, when Agostino stands accused before the judge, prudence makes him portray himself not as honour's rough devotee but as a law-abiding client of impartial justice.

Agostino portrays his in-laws as his foil. Honour's clumsy thralls, so keen are they for revenge that they seem sloppy plotters. In his tale, the Di Ricchi roar and grumble for months about killing him. It is true, 'He should be killed!' was the most banal of epithets, seldom to be taken straight. But, as Agostino tells the judges, Francesco and Ferdiano go beyond the usual bravado and speak in terms so precise and threatening that they alert the servants, Bartholomea, Giulio, and Vincenzo, and frighten their own daughters, who run tattling to Agostino's mother in the kitchen. The father's portentous gloatings would be foolhardy. The ears and tongues of servants are not to be trusted; their loyalties are brief, for they are always changing masters. Thus, their tattling tales swell the dossiers of many a trial. The brothers' recklessness bespeaks a passionate, reflexive love of honour. Whether or not it fits Ferdiano's true nature, it serves the moral of Agostino's pleas before the court.

Whether truth or semi-fiction, Agostino's and Bartolomea's testimonies show something of the powers of Roman women. Their pervasive subordination does not at all exclude them from the politics of family life. Although only one of them testifies in court, all the women of this story appear often in the words of others as busy interveners, messengers, counsellors and mediators. One sees this clearly in the conversation in the street between Bartholomea and Agostino. There, she tells Agostino to seek out Giulio as a witness and then takes on her own shoulders the task of tracking him down. 'Let me take care of it,' she tells him. Bartholomea's backing is newly minted. She claims some sort of kinship with Agostino, which might have moved her to take his side. But, at the wedding itself, when she smuggles in the pigeon, she acts against his interests, in the service of her employers of the time. Agostino's own mother is steadier in her partisanship. She gives her son counsel, warning him not to return to the Di Ricchi house and urging him, once he has healed, to let the whole matter drop. Ferdiano's own daughters are independent actors in the drama. Margarita's position is rendered delicate by her loyalty and subjection, on the one hand, to her father and his kin and, on the other, to her husband, whom she seems to cherish. Filial subjection does not stop Margarita, though she dares not spell out the danger, from warning the apothecary not to sleep alone in the house. Nor does it deter Caterina from running to the kitchen to alert Agostino's mother of her son's imminent danger. Caterina, we hear, goes so far as to tell her sister that to protect Agostino she will go to the Duke of Paliano himself, a papal nephew of great weight in Rome. Though we should not take such words literally, Agostino's story shows a young, unmarried girl who can imagine reaching out even to the public authorities to curb her wilful father.

The common thread of all this female action is the protection of the peace in a violent society. In some Mediterranean societies, women play the role of furies, egging the men on to redeem their honour through bloody deeds. They do no such thing in Rome. There, women do pick their own quarrels, which they pursue themselves, or through the hands of men. These squabbles, however, seldom spill blood. Female style is usually distinct, for women step in to curb male keenness for violence. Protectors of honour's victims, women subvert the claims of a retributive male social ethic. As pictured, Bartholomea's solicitude for the limping Agostino is thus altogether consistent with her earlier attempts, at his expense, to help his bride feign virginity. Thus, she helps him seek justice through the courts, the better to protect his skin. His mother, even more cautious, urges him to let the affair lie. The young women of the Di Ricchi do all they can to warn of danger and discuss appealing to the authorities to calm things down. Bound differently by the code of honour, women can distance themselves from masculine imperatives. To Agostino, the political instincts of Roman women offer a convenient image; he can contrast the peaceful, prudent females with the impulsive males.

Several other minor characters also serve Agostino's moral. Giulio, the ex-servant who testifies limply on Agostino's behalf and then recants, is a man caught in the middle. His rock is the law, his hard place the impetuous Di Ricchi. 'I have eaten the bread of messer Ferdiano. I wouldn't want to do him harm, nor be useful to You,' he tells Agostino in July, before giving testimony. Or so Agostino says in August, when he himself has to justify his methods of gathering evidence. If Giulio says such a thing, he may believe it, or he may drape his fear in the robes of the social ethics of good clientage. But Giulio's speech, as we read it, is a construction of Agostino's to serve himself before the court in that ticklish moment when Giulio has turned his coat and changed his story. There may be artistry in the contrast between the slithery Giulio and the voices of public justice. Agostino, who hopes to don the mantle of universal right, thus has every reason to paint the servant as a moral particularist, a client who would rather serve a patron than the impartial law. As everywhere in early modern Europe, the Roman magistrates strive to build up the state by defending the common good against just such narrow loyalties as Giulio's.

In this tale of Agostino's, Francesco the fish monger who walks with them serves as a foil to Giulio. For he is a chorus who invokes the values of the court and, by implication, of Agostino himself, who needs to seem a lawful man. The fish monger is made to say, 'Don't get fancy ideas. Even if it had been your brother, you should take neither one side nor the other. Tell what you know and what you heard with your ears.' In a second version, Agostino recounts how he said, '"Don't kid yourself!" and told him [Giulio] to tell the truth, and that he would always be considered a worthy man.' By implication here, fidelity to the truth and respect for the law can be every bit as worthy as is fidelity to your masters. That Francesco even has to make the argument tells us that, in fact, things are not always so. For many Romans, patrons come first and justice after. Agostino hopes to prove that he thinks otherwise.

The dialogue of the servant and the fish-monger points out a tension that tugged at sixteenth-century jurisprudence. In the face of inhospitable social custom, at least in theory, the courts hoist abstract justice above all lay obligations. Their cult of right procedures is designed to assure the autonomy and impartiality of the law in a particularist world. Agostino's and Ferdiano's trial displays some of the magistrates' scrupulosity in matters touching evidence. They thus abhor tainted witnesses like Giulio. They also measure with a seasoned eye special pleadings and inconsistent or too clever stories. At the same time, these tribunals, despite their fussy attempt at independent justice, are too weak to forestall the many bogus claims. Either Ferdiano, or Agostino, or perhaps both of them, make outrageous charges. It is difficult to assess their stories. What is clear indeed is how hard it is, in sixteenth-century Rome, to dig out the truth when justice is ensnared in social bonds.

the house while I was by the fire spinning. He asked where was madonna Giulia, his wife and my mistress. I answered him, 'I don't know. She's upstairs or in the loggia.'[2] And I went looking for her, and when I went into the *loggetta* and didn't find her, I went upstairs. I got just as far as over there, at the top of the stairs.[3] At that point, messer Gieronimo, my master, arrived and went upstairs and went in [the room], and I went downstairs.[4] And right away he came down, grabbing a halberd and asking for Ruggiero, his servant. He told him, 'Come, help me! I found someone upstairs!' So Ruggiero took the sword and the two of them went upstairs, going into my room, where messer Gieronimo began to poke around in the space over the ceiling. And he said, 'It's from here that the felon went out.' Then, while the servant stayed in the room, messer Gieronimo came down and left the house to look for messer Mercurio, who lives near here. They came back, and he [Mercurio] was carrying a light arquebus and a sword. And they went upstairs, he and messer Gieronimo, into a room and they talked together; what they said I don't know. And he left messer Mercurio there with orders not to leave and went out, locking the door with a key; he was a fair while coming back. In the mean time, along came Gentile, a servant of the bishop, who opened the door and came in. When messer Gieronimo returned, he said to messer Mercurio, '*Orsù!*[5] What should we do?' Messer Mercurio answered, 'I looked up in that ceiling space, messer Gieronimo. There's nobody here. I looked and I didn't see anybody.' Messer Gieronimo came down and, lighting a candle, went back up, he and the bishop's servant and the servant of messer Gieronimo. And again they began to look around to see if they could find the man whom messer said he had seen; when they didn't find anybody, he began to blame messer Mercurio, telling him he had let him escape. So messer Mercurio apologized for it and then left the house. When he was gone, messer Gieronimo came down again, relit the candle and went up once more to look. And when they found no one, all three came back, that is, messer Gieronomo, his servant, and the servant of the bishop. Messer Gieronimo said that he had found a hole that went through the wall above the ceiling, and they said about that hole or window that you could come in through it. By this time, night was coming on and the bishop's servant left, so they didn't do anything else that evening. *Adding on her own*: I have noticed that madonna Giulia, my mistress, ever since last summer, has always been flirting with someone who lives near here, next door to our house. I don't know his name. It is true that when some gentlemen passed by, I heard them call them 'Signore Ferrante,' 'Signore Camillo.' As far as I know, they are two brothers who live together. As for the name of the one she flirts with, I don't know it. I have seen them talk together various times, here from the window and from the loggia in back.[6] And I have seen him throw letters and I have seen her pick them up and read them. And those she didn't know how to read she had read by others. *Adding to a question*: She had a certain Fenice from Siena, a woman who once stayed with her, read the letters. And she had her own sisters read them. And I have also seen her throw letters to that neighbour with whom she flirted, from the loggia into his courtyard. This mistress of mine, ever since last summer, has thought of nothing else, and has turned her mind to nothing, so far as I can tell, except flirting with this man. It was all she ever thought about.

She was asked if she had ever seen that neighbour in the house of her master, messer Gieronimo, talking with madonna Giulia. Was it once or many times? And in what part of the house, by day or by night?

SHE ANSWERED: I have never seen him enter the house, nor have I ever seen them talk together except from the window and from the loggia, as I said.

She was asked if the neighbour had ever spoken to her. How often and about what matter?

SHE ANSWERED: To me he has never spoken. *Adding*: I have never spoken with any neighbour, neither man nor woman, except with the wife of the fiscale of the Campidoglio, and with the wife of messer Claudio della Valle.[7] Every now and again, they have sent me on some errand.

She was asked in what room or part of the house of messer Gieronimo she usually sleeps, and whether it is her habit to lock it with a key.

SHE ANSWERED: The room where I sleep is here upstairs. It is the middle room and locks with a key.

She was asked if there is any other way of entering the room.

SHE ANSWERED: I don't know that you can enter by any other place except the door, or the window if you put a ladder there.

She was asked if she knows that, six or eight days ago, someone entered that room. Who was he and how did he do it?

SHE ANSWERED: I have neither seen nor heard that anyone came in, except in so far as messer Gieronimo told me that last Saturday he saw someone and that he came in through the space over the ceiling and that a window had been made in the wall between the neighbour and us. But, as for the window, I haven't seen it.

She was asked if she heard anyone making a hole in the wall and any noise when he did it.

SHE ANSWERED: I heard banging but I didn't know where from, and I thought it was because they were building a wall at a new house near here, for they build in the daytime and sometimes at night by the light of the moon.

And I, the notary, said that it did not seem likely that she would not see or otherwise know of a window that was being made in and above her own room.

SHE ANSWERED: I never heard banging up over my room, but you could certainly hear the noise of the mice. Messer, on account of those mice, sometimes put the cats there.[8]

She was asked and warned to tell the pure and unadorned truth about the making of the window, and about who did it and how it was done.

SHE ANSWERED: I tell you that I know nothing about that window except what I have heard about it from messer.

Then, because of the lateness of the hour and for other reasons, the examination was suspended for now with the intention of continuing.

6 December 1559
Arraigned in Rome in the house of her usual habitation and in a room of that house in the presence of me, the notary, in the presence of lord Bartuccio, substitute fiscale: madonna **Giulia**, *wife of messer Gieronimo Piccardi, notary of the Rota, who, having sworn an oath about telling the truth, having touched [the scriptures] etc., said as follows.*

She was asked if she knows or in any way presumes to know the cause of her present examination.

SHE ANSWERED: Signore, yes, I know it because, through the bad advice that my servant Camilla gave me, I fell into a great error.[9] Because I believed her, I let myself be counselled and drawn by her to consent to make acquaintance and friendship with messer Camillo

Mantoano, who lives near here, next door to my house. Messer Gieronimo found out about it and made a great uproar about this matter; I think that that is why he had you come here to examine my servant Camilla and me, because he wanted to find out how this came to pass.

And the lord said that she should tell and lay out the true sequence of the events and all that happened.

SHE ANSWERED: I will tell you the whole truth, and I won't tell you a single lie. May God inspire Camilla to tell the truth, too! The truth is that Camilla, since last September, around the beginning of the month, said to me, 'Madonna, I have a lover near here. Every morning he greets me.' I asked her who was this lover of hers. She said to me that he was a neighbour and that he had told her that he wanted to throw her a letter. I told her, 'Don't pick it up! Give him a sign that you don't want it!' because I was afraid that it was some sort of trap for me. This discussion about the letter went on for three mornings. Then, when this neighbour threw it to her – it was messer Camillo Mantoano – in the yard behind the house, she took it and kept it hidden until my husband, messer Gieronimo, left home. And once he was gone, Camilla said to me that she had got those letters, and there were two of them, one unsealed and the other tied. I asked her, 'Where are they?' She said, 'Look! Here they are!' and showed them to me. But I didn't want to read them. I said to her that I didn't know how to read them and that she should throw them back. She said to me, 'Let's look at them first and then I'll throw them back.' I took the letters and, untying the one that was tied, I found inside a gold half-ducat. When I saw it, I said, 'Camilla, *ohimè!*[10] Didn't I tell you!'

She answered, 'Shhh! Shhh! This thing, he's not sending it to you! This one comes to me, because to you he would not send so petty a thing, for he would be ashamed of it.' I asked her, 'Camilla, do you think we are going to throw it back?' She said, 'No, not by my reckoning, because it could fall into the hands of some servant and that would be worse.' So she took the half-ducat and we burned the letters. *To a question she added*: I don't know what was in the letters because I didn't know how to read them; without having read them, I threw them in the fire.

About two days later Camilla picked up another letter that messer Camillo threw to her into the yard as before and she gave it to me. And, immediately, without having read it, I threw it in the fire. Then, afterwards, she spoke to me, telling me that messer Camillo had spoken to her early in the morning from the *loggetta*[11] and that he had begged her to be a go-between to me and to tell me that he was in love with me, and that he was my servant, and that he could neither eat nor sleep, and that he desired no thing other than my person, and words like that. And that I would be wrong not to consent, and many other such words, the way people do when they make such embassies. He urged me and beseeched me many times to love him, because he was a gentleman of worth and because good would come to me from it. Three or four days later, messer Camillo threw another letter with six gold scudi inside. Camilla gave it to me, and I took it weeping, saying, '*Ohimè*, Camilla, I ought not to want them. It will be my ruin!' And she said to me, 'Rest easy, madonna! It is your good fortune.'[12] I gave them to her to keep, and she answered him.

Some days later, she told me again that messer Camillo had talked to her once again, and asked her if I still had any of that money, and if I needed more. I told her I didn't need any more and that I didn't want any more. She answered me, 'Madonna, you will do better to keep him as a friend because you will have a gentleman. He will be all your entertainment. You have no entertainment at all,'[13] and many other fine words. I answered that I didn't want to do it, because there was no easy way, and that I was afraid of messer Gieronimo. But still she told me that I should do it, and that she was advising me like a daughter of hers, and that there was no need to be afraid. No one would ever know. She told me you could make a hole in the wall of the front room where we could talk and other people would never notice. I answered that I didn't want to do it, because messer Gieronimo would find out.

Finally, Camillo and Camilla were talking together, and Camillo wanted to know if there were any way to talk to me out of the house. Camilla told him, no, but that there was a place where you could pierce the wall between our place and his. They resolved to break the wall above the ceiling of the room where Camilla slept. Camillo gave Camilla a pointed iron tool to make a little hole where they were going to break the wall. And she did it without my knowing that she had made such a hole. I didn't know a thing about it until I heard the noise on our side when they broke the wall, where messer Camillo had us make a little window. He made us a wall of wood plastered over in such a way that you could barely make it out. It was big enough for him to come in through it. When I found out about this, I said, 'Camilla, *ohimè*! I don't want to put up with this. I want to tell messer Gieronimo.'

She said, 'Rest easy, madonna! This will be our amusement. There is not a woman in the world who does not do these things.' So I went to see it and I talked with messer Camillo, saying, '*Ohimè*, messer Camillo! What is this thing you have done without my knowing anything about it?' He told me, 'Don't worry! No one will know anything about it.' Camilla told me the very same thing. Messer Camillo asked me if it was messer Gieronimo's habit ever to go up there, over that ceiling. I told him, yes, sometimes he went there to put the cat to catch the mice. He said that he would rig it up with a board covered with plaster so well fitted into the wall that one would not notice a thing. And Camilla told me the same thing. And so it was set up the way you have seen it.[14] So, communicating through Camilla, we agreed that when messer Gieronimo, my husband, went out, Camilla would stand guard at the window and messer Camillo would come in by that window in Camilla's room. We were together there in the daytime eight or ten times. The last time – it was last Saturday – Camilla told me that messer Gieronimo had gone out of the house. She wanted to draw bean-lots to make messer Camillo jealously passionate. So she began to draw those beans, because she knew how to do certain things with them, saying certain spells.[15] She told me that messer Camillo loved me very much. After we had drawn bean-lots for a while, she said I should go up to the room. I told her that my heart was not in it to go there then, because I was afraid that messer Gieronimo would come back. She told me that I should go and not worry, for her heart told her that messer Gieronimo would not come back.

So I went there and from the window she made a sign to messer Camillo to come. So he came and entered. And just as he was coming down from the ceiling and was about to put his foot on the floor of the room, Camilla came up running, without her slippers. And she said to me, '*Ohimè*! Madonna, look, it's messer!' So I left the room at once. Coming down, I found messer Gieronimo halfway up the stairs. I tried to stop him, but he walked up and saw that Camilla was coming out of the room and closing the door to keep messer Gieronimo from seeing messer Camillo. But messer Camillo was not so very quick climbing up through the ceiling. So, when messer Gieronimo went into the room, he saw him from the knees down. At once he came back down and took a pike and called the servant, who took the sword, and they went up, thinking that messer Camillo was inside the ceiling. But they didn't find him, because he had gone back into his house and locked the window.

Messer Gieronimo called Mercurio, a neighbour and relative of one of his god-kin. He came with a light arquebus. At this point, Camilla wanted to flee the house. She said, 'Madonna, I want to leave because messer Gieronimo will kill me!' I held her back and I said, 'Ohimè, Camilla! You led me into this and now you want to leave me. If I die, I want you to die too!' When Camilla heard messer Gieronimo come downstairs, again she wanted to flee. Messer Gieronimo came down the stairs and said to her, 'Come, Camilla. Have no fear! Don't be afraid! Who is that man?'

She answered, 'It's that neighbour!' *Adding on her own: Ohimè!* How will God ever forgive her, having so sinned against me! And these are all the things that happened. And this is the pure and true truth and I have told it as it is, even though Camilla told me many times that I should never confess, that she would never confess, telling me, 'Madonna, if you confess it, I will tell so many things about you that I will ruin you and I will be your ruin, so don't let them chase it from your mouth.' And yesterday evening she said to me, 'Madonna, be strong this evening, because your husband will be preaching sermons at you, and he will try to chase it from your mouth. Don't confess anything to him.'

But I wanted to confess everything to my husband, and everything I have said to you I have said to my husband too, because I have put all my affairs in the hand of God. I have been assassinated[16] and betrayed by Camilla and by bad fortune. I ask of you a grace and I beseech you to do it for me and make messer Gieronimo pardon me, so that this thing doesn't go any further, because I promise never again to let myself get involved in such a thing. I will be a good wife to him, and as faithful as can be. *She then added on her own*: If I had been a saint, this bawd of a Camilla would have made me break my neck as she did with her pretty sweet-talk and with all the persuading she did. *Adding likewise*: I was assailed by her more than a month to agree to consent. If they hadn't made that hole in the wall, nothing ever would have come of it.

Then the examination was stopped with the intention of continuing.

7 December 1559
Arraigned to the same place,[17] in the presence of me, the notary, by man-

date, and in presence of Bartuccio, substitute fiscale: **Camilla**, *who swore to tell the truth and touched the scriptures and said as follows.*

She was asked if she has anything to add for clarity or greater truth regarding those things about which she was yesterday interrogated and examined.

SHE ANSWERED: It is my intention to tell you the truth about those things you ask me about, as I told you the truth in that other examination of mine.

I, the notary, said that she should tell the truth better regarding those things about which she was examined, because she had not told and expressed the truth.

SHE ANSWERED: I told the truth and, in truth, I cannot tell you in any other way about those things you asked me about.

She was asked if she was and is aware of those things about which she was interrogated and examined. And can she tell the story in full and in order?

SHE ANSWERED: All I remember is about the things that happened here in the house, that you asked me about and I answered you and told the truth.

She was asked what these things were that happened here in the house.

SHE ANSWERED: The things that happened are what I told you. That is, last Saturday, messer Gieronimo, my master, came back to the house and arrived in the room where I was by the fire spinning. He asked me where was madonna Giulia, his wife, and I said, 'I don't know!' Right away I went looking for her and I found her in the middle room, just this side of the room I sleep in, and I said that messer was asking for her. She came toward the stairs, and messer Gieronimo came up the stairs and went into my room and came out. And madonna and I went down, and he came down in a rage, took a halberd and called Ruggiero to get the swords. And they went up, as I said in that other examination of mine, where I said that Mercurio came with the arquebus. And they went up and searched, as I said.

She was asked if she ever had or received letters from the said neighbour. And to whom were they sent?

SHE ANSWERED: I have never had letters from that neighbour nor from anyone else.

She was asked if she ever had money from that neighbour. And how much and to what end?

SHE ANSWERED: Signore, No!

She was warned and asked to give the name of that neighbour about whom we have been talking.

SHE ANSWERED: I can tell you only that I have heard these two neighbours called Camillo and Ferrante.

She was asked whether she has ever, on behalf of the neighbour, said or expounded anything to madonna Giulia, her mistress and wife of her master, bearing, as the common speech says, 'embassies.'[18]

SHE ANSWERED: This neighbour has never told me to say anything to madonna Giulia nor asked that I bear any embassies. But it is true that a young man who, I have heard, is a nephew of Cardinal Pisano has sought me out to tell madonna that he was in love with her and the like. But I never wanted to say anything. And a certain Titta, who lives near Montecitorio, spoke to me. He wanted me to make love embassies in the usual way. I told madonna about this, asking who was this man, meaning Titta. Because, every time we went to Campo Marzio, he came along behind us showing off with the horses.[19] She said nothing, but did not deny that she knew him or that he was her lover. *Adding on her own*: Titta told me that he had had intercourse with her, and that he had had my mistress the second week of her marriage, and she couldn't deny this. And she confessed that before she married they flirted in the house of Giulia Santana, and he gave her scudi and they kissed each other dancing. This he told me, and so did she.

She was asked who this Titta is. And where does he live and how often has he spoken with her about madonna Giulia?

SHE ANSWERED: I don't know where he comes from, nor where he lives. But she herself has told me that it is towards Montecitorio and that he is the son of a very rich man. I have talked with this Titta various times because each time I went out, he came hanging around me talking about madonna, wanting me to make embassies to her. I told him that he was the devil coming to tempt me. And I never said a thing about it to madonna, except one time or two – I'm telling the truth! – when I told her what he had said to me. And she said that Titta had had her, and told what he did at the ball, and she couldn't deny it and confessed that once Titta had left her fifteen scudi.

She was asked whether she had a conversation last Saturday with madonna Giulia, her mistress. And what did they talk about?

SHE ANSWERED: We talked about household matters in the usual way. For you can't be in a house without talking together. But I don't remember what we talked about.

She was asked whether she and madonna Giulia, her mistress, had arranged and carried out any magical practices, or as common speech has it, any 'spell-casting'[20] against messer Gieronimo, her master, and of what sort was it.

SHE ANSWERED: Signore, no! I was never mixed up in such a thing. No, never! In good faith, no, really, no! But I've well and often seen madonna doing certain things with some beans, holding them in her hand and making the sign of the cross. What it was, I don't know, nor do I remember whether she was doing it on Saturday, nor do I remember whether she had them in her hand on Saturday or not.

She was asked whether she knows or has seen her mistress, madonna Giulia, to prepare any spells or poison for her husband, messer Gieronimo. And what was it, and what did this spell do or what could it have done? And did she, the witness, lend her hand to preparing and making it? And what did she prepare?

SHE ANSWERED: I have no knowledge that madonna ever prepared poison to give to her husband, nor that she ever did other magic or spell-casting, except that one day I saw certain little bottles of oil that her sisters had given her. I asked her what that oil was good for. She told me that it was good for making the husband of a woman humble when he was annoyed at her, if you anointed him and touched him a little with that oil. And she told me that she had used it, and that when she had touched and anointed her husband with that oil, that he, her husband, had been humble to her. She said that the oil also has the virtue that, if a woman anoints her husband with it, he must do what she desires. *To a question, she added*: I don't know, nor have I seen that madonna Giulia made any spells against her husband. Except, some days ago she told me that her sisters did a certain thing that was good to make her husband kneel before her and ask her pardon.

She was asked if she knows that madonna Giulia ever made arrangements to kill messer Gieronimo, her husband. And of what sort were they? She should tell everything she knows.

SHE ANSWERED: I have no knowledge that she has ever made any arrangements, but certainly, sometimes, when they are angry together, I have heard her tell him that she would have him killed. And she's said this to him many times, because they are always in fire and in flames. And they are like the dogs and the cats, never an hour in peace. And I've heard them arguing at night, and messer Gieronimo threw her out of bed, according to what she told me. But I certainly heard them arguing all the time, and many times when I got between them, I came out the worse for it.

She was asked if she knows that madonna Giulia gave some magic substance, or, as the common speech says, 'charm' to her husband to eat. What was it, and did the witness know about it?

SHE ANSWERED: No, signore, no!

She was asked if she knows that madonna Giulia had made some false keys for opening the strongbox of her husband Gieronimo in order to rob him of his money. And does she know that madonna Giulia did it? And did she ask her help in doing it?

SHE ANSWERED: I cannot tell you that. Nor do I know that she ever took money. *Adding on her own:* It's true I heard messer Gieronimo complain of it when they were shouting at each other.

She was asked if she and madonna Giulia took any sum of money or any other goods from messer Gieronimo, their master and husband, respectively. And what sort of goods, and what sum of money?

SHE ANSWERED: I have never taken goods or any money from him. Nor have I ever had anything else, except about two bowls of flour that madonna gave me some days ago, by the hand of the house-servant himself. She sent it to my daughter, who is in the monastery of San Giovanni dell' Isola.[21] And sometimes she has sent her *pizze.*[22] But I know well that some months ago madonna sold some shirts and some old sheets and certain other old clothes to the Jews.

She was asked if she knows a certain Antonia. And did this Antonia come here to the house of messer Gieronomo last Saturday? And what was she here for? And did she speak to madonna Giulia, her mistress? And what did she talk about? And where? And did she give anything to madonna Giulia?

SHE ANSWERED: I know Antonia, who does odd jobs at the monastery of Campo Marzio. On Saturday, she came to the house and talked to madonna down here at the door of the house. She couldn't come in because the door was locked with a key, because messer always locks it with a key, and he carries the key. What they talked about I do not know, because I didn't go down to the door. But I saw clearly that madonna took from the door slot a little thing, nothing much, a paper packet, or a small object, that Antonia gave her. And, when Antonia went off, she said something or other about eating. And, because I was afraid that it was some bad thing to give to messer to eat, I spoke to the servant and the servant told messer. And when he asked me, I told him what I had seen and what I had heard. *Adding on her own*: The thing Antonia gave to madonna – she had it and I believe that messer has it now.

She was asked and warned and strongly urged to speak the pure and whole truth about all the acts done by her between Camillo Mantoano, their neighbour, and madonna Giulia, her patroness and mistress, and to tell the whole story.

SHE ANSWERED: I tell you, signore, I don't know anything about anything between them. I never got involved in any matter between them; all I know is what I have told you above.

She was asked and warned again to tell the truth. Is it true that she was aware and cognizant of a conversation between Camillo and Giulia and of the carnal knowledge between them that followed upon it? And did she receive several letters, along with money, from signore Camillo and give them to Giulia, her mistress? And did she not many times urge Giulia to consent to receive Camillo as her friend and to permit herself to be known carnally by signore Camillo?

SHE ANSWERED: I tell you, signore, none of these things are true! I knew nothing but what I told you. If she did wrong, she's the loser by it! I informed messer Christofano, an apothecary in Piazza Colonna, who is madonna's guardian.[23] I told him that I had been seeing some things that madonna Giulia did with the neighbour, in front of and in back of the house, which I didn't like and I told him to come and set things right. I also told and warned suor[24] Arcangela, her sister; she said that the serving women always misjudged matters. *Adding to a question*: I was aware that she flirted with this neighbour, but I have neither seen nor heard that anyone entered the house or had intercourse with her here in the house.

She was asked what she would say if it were said to her face by madonna Giulia that she herself had been the go-between; and that it was through her and by her efforts that madonna Giulia made friends with signore Camillo, the neighbour; and that she was known carnally by him in her [Camilla's] very room; and that she knew of all the doings between Camillo and Giulia; and that it was by the advice and deeds of her herself that Camillo made a hole in the wall over her room to be able to enter and there to know Giulia carnally; so that, very often, he came in and knew her in the past four months, while she [Camilla] stood on guard lest messer Gieronimo catch Giulia in adultery.

SHE ANSWERED: If she says such a thing, she will say it because she is spiteful, not because it is the truth, and I will tell her that she is not telling the truth.

*Then **Giulia** was brought face to face with Camilla and, having been put under oath, she was asked whether what she said and confessed in her examination yesterday was and is true, and whether she said it as the truth. And does she remember it, and does she wish to add or diminish or remove anything for the sake of the truth?*

SHE ANSWERED: Everything I said to you and confessed yesterday in my examination is true and I told it to you as the truth and I do not wish to add or subtract anything. And I remember well everything I said and I told you everything. Except I don't remember having told you that Camilla said to me that she would get me to buy a pair of strong-boxes from messer Camillo and have them filled with woollen clothing and that she would hide them for me in the house of a woman-friend and companion of hers and keep them there for me.

Then the examination and deposition of madonna Giulia was read by me, the notary, in an intelligible voice and understood by Camilla and she was asked whether what was read to her in the common speech was true in the way and form in which it was said. And she was warned and urged to tell the pure truth.

SHE ANSWERED: Signore, no! Signore, no, they are not true, and they never were true! And she said them and is saying them out of spite.

THEN MADONNA GIULIA ANSWERED and said in the face of the witness: These things, all of them are true, and they are Gospel of

God. *She added*: She should have as many ills as holy Lazarus; just so many times did she say that I should love messer Camillo. And then once she said to me – it was one evening by the fire – that once, when she got married, a niece of the bishop of her town was wedded at the same time. And there was a count who was in love with that niece of the bishop; he told Camilla that he was in love. And she talked about it to a cousin and carried it off in such a way that she brought to its goal that love of the count's and of that young woman. Camilla told me that she didn't do it as procuring, but she did it to please a signore.

THEN CAMILLA ANSWERED: These are things that you are dreaming up and they are not true.

Then madonna Giulia was sent off and Camilla was again warned to cease her lies and to speak the pure and entire truth.

SHE ANSWERED: I have told you the pure truth; I am neither willing nor able to say other than what I have said.

Then the examination was dismissed for now with intention of continuing.

7 December 1559
*Arraigned in person in the same place and before the same person as above. In the presence of Bartuccio, substitute fiscale: **madonna Giulia**, about whom as above. The oath about telling the truth was sworn by her and [the scriptures were] touched, etc. She said as follows, viz.*

She was asked if she has thought of anything more to enlarge upon the truth, beyond what was in her previous examination.

SHE ANSWERED: I have not thought of anything else to tell you because I have told the truth, and everything I told about it is true. I have been led to this great error by the counsel of this traitoress, Camilla, my servant. God knows my soul, and if God will prolong my life, I will never have any thought but to stay in His grace and in the grace of messer Gieronimo, my husband.

She was asked if she ever, on her own or on the counsel of others, prepared any charm, any spell for the poisoning of her husband, messer Gieronimo. And how many times, and what, and of what sort?

SHE ANSWERED: I will tell you the whole truth. And if I say anything else, I pray that God make me the sorriest woman in the world. And if I have ever thought to make or give poison or to do any hurt to my husband, whom I have loved and I love more than my life, even if I have done him this wrong with this Camillo Mantoano, about which I have grieved so bitterly with Camilla, telling her, 'Camilla, *ohimè*, what wrong is this that you have made me do to my husband!' And she kept saying, '*Ohimè*, madonna, why are you getting so squeamish? There is this one, and that one!' And she named me many noble ladies and great ladies who did this thing with an easy mind. And she told me that the Lord God was helping me, and he was doing it by way of a miracle, because I knew how fierce-tempered my husband was and because I didn't have any fun. And, in taking up the company of messer Camillo, I would have all the pleasures.

And because she said these things sobbing and weeping, I, the notary, asked her to return to the question.

SHE ANSWERED: I never thought to prepare poison for my husband, for whom I desire life, and not death. It is true, though, that, desiring the love of my husband, when I had gone one day last year to the monastery of Campo Marzio to see my sisters, I found a woman there. When I spoke of some standoffish things my husband did to me, she told me she would give me some sort of honey in a little flask. And she taught me that I should put it under the altar on Christmas night and have them say three masses in honour of the Trinity.[25] So I took it and put it under the altar and had the masses said, as she had told me to do. And she told me that any time I wanted an honest grace from my husband, anointing him with it, I would have any honest and licit grace. *Adding on her own*: I forgot to say that my own sisters, the nuns in Campo Marzio, had the honey fetched and they had the three praises of the Holy Trinity said. And that same woman gave me a little bit of magnet; if I had worn it, messer Gieronimo could not have done me harm and would have always loved me. And it was always for this end and effect that I have had these things. Look, here they are! *She showed some little bottles in which was honey and some beans and a magnet, saying*: If you are afraid that these things are dangerous because of poison, put them in my hand, and I will take them in my mouth to certify to you that I do not believe that there is anything poisonous or dangerous. If I had known such a thing, I never would have used them against my husband, except to the end that I told you about before. *And to a question she said*: I've never used these things – except the honey, one time only – on the person of my husband. It is true, though, that, as for the bean thing, Camilla did it many times in my presence, for Camillo. If she had done it for my husband, I would tell you, as I told you about the honey.

Then, because night was coming on and the hour was late, the examination was stopped for now with the intention of continuing.

8 December 1559
*Arraigned in person as above and in the presence of me, the notary, and in the presence of lord Bartuccio, substitute fiscale: **madonna Giulia**, about whom as above, by oath, touching [the scriptures] etc., she said as follows, viz.*

Asked and warned that, for greater and clearer truth, as said above, she should say and express by what means and how, by her consent and order, Camillo Mantoano broke through the wall and made a window, as is said above, and by what means and how often he came in through it to know her carnally.

SHE ANSWERED: That window that you have seen, which is built above the ceiling of the room where Camilla, my servant, usually sleeps – messer Camillo had it made by the arrangement and with the knowledge of Camilla. Since that window was not very commodious, he had it walled up again. When it was made, I did not know anything about it. And he came by day; he came down from the ceiling of the room and we had intercourse together and then, as I have said, he had that window walled up and had another made, more comfortable, and this one I knew about. And he had the wall fashioned in such a way that you could barely see it. By this means, he entered in the daytime and Camilla stood guard at the window of the stairs on the look-out for my husband.

I, the notary, along with Narcisso Rosati Bizzari di Trevi, saw and inspected this window, and also messer Vincenzo, chancellor of the bargello, saw it and inspected it.

15 December 1559
*Arraigned in Rome in Tor di Nona[26] in presence of the magnificent lord Romolo de Valenti, lieutenant, in my presence, and in the presence of lord Bartuccio, substitute fiscale: **Camilla**, as above, who was given the oath about telling the truth, and she swore and touched [the scriptures] and she was asked by the lord whether she is disposed to tell the truth more and better than she did in her other examinations.*

SHE ANSWERED: My signore, I am disposed to tell the truth and I told it in all those things they wrote down there in messer Gieronimo's house where I was examined two times.

And the lord said that, unless she was disposed to offer more truth than there was in her earlier examinations, the truth itself would stay hidden, for not a trace of the truth appears in her examinations, so far is what she has said from the truth.

SHE ANSWERED: I tell you, signore, that I did tell it! *And she said this several times.* My master and my mistress want me to lose the little I have in their house, that's what they want to do. Because I think that my master is a man who would divide a louse in half [for stinginess], and everything he does, he does to win for himself the property of that poor thing of a madonna Giulia. And he told me this. For one evening he kept me more than four hours in his office, asking me to tell him if Giulia had had it done to her. And I told him that, truth to tell, I couldn't say, because I hadn't seen a thing. And messer Gieronimo went after madonna Giulia several times, with daggers to her throat. I tell you, signore, whatever Giulia confessed, he made her confess it by force and fear. And this I heard myself. If you knew the bad treatment this messer Gieronimo gave her, you would be astounded. You could barely believe it. I swear to you, I have seen him take away the bread in front of her and other foods, because he didn't want her to eat. And sometimes he made her get out of bed in the middle of the night, because he wanted to sleep on the tile floor or on the chests. And he kept her locked in her room and he did other such doggish things to her. And a thousand times he has kicked her, and I had to separate them and at times I got hurt. The poor thing gave him a good dowry. If I have heard right, between house, money, and other movable goods, she gave him a good three thousand scudi.[27] And all the goods in this house come from that poor dear, according to what she said, because in the house he didn't have anything, except certain goods of a woman-servant who had lived with him, and which he never would let her have back. And think! That poor madonna Giulia has no wish to say these things because she is in his hands. But they are very true. And I didn't say them in my other examination because I was in his house and I was afraid of him.

She was asked how she knows that what madonna Giulia confessed in her other examination was said because of fear and force.

SHE ANSWERED: I know because I heard it, and I heard them quarrelling in the night.

And the lord said that she should specify what her master and her mistress were quarrelling about.

SHE ANSWERED: I couldn't hear all the words, but the substance of what they were arguing about was that messer Gieronimo said, 'Tell me! Confess it to me! If you confess it to me, I will pardon you. I want nothing more from you. If you don't confess it to me, I will make you confess anyway.' And then I heard madonna Giulia scream, 'Leave me alone, traitor, traitor!' so that I thought he had his hands at her throat. But I don't know if that poor thing of a Giulia will confess these things, for she is afraid of her husband.

She was asked what this thing was that messer Gieronimo so insistently wanted his wife to confess.

SHE ANSWERED: I can't tell you any more. He wanted her to confess what she has confessed. I couldn't hear all the words.

And the lord said that she should go into the particulars of accusations made and objections offered between madonna Giulia and her husband, messer Gieronimo.

SHE ANSWERED: All I can tell you is that messer Gieronimo said that he wanted madonna Giulia to confess, that he had found someone in the house, and she should tell him who it was. And she has confessed what the notary wrote down, but I know neither who nor how, because I didn't see anybody.

And the lord asked again if she does not know the name of the person who is supposed to have been in the house of messer Gieronimo with madonna Giulia.

SHE ANSWERED: I don't know what his name is. I don't know who he might be. I've never seen him; in the house I have seen neither him nor others. *She added*: I don't know anything more, except what was read to me in messer Gieronimo's house in the examination of madonna Giulia. And as for her, I have no knowledge that she ever talked with anyone in the house. But she certainly talked with men or with women, as pleased her fancy, there at the door by the stairs. But it was locked with a key and you couldn't come in. *And to a question of the lord she said*: I had no traffic with the neighbours, except in the house of the fiscale of the Campidoglio and in the house of messer Claudio della Valle.

She was asked who inhabits the house contiguous to the house of messer Gieronimo.

SHE ANSWERED: There were some gentlemen. I don't know. I don't know them. I've heard tell they are two brothers, but I don't know what they're called. But I've heard them called by other gentlemen signore Camillo and signore Ferrante, when they came to ask if they wanted to go riding. And they rode for pleasure. But that's all I know of them.

His Lordship asked who is the elder of the two brothers.

SHE ANSWERED: This I don't know, because I don't know which is Ferrante, nor which is Camillo, except that I have heard them named. And several times I have seen them from the window, and sometimes by chance in the street. But I don't know them by name.

She was asked with whom madonna Giulia was talking at the door as she said above. Did she talk with one or another of these brothers at that door or elsewhere, so far as she knows?

She answered in the negative.

She was asked whether messer Gieronimo was suspicious of one of the two brothers. And of whom?

SHE ANSWERED: I don't know anything, except what his wife confessed. She named this Camillo.

She was asked if anyone could get into messer Gieronimo's house by any other way, ordinarily, than the door. And where?

SHE ANSWERED: I don't know that there is another entrance or way of entry except by the door, or by the windows if you put up a ladder. Except that messer Gieronimo has said that he found something or other in his house. But I don't know what it is and I haven't seen it. *Then she added on her own:* He says he found a window, but I don't know, except from his mouth, because I haven't seen it.

And the lord said that she should indicate in what part of the house the window was made.

SHE ANSWERED: I tell you that I don't know, save from the mouth of messer Gieronimo. And he was the first to tell me that it was a window, or hole – I don't know what it is – that was made over the room where I slept. I left that room in the morning when I got up and I never came back, except in the evening when I went to bed. Over my room was a loft and a hole to go up there. Messer went up to put cats there, but never went up inside. But I never went there.

She was asked what made messer Gieronimo fall into suspicion of his wife.

SHE ANSWERED: Messer came to the house and found me by the fire and said to me, 'Where is Giulia?' I said to him, 'I don't know,' and went looking for her in the *loggetta* and, not finding her, I went up to the middle room and said, 'Madonna, messer is asking for you!' And she came out, and we encountered messer at the top of the stairs. He said to us, 'What are you doing?' And madonna answered him, 'Nothing special.' And messer went into the room and we went downstairs and he said that he had found a man. And that's what brought on all this uproar. *Adding to a question*: It is true that, when I went to call madonna Giulia, I left my clogs by the fire because I had been warming my feet and I had them out of the clogs. When I have to go upstairs, I always leave the clogs off so as not to break my neck, or my legs, or get hurt.

She was asked how long before the return of messer Gieronimo had madonna Giulia gone upstairs. And did she often go up?

SHE ANSWERED: Giulia went up a little beforehand. And she went whenever she felt like it. I didn't go up after her, because I had other things to do. And because I have been in that house sixteen months and my life's been total misery. I've never had it worse.

And the lord asked what madonna Giulia was going to do when she went up to the room.

SHE ANSWERED: If she knows the answer, I don't. I don't know if she went there for the oakum, or for the flax, or for lovemaking. She went any time she wanted to. And she went when her husband wasn't there, and, when she felt like it, she went when he was there too. I don't know any more about it. That's all I know. You can keep me here a thousand years, because there is nothing more I can tell you.

And the lord said that she is audacious so boldly to deny what was affirmed by madonna Giulia, and which concerns more Giulia's situation than her own. That fact makes it seem that madonna Giulia is not lying.

SHE ANSWERED: I tell you that whatever madonna Giulia told you is a lie. She said it to please her husband, who wanted her to confess. She thought she would get back into his good graces. Rather, she confessed what he made her say. Or rather she wanted to put the blame on me and to excuse herself. Or because she hated me because that day I said something really bad, and because messer Gieronimo made all this fuss. Madonna Giulia had taken something or other, I know not what, from the serving woman of the nuns of Campo Marzio at the slit in the door, and, when I told on her, madonna took to hating me and said against me what she has said, but she was wrong. *Adding to a question* : This thing that the woman brought her, I said in the other examination that I don't know what it was, but the notaries found it. That thing was given her from the slit in the door and I believe it had to have been that woman from the monastery in Campo Marzio.

She was warned to make up her mind to tell the truth about the whole affair, without any distortion, and about the deed that was undertaken and accomplished by madonna Giulia and her. And she should avoid all lies. Otherwise, the truth will be had from her by rigorous examination and extraordinary measures.[28]

SHE ANSWERED: Signore, you should know that I have told you the truth, and with all the martyrdoms in the world you will not make me say anything but the truth. I can't say anything but the truth. I tell you, she has lied to you. She said it from fear, to excuse herself, and there is no truth in it. You will never find that I know a thing like that. And if she did it, she knows it. I don't know it. I know indeed that her husband treated her terribly and barely let her go to mass. And, after the Pope died [23 August], she has never gone. Even the day of St Andrew [30 November], with her husband's permission, she was dressed to go to the parish church to mass, and Gieronimo, when he saw her, because she looked too comely, put his fingernails in her cheeks; I believe that even today she bears the marks.

The lord then dismissed the examination and ordered the witness to be put in the public part of the jail with the intention of continuing.

THE COMMENTARY

This trial feels immured. Not only almost all the events it portrays but also all save the very last of the six testimonies collected by the court take place within the confining walls of one unhappy household. In this domestic tale, there are four chief protagonists. One is the master of the house, messer Gieronimo Piccardi, a notary of the Rota, a major papal court. He is a rough and restrictive husband. Another, madonna Giulia, is his unhappy wife. A third, Camillo Mantoano, is a gentleman, a next door neighbour, and Giulia's lover. Fourth, and surprisingly central to events, is Camilla of Parma, a middle-aged servant of scant wealth or station; as wily as she is marginal and poor, she is the linchpin of several plots and thus, eventually, the butt of the court's investigation; it is she, and not the adulterous wife, who figures on the title page of the manuscript, charged with 'procuring.' Why so, when both do wrong? Clearly, social standing counts; the respective fates of the two women illustrate the play of status, for legal and social blame often flow readily down the course of least resistance. This trial thus brims with lessons about the domestic politics of gender and of status. It illustrates, in particular, some of the power that weak but resourceful women could contrive to grasp. In this case, both wife and servant construct a fragile alliance against the husband. But, in the end, it collapses ignominiously. The collapse itself offers an interesting commentary on the limitations of female strength in a world where most power lies in the hands of males.

The events span four months. August 1559 sees madonna Giulia shut in at home. Always tumultuous, the Vacant See which then celebrates the death of Paul IV is especially violent, chasing many women more than ever into the somewhat greater safety of their houses. Since then, it seems, madonna Giulia has been confined at home, locked in by her husband. Not long after, in September, the love-plot begins; serving as a go-between, Camilla approaches her mistress on behalf of Camillo, the gentleman in the house next door. But, if we can believe Giulia, Camilla does more than carry amorous messages, for on love's behalf she urges, plans, conspires, counsels and consoles. Indeed, Giulia would have the court believe that Camilla has been the instigator and guardian spirit of the whole intrigue. Maybe so. Certainly, with Camilla's help, Camillo pierces the wall between the houses, fashioning a cunningly disguised window that opens into the air space above the ceiling of the middle room upstairs, over Camilla's bedroom, where Gieronimo is wont to put the cat to chase the mice. In the servant's chamber, while she stands guard, the two meet for love's pleasures. Some eight or ten times they enjoy their trysts before, on Saturday, 2 December, Gieronimo's too swift return and Camillo's too slow escape expose the women's plot and shatter their alliance. The former allies swiftly turn on one another, each hoping to shift blame onto the other's back. Within hours, Camilla, despite her erstwhile protestations of loyalty to her mistress, blurts out a confession to her master. Before the magistrates, mixing calumny with syrupy commiseration, she blackens her mistress. Meanwhile, protesting devotion to her husband, Giulia does her best to convince the court that the blame is all Camilla's.

Three days after the plot's discovery, the envoys of the court arrive at the Piccardi house, summoned by the husband. On Tuesday, 5 December, they question Camilla, who strives to obfuscate and to deny. But, the next day, Giulia gives a long confession in which she claims to tell all about her adultery, but recounting the story as if Camilla has been the principal instigator and she, the adulteress, a mere reluctant accomplice. On Thursday, the magistrates return with further interests, for someone, probably Gieronimo, has denounced the women for thefts, magic, and a plot to poison him. Camilla remains obdurate in the face first of very precise questions based on Giulia's confession and then of Giulia herself. When the court brings the wife in for a formal 'confrontation,' it ends in mutual recrimination, Giulia citing Camilla's earlier amorous mediations and the servant accusing the mistress of spite. The court, having dismissed Camilla, then brings Giulia back to answer terrifying accusations of spell-casting and intent to poison, which she denies with tears and supplications for aid in reconciliation with her husband. On Friday, the wife appears once more to testify about piercing the wall. The officers of the court, having inspected Camillo's secret door, depart, leaving Giulia to the mercies of Gieronimo. Camilla, on the other hand, at some point is hauled off to jail at Tor di Nona. There she appears, one week later, steadfast as usual in denial and blame. The court threatens her with torture but, refraining, releases her into the public section of the jail to prepare a legal defence. As often, no sentence survives; we cannot be sure if the trial ever goes forward.

It often helps to unravel a political event, even one so small as this, if one catalogues the goals, the assets, and the liabilities of the several parties. Let us survey the four chief actors, starting at the top with Camillo, the most privileged, and then descending stepwise to the servant.

Camillo is a gentleman. That fact distinguishes him in the women's eyes. Indeed, we know little else about him, save that he lives next door, for in this story we, like Gieronimo, see him only from the knees down. Camillo's most concrete asset, in this intrigue, is a convenient lodging on the other side of a frangible wall. More important are his wealth and standing, both for winning Giulia's assent and for warding off the law and the wronged husband's wrath. Gieronimo seems to have lacked the nerve to take him on. His lower status may have discouraged violence, for, in general, the Roman sense of honour frowns on attacking one's betters or one's underlings. It only favours horizontal challenges. Consequently, Camillo's liabilities are few. Although law and religion deplore adultery, they pose him little danger when the ethics of everyday life regard phlegmatically the seduction of the women of one's inferiors. But what are his aims? Why make a play for Giulia, a wife, when Rome is full of courtesans, serving girls, and other women too weakly placed to deny a gentleman's desire? Locked away by a jealous husband, Giulia may have posed a delicious challenge. We suspect that the thrill of stealing honour from a man of substance may have whetted the lover's intent.

Though below Camillo on the social ladder, Gieronimo too has many assets on his side. Law, religion, and custom all accord him, as husband, the headship of his house. All three thus sanction his unquestioned command over its womenfolk. Against them, he can also wield the force of hands and arms. By law, all property is his. In his serving man and in the neighbours, he has allies ready to defend him from intruders. A man of the law, he has easy access to the courts. To what end does he use these assets? Primarily, to protect his honour, which is intimately bound up with the integrity of two enclosures, his dwelling and the body of his wife. Thus it is that Gieronimo locks her in and carries off the key. But honour is at once an asset and a liability, for it is fragile and its breach is costly. The two enclosures, house and wife, prove all too permeable. Around the city go the servants, Camilla and Antonia, messengers across the thresholds of private space. Into the open yard sail love letters. Through the windows come words and signs and glances. Through the door come dangerous packets. Through the very wall comes Camillo, violator at once of house, of matrimony, of woman, and of honour. But how could Gieronimo's honour, which gives him social credit, at the same time be a burden and a hinderance? Honour constrains Gieronimo. It leaves him vulnerable through his wife, who could thwart his vigilance. Fear of disgrace might deter some men from availing themselves of neighbours and of the court to chase off an adulterer; Gieronimo, however, seems to have been willing to risk the shame to gain some allies.

At first glance, only the weakness of Giulia's position catches the eye. Law, religion, and custom dictate her subservience. Her honour, as a woman of worth, keeps her tightly confined. To make things worse, fortune has left her few social allies. Her parents must be dead, for she has a guardian, an apothecary. We see no trace of brothers, or even of brothers-in-law, for her sisters are nuns together in a Roman convent. We do not hear even of a network of friends. She is locked up at home. Thus she falls back on Camilla and on the supernatural for support and aid. So long as he lives, Gieronimo is master of her dowry and her fate; yet, even against this harsh and overbearing husband, Giulia is not completely defenceless. She discomfits Gieronimo, screaming at him when they fight 'like the dogs and the cats.' She can filch money from his strongbox. Perhaps she could take a wife's sullen revenge in bed, though we have no hint of that. Against him she can use magic, no mean threat in a credulous world. Geronimo seems to suspect that she could even resort to poison. One great source of Giulia's strength lies in the vulnerability of Gieronimo's honour. Her power to destroy it through adultery may have tempered his behaviour. Still, when she carries out the threat, Giulia turns to her servant for help. With Camilla, too, she has assets. Giulia is a benefactress with a broker's powers; she can intercede with the husband on her maid's behalf.

We can only guess at Giulia's goals in pursuing a love intrigue, for she discreetly hides them from the court. There must have been the obvious pleasures of love itself, of flattery, of sympathetic company, of pocket money. Giulia may also have enjoyed a taste of revenge. But uppermost in her mind may have been the fun of it all. Several times in the trial, Giulia quotes Camilla as telling her that she has no fun at all. 'This will be your entertainment.' The term is active. Camilla, in Giulia's mouth, has said not 'He will give you pleasure' but 'You will entertain yourself.' The phrase suggests the playfulness of the whole affair. Love, like other games, has its trodden rules, its roles, and its etiquette, which guide the lover, the beloved, and the go-between. Each stock character has a familiar part to play. If this love affair seems almost plagiarized from a Renaissance novella, is it not because art and life shared many of the same conventions?

Camilla has unexpected assets. Of course, her weaknesses are legion, her means paltry. She has no family, save a daughter in a nunnery on the Tiber Island, for whom she scrounges flour and *pizze* from her mistress. Unlike Giulia, she can barter neither looks nor youth nor reputation. She has little property, status, strength, or security of employment. But out of these weaknesses, she can forge some strengths. Because low in status, unlike her mistress, she has scarce honour. That fact gives her great franchise; she can come and go at will. Not only that, but it allows her the inverse of honour, shame-lessness, which lets her bear disgraceful propositions, betray her master's trust and dabble in black arts. Camilla, thus, is free to play the scamp and go-between. Her liberty of movement lets her build up a network of women and men for whom she does errands and favours. There is thus a complementarity between mistress and servant; while Camilla depends on Giulia's patronage, Giulia needs Camilla's lack of honour. She has other assets too. Camilla enjoys a worldly wisdom, a savvy about love matters that seems to have given her a kind of ascendancy over her young mistress, whom she counsels 'as a daughter.' Camilla also has a more sinister power: blackmail; she knows about her mistress's trespasses. Giulia quotes her as threatening her with ruin. Leading her mistress into misdemeanour, Camilla has garnered leverage against her. Of course, Giulia could also have exposed Camilla, who is in as deep as she. But this, as a woman of honour, she cannot easily do, for she has far more at stake. Where Camilla risks punishment and dismissal, Giulia risks her position in society.

Operating as she does from a position of social weakness, Camilla, a restless and instinctive political machinator, brings to bear her every asset to building an alliance with her mistress. Like politicians everywhere, she traffics in secrets. We see her 'one evening by the fire' telling madonna about her past exploits as go-between. In exchange for confidences, she receives like tokens from Giulia, tales of her earlier indiscretions. But Camilla always plays a double game, for, both during and after her alliance with her mistress, she betrays these confidences and tattles on her doings. Lacking honour, she is little bound to fidelity; necessity and licence combine to make her a rascal.

A love intrigue offers Camilla several boons. There are the tips and gifts she earns for errands. There is the fun of it, the pleasure of the game. In addition, there is the ascendancy she gains over her mistress, who comes to depend on her for advice, for services, and for discretion. For both servant and mistress, there is yet another benefit, the conspiratorial intimacy born of the thrill of shared enterprise and danger. We cannot prove it, but suspect that Giulia and Camilla may have enjoyed together an emotional exchange more potent, keener, and more satisfying than anything imparted by the furtive, fleeting lover.

Although their assets and their goals diverge, the two women can build an alliance that crosses the boundaries of status. An exchange of favours and threats cements it. To Camilla, Giulia gives protection against the master, small gifts of food and household objects, the lover's lesser tips, some of her secrets. To Giulia, Camilla gives her conspiratorial companionship, her worldly wisdom, her freedom of movement, her access to the supernatural, and her wider network outside the Piccardi doors. Against Giulia, Camilla holds the threat of exposure. Against Camilla, Giulia holds her authority as mistress of the house. Although cemented by no formal oath or treaty, this alliance has much of the nature of the alliances built by the men who rule city states and principalities. There are the same half-sincere protestations of shared fate and sentiments, the same betrayals and double dealings. Sometimes, the women even evoke the male rhetoric of state. We hear this best in Giulia's epitaph for the love conspiracy: 'I have been assassinated and betrayed by Camilla and by bad fortune.'

Camilla has betrayed her mistress all along. She has run to Giulia's guardian and to her sister, suor Arcangela, to tattle on madonna's indiscretions with Titta. Camilla's greatest betrayal comes the very morning of the dénouement, when, glimpsing what she thinks is poison passing through the slot in the street door, she informs first the servant, Vincenzo, and then, on questioning, her master. Does Camilla really fear for messer's life or, as is more likely, does she merely wish to curry favour? Her news may have provoked Gieronimo's disastrous return that afternoon. The contents of this recent packet are never made clear. Notice that Giulia's testimony seems not to deal with it; the potion she offers to swallow had been, she says, under an altar at Christmas, almost a year ago. Nevertheless, the court, which seems not to take the chance of poison seriously, lets the matter drop.

Under the pressure of discovery, the alliance between the two women collapses ingloriously. Within hours, cajoled by Gieronimo, Camilla blurts out the lover's name. The betrayal is mutual. As her secrets come to light, Camilla loses all her hold on her mistress; Giulia takes to serving her husband's purposes, collaborating in his attempt to throw all blame on the servant, and hastens to blacken Camilla to the court. Camilla responds in kind, painting her mistress as an inveterate ribald and casting doubts on her veracity. By the formal logic of the situation, the women almost have to welch on one another, for collusion is not easy under Gieronimo's angry scrutiny, and their culpability is too clear. Although stubborn mutual silence might have served them both, in the absence of mutual trust, they can make good some losses through betrayal. Giulia, who has to make peace with an intemperate husband, can best do so through humble supplication and help in finding a scapegoat for the disgrace. Under stress and in real danger, she assumes a suppliant pose at once Christian and secular; she throws herself at the mercy of those who, on earth as in heaven, might spare her. Camilla, for her part, has too much to fear from the state and too little to gain from heaven or from Giulia, whose service she must quit. In the light of day, most of her assets vanish. Like guerillas, women can work only clandestinely for power. Under the pressure of male power, Gieronimo's and the court's, Camilla and Giulia can only turn against one another.

CHAPTER SIX

Lucrezia's Magic

THE TRIAL

[This is not a proper trial, but a preliminary investigation that may or may not lead to more formal proceedings. Lucrezia the Greek is under suspicion of magical practices. Three of her servants and a friend testify.]

Concerning Lucrezia the Greek, a courtesan[1]

20 April 1559
There was examined in the office of me, the notary: **Caterina Nanzi** *of Lorraine, who lives at San Lazzaro, witness for the information of the court, who, having touched the scriptures, said as follows.*

She was asked whether she knows or presumes to know the cause of her present examination.

SHE ANSWERED: I believe your Lordship wants to examine me on account of one Lucrezia the Greek, against whom I was examined one other time.

And I, the notary, asked about what things the witness was examined elsewhere against Lucrezia, and where, and by whom.

SHE ANSWERED: About certain follies, prayers, and spells that she caused to be done by a boy named Christoforo, whom she had in her house.

She was asked whether she can remember what she said in her other exami-

nation. And she should tell it again, as the truth, without straying from the tale.

SHE ANSWERED: I said that I was with Lucrezia for the space of eight or ten days, and in that time I saw that Lucrezia made that boy of hers, Christoforo, who was some thirteen years old, say certain prayers written on [...] paper with a blessed candle, lit, in his hand, in front of an image of St Daniel in an upstairs room. I heard the boy reading that prayer with that blessed candle in his hand in front of St Daniel.[2] He said to St Daniel on the part of God, of the Virgin Mary and of all the male and female saints of God, of the sky, of the earth, of the air, fire, and water, that St Daniel should work magic on one messer Giovanni Maria, a servant[3] of the pope, to make him love Lucrezia. I saw this several times, for Lucrezia ordered the boy to say it. The boy told me that at Lucrezia's orders he had said that spell twenty or thirty times. As for that prayer, Lucrezia told me that she had bought the prayer from one Imperia who used to live at the Ripetta[4] in a house near the Inquisition, and Imperia has a mother who had it. This was two years ago and Imperia often came to Lucrezia's house. *Adding*: Lucrezia told me that she had bought that spell from Imperia for five scudi. *Adding*: That prayer was two written pages and I don't know what it contained besides what I have said. *Adding*: I have also heard from one Laura the Sienese, who was then living with donna Lucrezia the Greek, that the Greek went to cut the cords of the bells and that she had them burnt in a lamp with oil and holy water so that messer Giovanni Maria might love her, and that she had earth taken from in front of the doors of the famous courtesans and brought to her house, saying that in such a way she would have good fortune come into her house.

She was asked whether she knows or has heard said that the aforesaid Laura is angry with Lucrezia the Greek.

SHE ANSWERED: This is what that was all about. Madonna Laura told me that Lucrezia said some insulting things to her, I don't know what, and that she called her a whore to her face, though she is a respectable woman.[5] They became acquaintances because Lucrezia fled to Laura's house, for a captain Tomasso wanted to kill her, as I have heard. *Adding*: I said all these things to Lucrezia's face and I will say them to her again when the need comes. And I said this in my other examination, for the truth, to her face, in Corte Savelli.

[She was sworn to] silence with an oath.

In the same case

The same day
There was examined in the same place and by the same person: **Lucrezia,**[6] *daughter of Francesco of Siena, widow of one Giovanni di Domenico di Pontremoli, witness for the information of the court, who touched the scriptures etc. and said as follows.*

She was asked whether she knows or presumes to know the cause of her present examination.

SHE ANSWERED: I think it is on account of Lucrezia the Greek, and if not, I have no idea for what other reason.

And I, the notary, asked why she believes it is rather on account of Lucrezia than for another reason.

SHE ANSWERED: I think that is the reason why, for I have been examined other times on her account.

She was asked for how long she has known Lucrezia the Greek. And what was the cause of her knowing her?

SHE ANSWERED: I met her on St Bartholomew's day, going on two years ago now.[7] And the reason was that I went to live with her as a servant and stayed with her for nine months.

She was asked how many times she was examined against Lucrezia and in what court.

SHE ANSWERED: I was examined against Lucrezia one time in my house by a notary of the vicario. I think his name was messer Camillo.

She was asked whether she remembers what she said in her other examination. And can she tell it truthfully, without lies?

SHE ANSWERED: I certainly can remember something of what I said. *Adding*: When I lived with her I saw that she used a spell that she had said daily by a boy of hers called Christoforo, in front of St Daniel, upstairs in a room. She made him hold a blessed candle lit in his hand. I saw this several times. Lucrezia would send me away and didn't want me to see it. But I didn't hear the words. She made him say this spell eight or ten times a day. She told me that she had this spell said because she wanted to make one Giovanni Maria, servant of the pope, fall in love with her, and others too. Then one day the Greek wanted me to go fetch the rope of a bell. And she gave me a pair of scissors because she wanted me to [...] go cut the rope with them. So I pretended to go do the job, and I [took?] those scissors and went to my niece's house, where I am living now. I went upstairs and found some window-blinds of mine that were in a room, and on them I found some rope. I took a knife and I cut a palm's length of that rope, and I took it to the Greek. She said to me, 'You've been gone a long time!' I answered her, 'Eh! What did You want me to do? Did You want me to be seen cutting the ropes of bells?' So she began to believe that it really was 'cord,' and she gave me money to go buy a lamp, and said that I should do what she asked me to, without further talk. So I brought her the lamp, and she began to light it with that cord. And she made me buy a jug of oil just for that.[8] And she left that lamp burning both day and night on a hearth so that that Giovanni Maria would love her. And it was she who lit the lamp, and she said certain words over it, but I couldn't hear them, but I saw her move her mouth.

Afterwards, whenever she slept with someone, and above all with cardinal Strozzi, she gave me certain ragged handkerchiefs, telling me, 'Put this aside. I sponged my genitals with it because I slept with the cardinal.' So I put those handkerchiefs aside. Later, she made me find those handkerchiefs. And I gave them to her, and she took them and tore them into little bits and made wicks out of them. And with them, she took a lamp with oil and made those wicks burn, sometimes under the bed and sometimes at the fireplace. And she said certain words over them, like the others, or like them in meaning, to kindle the heart of Giovanni Maria, or some other heart [...] And I have seen her do this several times. *Adding on her own*: Several days before I left her, all one night long, Lucrezia was crying. I asked her what was wrong, but she didn't want to tell me anything. But, almost at daybreak, in tears, she told me that she had had intercourse with a gentleman, a *cameriere*[9] of His Holiness – I don't remember his name – and that she had attached her 'cloths' to her.[10] So she let me see, and I found that she had two 'cloths' attached to her bottom, down by the genitals, and there was one that was big. She had tightened it [?] with a silk thread and this 'cloth' was swollen up and it was causing her pain.[11] So she had me get a pair of scissors, and she had me cut that thread. And I was at it, cutting that thread from before daybreak up till the hour of the mid-day meal. I asked her how it had happened and how they came to be there. She answered me that she had had intercourse with that *cameriere* and that the sperm had syphilitic traces and that was why those cloths were there.[12] That is all I can tell you. *Then she said*: One Francesca, who lives with Caterina the Greek, behind [Santa Maria della] Pace,[13] who also lived with Lucrezia the Greek, told me once that the Greek had sent her to collect the dust from in front of the doors of the most favoured whores, saying that she was carrying off the good fortune from that whore and carrying it to her house. I think she could tell you something, as could that boy, Christoforo, who lives near Sant'Ivo[14] in that alley – he lives there with the colonel, also known as Salustio Borghese – in a house where there are rooms for rent. *Adding*: These things that I am telling You, I have told as the truth and as the truth I will maintain them.

[She was sworn to] silence with an oath.

24 April 1559
Against Lucrezia the Greek, courtesan.

There was examined in Rome in the office of me, the notary, and by me: madonna **Imperia**, *daughter of the late maestro Giovanni di Caravaggio, living near the embassy of the king of France,[15] witness for the information of the court, who touched the scriptures and said as follows.*

She was asked if she knows or presumes to know the cause of her present examination.

SHE ANSWERED: I was summoned yesterday morning, and all yesterday and last evening I have thought about it and I have not been able to imagine why.

She was asked whether she knows madonna Laura Mosti. And since when? And what has been the cause of their acquaintance?

SHE ANSWERED: Signore, I do not know this madonna Laura Mosti. *Adding to a question of me, the notary*: I have been a widow for four years now, since they knocked down the houses at the Madonna dei Miracoli.[16] *Then she said*: I have never had a husband, but that friend of mine died then. His name was messer Francesco the Spaniard, a solicitor of the cardinal of Santiago. By him I had four children, two boys and two girls. And one boy and one girl are dead, and the other boy is in Spain and the other girl lives with a boatman named Antonio da Carpi, who also is a wood merchant and lives in the street called Vantaggio as you go by San Giacomo degli Incurabili, the first alley you find on the left as you go toward the Popolo.[17]

She was asked if she knows a certain Lucrezia the Greek, a courtesan. And since when? And what was the cause of their acquaintance?

SHE ANSWERED: Signore, yes. I know this madonna Lucrezia the Greek, and this is how. Four years ago, already, before they knocked down the houses at the Madonna dei Miracoli, I was at my house. I had a pretty garden. This signora Lucrezia happened one day to pass by my house. And she said, 'Oh, Madonna, You have a pretty garden!' and things like that. So we made friends. Then along came the war and I heard she had as a friend one messer Salustio Borghese, a Sienese, called 'the colonel.' One day, this Lucrezia showed up at my house saying that the colonel had thrown her out. She stayed for a month, and she came naked and barefoot to my house. And if she wanted to go out, she put on my clothes, even down to the stockings.

She was asked if she yet knows or even can presume to know the cause of her present examination.

SHE ANSWERED: Signore, no! I do not know, nor can I even guess.

She was asked whether she usually keeps the company of Lucrezia.

SHE ANSWERED: I saw a lot of her while she was living with the colonel. And, at the time, I slept with her several times.[18] At the time, I lived at San Salvatore alle Coppelle.[19] I can't tell you how long I lived there. I believe I only lived there a short while. As for the rest, after that, I had no dealings with her, except when she lived there. I went once to her house to fetch back a mirror and a pair of sleeves of mine that she had carried off from my house. *Adding to a question*: I know that she had as a friend cardinal Strozzi and messer Salustio, as she told me.[20] As for the rest, that is all I know.

She was asked whether she knows or can guess the cause of her present examination.

SHE ANSWERED: I do not know, nor can I even guess. *Adding to a question of the notary*: I never knew that Lucrezia did things to draw to her any man, or that served the cause of love, because I never have been close with her.

She was asked whether she knows that Lucrezia had in her service a certain boy named Christoforo.

SHE ANSWERED: I never knew that she herself employed this boy, but I heard it said that the boy was with the colonel, in so far as he [the colonel] was in her house.

[She was sworn to] silence with an oath.

In the same case

On the same day
There was examined in the same place and by the same person as above:
Christoforo, *the son of the late Bartolomeo di Sintoni, of Padua, witness for the information of the court, who touched the scriptures and said as follows.*

He was asked if he knows or can presume to know the cause of his present examination.

HE ANSWERED: I do not know the cause, nor can I imagine why.

He was asked if he was ever examined, and for what reason, before whom, and in what matter.

HE ANSWERED: I was examined, some days past, in Corte Savelli, by the judge and the notary – I don't know what court they belong to – on account of a signora Lucrezia the Greek. *Adding:* They asked me if I knew that she was a caster of spells. I answered that I did not. *Adding to another question of me, the notary:* All day yesterday, I thought over the reason why I had been summoned to inform the court. For the life of me, I couldn't guess.

He was asked how long has it been that he has known Lucrezia the Greek. And what was the cause of their acquaintance?

HE ANSWERED: I have known Lucrezia for four years. The reason was that messer Salustio, my master, kept her at his house, and then, when I fell sick, I spent nine months at her house.

He was asked if he knows or has even heard it said that madonna Lucrezia used anything for magical love craft.[21]

HE ANSWERED: I do not know that she ever used such a thing, nor that she amused herself in such a way.

[He was sworn to] silence, with an oath.

THE COMMENTARY

Like madonna Giulia and her conniving servant, the courtesan Lucrezia the Greek makes alliances and uses magic to conduct the risky politics of love. We have met Lucrezia before, as the old rival of

Camilla the Skinny, who may have burned her door. Clearly, the Greek is a substantial courtesan, rich enough to employ at least two servants and attractive enough in body, clothing, and domestic furnishings to entertain a cardinal who is otherwise known, says the famous papal historian Pastor, for his zeal against Calvinism. But even a fancy prostitute's lot is not an easy one. The many books that celebrate the glories of the Roman courtesan often overlook the tawdrier side of her life. Lucrezia is secure neither in her alliances, nor in her status, nor in her house, nor in her body. The firebrand Camilla the Skinny is the least of her worries. For example, angry lovers can chase her 'naked' into the street. The virulent syphilis of the sixteenth century can ruin her. Against such danger and insecurity, Lucrezia, as did madonna Giulia, turns to friends and, through magic, to supernatural allies.

Her friends are both women and men. The neighbour, madonna Imperia, is a 'widow' who has never married, neither wife nor whore, but 'woman' [femina] of a man now dead, a mother of four who claims respectability. To the courtesan, she offers shelter and clothing when trouble strikes and, for cash, the prayer for love. Imperia proves what is clear from other trials, that the prostitute, though of dubious repute, is no outcast in her neighbourhood.

As for males, although we know far less of Lucrezia's friends and allies than of Camilla the Skinny's, clearly, for her as for Camilla, the ties with clients were complex. These bonds might engage not only mercenary interest, but also obligation and sentiment. Thus, we hear of the Greek's intense desire to secure the love of certain men. Camilla the Skinny, in the Di Grassi trial, describes her as 'in love' [inamorata] and as driven crazy over a man. Talk of love is not uncommon in the profession. As Camilla's colleague, Paola da Forlì, says, courtesans talk of lovers and little else. Rome has go-betweens, but, seemingly, few pimps who extort money in exchange for protection. Rather, there are 'firm friends,' regular clients who offer not only cash and companionship but also political support. Thus, lacking the shelter of a husband, who is held by the staffs of religion, law, and custom to protect his wife, most courtesans are forced back on the much thinner reeds of affection and lust. Such 'friends' can be abusive; witness captain Tommaso's chasing Lucrezia from her house. Still, when things get rough, the prostitutes must turn to the strong arms of allies like Paolo di Grassi and to the subtler powers of men of state like the cardinal Strozzi. Thus, women like Lucrezia, Paola, or Camilla have good reasons always to be thinking and talking about lovers or to be fighting one another for them. The competition for their hearts is an earnest, urgent business. Still, as here, feeling sometimes skews the calculation.

Not all Lucrezia's support is human. She also turns to magic, both to steal the fame of rivals and to win a man's affection. As in the cases of Camilla the go-between and of Danese and Cassandra, in the trial below, so here, the learned magistrates share the practitioner's belief in the power of the spells and charms. This, to them, is 'superstition,' not because erroneous and impotent, but because esoteric and diabolically efficacious. Here, as always, magic has its own symbolic logic. Why candles, lamps, and such prayers as these? Why dust from doorways, why bell-ropes, and why a cardinal's seed? Here, vernacular magic has borrowed from high culture, for, the dust excepted, everything in use, even the purloined sperm, has a Christian tinge. Sixteenth-century magic is not the negation of an orthodox religion that itself often conjures the supernatural for terrestial good, but its extension into a zone outside clerical control. In prosecuting magic, the state's court thus polices the boundaries of religion and wards over the church's prerogatives.

Nothing better illustrates the interpenetration of magic and religion than the prayer to 'St Daniel.' In 1883, the antiquarian Bertolotti published extracts from a very similar prayer seized by sixteenth-century Roman magistrates. It is worth quoting at some length, both for what it shows of Christian motifs in magic and for what it suggests about the psychology of the war between the sexes in a world where most power wore swords or cassocks.

> I see you, [Here one names the man. Lucrezia would say 'Giovanni Maria'] and you do not see me. I am sending you three good messengers, Oh [Giovanni Maria]. The first is Jesus Christ, the second is the Virgin Mother Mary, and the third is Daniel, which is the one of my love. May they bind you and squeeze you and may they inflame you so that they give you a jealous love sickness in your heart, so that no good may come to you until you have done my will. Oh, St Daniel, I conjure you by the whole Trinity, by the power of the Father, by the wisdom of the Son, by the virtue of the Holy Spirit.[22]

The prayer goes on for some seventy lines in all, calling up the six days of creation, the seven angels who came to raise Eve up at her birth, Abel, various details of the Gospels and the Apocalypse, the seven churches of the Roman pilgrimage, and the wand of St Joseph. The devil never appears; all power comes from sacred things. Love, as represented here, is not sweetness, but power. In the politics of daily life, women in general, and prostitutes in particular, can exploit male love and lustful passion as they can little else. To secure full-blooded allies and protectors in the city, Lucrezia thus turns to other allies in the supernatural realm.

Lucrezia's spells depend on more than folk memory. For early modern magic, like much else in vernacular belief and practice, combines in subtle ways elements of written and oral culture. Lucrezia, like Cassandra, uses charms wrapped in the allure of a print she cannot read. Rather than learn the spell by heart at the knees of some old wise woman, Lucrezia has had to buy it, penned on a sheet of paper, in the clandestine magic-market. Thus, she cannot master the charms herself, but must rely on the literate skills and dubious loyalty of Christoforo, a servant boy not even in her employ.

The testimony of the servant, Lucrezia, about her mistress's painful 'cloth' shows again how, for this household, the practical is laced with magic. Evidently, the Greek is using some sort of device akin to a diaphragm to ward off syphilis. It is clearly hard to rig. When the threads snag, Lucrezia needs a woman ally to set things right. A vignette of hurt, fear, and female intimacy, the scene has its pathos. But why does the servant volunteer this story, which does not at first glance seem incriminating or relevant? Yet, clearly, to the witness, it belongs with the others about magic. Like the dust, candle, lamp and bell-cord, the 'cloth' inhabits the sphere of secret objects serving hidden practices ordained to guard her mistress's welfare. Like the post-coital swab, it catches potent body fluids. Lucrezia the servant clearly takes conjuring seriously; that is why, to protect herself, she is careful to tell the court that she fetched only a fraudulent bell-rope. To the minion, what her mistress is using against the fearsome power of syphilis is thus, by cultural logic, not hygiene, but magic.

The Greek's alliances are rickety, for in court Lucrezia the servant betrays her mistress with tales of suspect deeds. Like Camilla the go-between, she proves a fragile ally. Women seem constrained by their weak position in a risky world to make use of unsteady friends, both male and female. In the face of such vulnerability, the allure of magic may be the illusion that, at least with the supernatural, one has some sway. Yet that temptation leaves the spell-makers at the mercy of the all too human rigours of the courts and a church bent on reformation.

suffe e capelli

CHAPTER SEVEN

The Exorcist
and the Spell-Caster

🜚

THE TRIAL

[The wife of Agostino the saddler suffers from demons. Danese, a cobbler, has attempted lay exorcism to cure her. The police have jailed him in Tor di Nona as a sorcerer and have locked up two fellow shoemakers as possible accomplices. At the same time, they have brought in Cassandra, the ex-mistress of the saddler, on the suspicion that old jealousy had led her to bewitch the wife. While Cassandra testifies over four days, Danese undergoes three weeks of questioning that end in torture.]

Rome, Casting spells
Against Camillo and Danese, shoemakers, and Cassandra of Ferrara and others

23 January 1559
Arraigned in Tor di Nona before Francesco Salamonio, substitute auditore, and me, the notary: **Camillo**, *the son of the late Sebastiano di Visso.*

He was asked if he knows or presumes to know the cause of his arrest and his present examination.

HE ANSWERED: I can't tell you, except that a neighbour of mine named maestro Agostino came to call me. He lives a little up the way and is a saddler. Maestro Agostino said I should go to his house to see his wife, who is possessed, or crazy, I don't know which. So I told him I couldn't go. And he said I should. So I went, without my cape.[1] And he told me, I mean Danese[2] told me, 'You'll be back in no time.'

So I went, without the cape, without anything. When they said that Danese would be there, I thought, 'He'll want me to help hold her! He'll want to call up spirits.'[3]

So I went upstairs into maestro Agostino's house. I found Danese there, by the fire. He was standing and maestro Agostino's wife [Maddalena] was sitting down. So I arrived and I said, 'Good evening!' and the possessed woman turned to me and said, 'What do you want?' I said, 'I have come to see Maddalena.' She said, 'What have you to do with Maddalena?' She then left me alone and turned to Danese. I sat on a chest and didn't say another word. I let her argue with Danese, because I don't get mixed up with these things. So the captain arrived.[4] And the captain said, 'What are You doing here?' I said, 'Maestro Agostino brought me here.'

Then they [the police] turned to Danese. 'What are you doing here? You are here to do things to her!' They asked him about many things. Danese answered that he had come with good intentions and that he didn't know how to do anything. And the captain told him to make her speak, and Danese said that he didn't know how to make her speak. They argued about that for a while. The captain took me out of there and led me down below. And so they took me to jail.

He was asked what adjurations[5] did Danese make with Maddalena, in his presence, before captain Ventura appeared.

HE ANSWERED: He said no spells in my presence. But I've been there three times in the presence of certain shoemakers, who were all standing there together. Danese said to that spirit, 'You gave me your faith that you would leave and you didn't keep your promise, so I intend to go to as many masses as I can.' And at these words the captain entered.

He was asked what deeds and conversations took place between the aforesaid spirit and Danese.

HE ANSWERED: I was not there at the beginning when the two of them gave faith together, but this is what I know about it. The first time I was at maestro Agostino's and Danese was there too, because we had run into each other on the way there – I was coming from the Consolazione[6] and we arrived together at the shop of those shoe-makers and from there we went to maestro Agostino's where that possessed woman was – and there Danese and that possessed woman began to talk together. They traded insults. And that spirit said to

Danese, 'You made me come in, you here and Cassandra!' and Danese said, 'This is a big lie. You are an accursed devil and you never tell the truth, you!' After they had chatted a piece, Danese said, 'Didn't you promise me to come out of there? And you gave me your hand. You are a breaker of faith.'

The spirit answered that he [Danese] was the one who was a breaker of faith, because he hadn't kept his promise. And Danese said, 'I have indeed kept my promise to you and I will keep it, if you are willing to come out.' And the spirit said, 'If you keep it, I will keep it.' And they gave faith to one another again, in my presence and in the presence of those shoemakers, to the effect that Danese would not go to high mass and the spirit would come out. And Danese said, 'I don't want you to catch me up on some quibble. Don't go finding little excuses. You always find some sort of excuse.' And Danese said, 'I will not go to high mass on holidays, but if I find myself at low mass and the high mass begins, I'm not going to plug my ears not to hear it, but I won't go on purpose.' And the spirit said, 'Yes, yes. This is not the point.' Danese asked, 'What is the point?' The spirit said, 'You know very well, you scoundrel, you bastard!'[7] Finally, they gave faith together, agreeing that Danese would not go to high mass and the spirit would come out.

And other times as well, I was present when Danese spoke with this possessed woman, but I was not present at other pacts and other conventions between them.

He was asked how he made the acquaintance and friendship of Danese. Since when and by what means did they begin to have a friendship together?

HE ANSWERED: This Danese is from Visso.[8] Because I was born in the village, I have known him since we were little children. I have not seen much of him until just under a year ago. It was several months ago that he came to stay with me to work on shoes. He stayed with me five, six, or seven months, really! He left and went to stay with his master, Persio the cobbler, in Campo dei Fiori.[9] After he left, we went several days without seeing each other, because we'd quarrelled. But after that he came many times to my shop and he stayed there with me once or twice. That is how we see each other now. Most recently, he has worked at my place three or four times. Then he was arrested. Our friendship began because we are from the same village and he is of my trade.

He was asked if he had and has knowledge of and acquaintance with the aforesaid Cassandra, about whom the possessed woman said that she [Cassandra] was with Danese in the same place when the spirit went into the body of Maddalena.

HE ANSWERED: I have not known her, nor have I ever seen her, nor do I know who she is, but that spirit said she that lived in Via Giulia.[10]

He was asked whether he and Danese ever happened to converse together about how that evil spirit went into the the body of Maddalena.

HE ANSWERED: Signore, no! He never said these things to me. But when I told him that I didn't believe that they were spirits, but that I thought that she was crazy, Danese said that they were spirits because you can tell when someone is crazy and when someone is possessed.

He was asked whether, when he and Danese were in maestro Agostino's house, he in any way took part in dealing with the possessed woman and helped Danese conjure the spirit.

HE ANSWERED: Signore, no! How could you possibly think that I should help him! Rather, I stayed to one side to watch, because they were doing some outlandish things and because I had gone there to listen, for I had never seen people who were possessed, but I didn't believe in it.

He was asked where Danese stays.

HE ANSWERED: He lived at Ponte Sisto along with his brother, whose name is Felice. He used to go back there to sleep but, according to what I have heard, he ate sometimes in one place, sometimes in another, wherever he happened to be.

He was asked whether Danese ever told him that he has the skill of doing magic and conjuring demons and doing other diabolical acts.

HE ANSWERED: I have never heard that he got involved in things like that. It is true that several times he has been with me at night and the man-waker screeched and he said that he thought he saw the devil.[11]

He was asked about the company and conversation Danese had with Cassandra. Had Danese talked to him about her? And what did he say?

HE ANSWERED: Danese told me that he didn't know her and didn't know where she was, and he swore to me. He told me that it's not worth writing down what they [the demons] say, for those who say it never speak the truth.[12]

He was asked if he knows or has heard what items were found by the watch in the house where Danese lived.

HE ANSWERED: I don't know anything about it.

He was asked whether Danese told him that he had observed a pact and agreement with the evil spirit about not hearing or going to sung mass.[13]

HE ANSWERED: He told me, because I remarked that up till then he had not gone to high mass, 'But if the spirit came out, I would keep away for another month or two.' And I told him that never had I taken on an obligation like that.

He was asked whether Danese is married or not.

HE ANSWERED: He has a wife. *Adding to a question*: Danese keeps his wife in the village. I don't know what she is called.

He was asked whether Danese was acquainted with Maddalena, the possessed woman, before she fell into this illness.

HE ANSWERED: I cannot tell you.

He was asked how many times he was with Danese in the home of maestro Agostino to talk with the possessed woman. Let him tell in order what both of them did and said on the several occasions.

HE ANSWERED: I was there four times. The first time I went there, I went in, as I said, with Danese, who was coming from the Consolazione. We went to the shop of a maestro Marco, a shoe-maker. We went in. There we found maestro Agostino, the husband of that woman who is possessed. So we talked there about the wife of maestro Agostino, though I stood there and said nothing. I said, 'Let's go for a bit to see, because I have never seen possessed persons.' So we went and we sat there in the house and the moment that the possessed woman saw Danese, she rose up and went right up to him and said, 'What are you up to, you rascally scoundrel?' And Danese said to the spirit, 'What put you in here?' And the spirit answered, 'You put me here yourself.' And the spirit said, 'I think that you put me here, you and that whore of a Cassandra,' and they quarrelled a bit, insulting one another. And they gave faith to one another. And I didn't do anything; I just stayed watching. They finished giving faith and they spoke together for a little, in the ear, softly, softly, so you couldn't hear. And so we went home; after they remade their pacts anew, I went off home. As for Danese, I can't tell you if he left.

The second time, it seems to me, was in the bath house. We found the possessed woman there. I went off to one side and the spirit began to talk with Danese. Danese said, 'These are not the promises you gave us. Didn't you promise to go away?' According to the others, Danese had been there other times, when I wasn't there. This was because, Danese told me, the spirit had promised him that it would leave, half on Monday, and the other half the next Monday. And they chatted and they quarrelled a while – I don't remember how long – and then we left.

The third time he said that one part of them had gone away and Danese said, 'You have promised me that You would all go away.'

The last time, we found her and she was in her right mind and we talked sensibly. Danese asked the husband and Maddalena if they had gone on Sunday to the Popolo.[14] They said that they had. And Danese asked if they had seen anything happen. And that woman said that on the trip up to the Popolo, it felt to her as if she had a weight on her back pulling her backwards. He asked if she had gone there willingly. She said, 'Willingly.' And Danese said, 'Recommend to St Bernard, who is there on the left-hand side when you go in to the Popolo, that he hold the demon tied fast.' And Danese asked if anything else happened. She answered that when they raised the body of the Lord, it seemed as if it stank. Danese said, 'The next time You go there, summon me to come see what happens.' And, all of a sudden, that woman jumped up and said, 'Ah, you rascal, what do you want to do? Ah, rascal, rascal!' And they began to wrangle. Danese said, 'What are you doing to us? I want to hit you in the neck.' Nothing else happened.

The last time, which is when we were arrested, was in maestro Agostino's house. When I got there, I found Danese, who was on his feet. I said, 'Good evening.' Danese answered, 'Good evening! Good evening!' That woman turned around and said, 'What do you want?' I said that I had come to see Maddalena. Then Danese began to say a heap of insults, 'Devil of the Inferno, liar!' And that spirit said to him that I was a great scoundrel.

He was asked whether Danese had ever conjured a spirit in his presence, either with that possessed woman or elsewhere to some other purpose.

HE ANSWERED: I have never seen him do anything except pledge faith; neither before nor after have I seen Danese do anything, nor do I know anything else about him.

He was asked what friends Danese has, with whom he keeps close company.

HE ANSWERED: He is not a sociable man, but I don't know what his regular friendships are. I think his friends are like me; I am of the same craft, and I pay him when he works for me.

He was asked whether he ever kept at his house articles useful for doing magic or other diabolical acts that either he or Danese used.

HE ANSWERED: I have never had anything. It could be that Danese had given me something to keep, but I don't remember his ever giving me anything to keep.

*Then the lord ordered him to be put back in his place of imprisonment with the intention of continuing and ordered to be brought in the aforesaid **Danese**, son of the late Giovanni Francesco of Visso, who was brought in and who swore to tell the truth and touched the scriptures and said as follows.*

He was asked about the cause of his arrest and his present examination.

HE ANSWERED: I don't know. I was arrested by Ventura, who took me in the Via del Panico in the house of one maestro Agostino, a saddlemaker. *Adding on his own*: I will tell you everything the way it is, for I am known in Rome.

He was asked what is it that he says he can say so freely.

HE ANSWERED: I want to say this, that when Ventura arrested me, I was talking with the wife of maestro Agostino, who said that she was possessed. We began to talk with one another because I came to know maestro Agostino in the week before Christmas. I chanced to be in the shop of maestro Marco, a shoemaker. I was there, talking with a worker of that master and he [Agostino] said that he was ruined because for three years he had had a wife who was possessed. He had tried three cures that are required in such affairs, taking her to St Peter's, to San Giovanni, and to the Popolo, and it hadn't helped her a whit.[15] He also said he had written a letter to a necromancer named Coccio, the one in Palestrina who chases away spirits, and that, when they were coming back from up where they make the fire, his wife asked him where he wanted to send that letter. He said that he wanted to send it to Florence.[16] His possessed wife replied, 'You want to send it to Coccio!' Maestro Agostino answered her, 'If I send it to Coccio, will you be willing to go?' The possessed woman answered, 'Coccio is the master there and he can command everyone.'[17] I asked him, 'Ah, brother, why doesn't it seem to you a good thing to go to Coccio?' He told me, 'I have already been to a friar for a month and five days, and every day I gave him four, five and six giulii, and I have gone broke.'[18] I said that it was a sin and not the way of Christ to go find the Devil to chase away the Devil.

He asked me, 'What do you want me to do?' I told him, 'Turn to the arms of Jesus Christ and of the Madonna. Come to the Madonna of the Popolo. Commend yourself devoutly and seek in a holy way to have God accept you.' And I told him that he should say the verses of St Bernard that begin, 'Oh, good Jesus, illumine my eyes.'[19] I said that he should say them many times when near the Madonna, because it would help her. And I showed him those verses in his breviary.

He said that he would do it and went off saying that he would go to his house and tell his wife, 'Listen to me! A certain Danese has told me to say these verses to you, and I know this Danese.' And he said that his wife said, 'Ah, Danese! You told him that I am here! You have given me a dagger-thrust in the heart.' And he replied, 'Do you know Danese?' And she answered, 'He could be quartered and I'd know him, and he can have tribulation the way we give ourselves tribulation.'

So maestro Agostino sought me out and begged me to go see that wife of his. I told him, 'What do you want me to do? I could not do anything for her. Rather commend yourself to God and live virtuously and be sure to confess and take communion at least once a month and God will help you.' And I exhorted him to have patience and not despair. He insisted that I go there on the feast of Christmas. I told him that those days were holy holidays and that they said mass at night and that I didn't want to go there. And we agreed that I would go there on the day of St Stephen [26 December]. So I went there together with him, with maestro Marco, with Fra Perusino,[20] his shop assistant. I went there down the street, going along saying those eight verses of St Bernard. I stationed myself on top of a chest and I saw before me a woman who I didn't believe was maestro Agostino's wife. I asked maestro Agostino if that was his wife and that woman turned to me, 'Ah, you pretend not to know me! I know well what spices you gave Cassandra.'

I said, 'These are the first words I have heard about this. From tomorrow on, no more lies!' And she said again, 'You are pretending not to know me! You've been here, because you have made us come in here, and you pretend not to know me!'[21] And, as we talked, I said, 'What spirits are you?' And the woman said, 'You know!' I said, 'What's your name?' and she said, 'I will never tell. I've been conjured other times and I've never been willing to say.' While she was talking to me, she always kept her eyes shut, for she never was willing to look at me. She told me that I stank to her, and that if I hadn't had those words that I always kept saying, she would have done me harm, but that in any case, one day, she would have shown me a thing or two, et cetera.

That time, nothing else happened. When I left there, her husband begged me to give him some remedy. I told him that he should go to the Madonna of the Popolo, that he should live virtuously, and that he should take communion once a month.[22] And I said that, since I habitually had certain needs in the night, when I felt that I could not catch my breath in the night, I had gone to the Madonna of the Popolo and that it had helped me.[23] So he should do that, too.

I went back there another time and I found that woman downstairs, in the shop, saying her rosary. I said, 'Good day! What are you doing, Maddalena?' She answered, 'I am saying my rosary.' I asked why she didn't join the Company of the Rosary, which is so devout. She said that she belonged to the Company. I asked her if she recognized me. She shrugged her shoulders to say that she didn't know who I was. So nothing else happened and I left.

Her husband was always pestering me to teach him some remedy, and I always said that he should live virtuously. And he took me to his shop and sent for his wife, who was at her father's house, and thus not at home. When she arrived, she said to me, 'You are here!' She picked up the scissors and tried to stab me with them. She was held by some of the others, but then she hit me in the head with her fists and said that I stank to her, that I shouldn't get close to her, and that she couldn't bear to look at me.

I was very eager to see her freed for love of that poor fellow, her husband. When we got to the end of this conversation, I told her, 'I want you to do me a favour.' She replied, 'I want you to do one for me, if you want me to do one for you. Say the favour that you want from me, and then I will tell the one I want from you.' I told her, 'You will have any favour from me, but don't ask of me anything that can harm the soul.' She said, 'It will not lead to the damnation of the soul.' And I said to her, 'You have all given this poor maestro Agostino such a working-over that he no longer knows where he stands. I want you to stop tormenting him. And I want you all to get out of there and to leave the body of this woman free.' And she said, 'The favour I want from you is this, that you never go to a sung mass.' I replied, 'Oh, you said that you wouldn't ask of me anything that would harm the soul!' She answered, 'This won't hurt your soul. Go to the low masses whenever you want.' And I said to her, 'This task is one that maestro Agostino, the husband of Maddalena, can perform.' And the husband said, 'Would that it were the will of God that I did this thing and she were free.'[24] She said, 'In this affair, I want you and not him.'

And a man who was there, who I think is called Lazzaro, told me, 'If, by not going to high mass, You could free the possessed woman, You could make the promise, and with promises like that you could cure all the possessed people in the world.' I said to the possessed woman, 'There is no need to keep any promise I make to you fellows, because you are the fathers of lies and never keep to anything you promise.' So we gave faith one to the other and she said to me, 'And so I will leave here.' And she said, 'I want you to promise never to go to mass, if they say it singing.' And I said to her, 'I want you to leave here first.' But I didn't want to promise anything. *Then he said*: Write it down that I promised her never to go to sung mass, but that I promised it with my tongue and in order to liberate maestro Agostino, but not with the heart, and that, if someone had given me ten thousand scudi, I would not have promised with my heart. So we gave one another our hands in faith. And she said right away, 'Give me the striped cloth, for I want to go accompany the corpse and come back sane.'

I went away, but the next morning, to tell the truth, I went to San Lorenzo to a sung high mass because I didn't want the Devil to win, nor to boast that he had bested me.[25] And, after that, her husband asked me many times to come back to work some sort of cure. Finally, the day before the feast of St Sebastian [20 January], I had been asked by maestro Agostino to go to his house – it was early in the morning – and that day he begged me two or three times to go. So, that evening, after dark, I went to maestro Agostino's house and I started to speak with the possessed wife, saying to those spirits, 'Well, you're still here!' And she said, 'You still don't want to get us out of here. Because you are the one who put us here, and you don't want to get us out. Take back the words that you have said.' I said, 'The words I said were said only in the praise and glory of God. I will never take them back, for eternity.' She said, 'You put us in here.' I said, 'If I put you in there, isn't it a disgrace to God that he doesn't give you licence to come out of there and carry yourselves off, body and soul?'[26]

At this point, captain Ventura turned up and told me to make the woman speak. I told him that I wasn't a saint or a person who could make the spirits talk. And he began to slap me so that I would make her speak and tell her name. I said, 'What's your name?' She answered, 'As he should know, my name is Maddalena, wife of Agostino.' And Ventura began to strip me, saying to his men, 'Strip this sorcerer.'[27] I begged him to let me keep the rosary that I had in my purse and a prayer that I had composed to the Madonna, which I wanted to place, with a picture, at the Popolo.[28] Ventura tied my hands and gave me to the policemen and they brought me here to jail.

He was asked whether that possessed woman had ever said anything to him about another woman named Cassandra.

HE ANSWERED: Signore, yes. She told me something or other about this Cassandra, as I said above. That is, she asked me if those spices I had given Cassandra were good.

He was asked to whom this Cassandra was married and of what family she was by birth. And where does she live, and how long has he known her, and what was the cause of their acquaintance?

HE ANSWERED: I swear to you by this Gospel, holy to God, that I don't know her. Maddalena said to me that she lives in Via Giulia, or by Santa Caterina da Siena, but God keep my soul, I don't know who she is and I've never seen her.[29] *Adding to another question of the lord*: Signore, no! I have never given spices, or medicines, or powders, or anything else to any woman named Cassandra, nor to any other woman.

He was asked of what family and trade he is.

HE ANSWERED: I am a cobbler and I make the forms for the shoes.

He was asked where and with whom did he and does he live. And for how long has he resided in Rome?

HE ANSWERED: It's more than twenty years that I've been in Rome. It is true that sometimes I have been away for a month, or two, or three, or a year. And I went to live at the house of a brother of mine, where there is a woman who has beds to rent out. And, later, I slept in Via del Panico at Camillo's two or three nights, because I was helping him to make wooden shoes. And that's what made me end up here in jail, for if I hadn't gone to Via del Panico, I never would have gone to that house where I was arrested.

He was asked if he had ever, anywhere else, been summoned to cast out evil spirits from the body of anyone who was tormented by them, as Maddalena was.

HE ANSWERED: Never, never, in eternity, have I been with others besides this lady.[30] She was the first, and I hope she will be the last. And I have never conjured. I don't know how to conjure, and I don't know what conjuring is. *Then he added on his own*: No, no, signore judge, I don't want anything to do with this business of conjuring.

He was asked whether he had or has any remedies for evil spirits, or charms,[31] or anything of the sort.

HE ANSWERED: I couldn't give You any other remedies than living virtuously with Christ and with the Madonna and confessing and communing often.

He was asked whether he had ever been conversant with any remedies to foster love.

HE ANSWERED: I don't get mixed up in things like that, for I don't get mixed up with other people. That fellow called me and begged me for the love of God to go to him. And for the love of God I have to suffer this.

He was asked if he had ever seen virgin paper. And does he know what it is good for and what virtue it has?

HE ANSWERED: I don't know what virgin paper is.[32] I have never before heard of it.

He was asked whether he knows that Ventura carried off some things of his. And what are they?

HE ANSWERED: I don't know that he has taken any goods from me.

He was asked what things he has in his house where he goes for sleeping, or elsewhere in Rome.

HE ANSWERED: I have a chest without a key where I have a knife, one or two shirts, a hammer for nailing wooden shoes, and a white book where there are written down certain recipes for treating the bloody flux and things like that, which I do not use. And it was two years ago that I wrote them down. I don't remember that there is anything else. I have some forms for making shoes, but I am in debt for them.

He was asked again whether he had ever been engaged in magic matters and in making charms or evil remedies for inducing love or taking it away.

HE ANSWERED: You will never find any such thing on me. On holy days, all I do is go to the churches to mass at vespers. You can make inquiries about me.

He was asked whether, in his conversations with Maddalena, the possessed woman, he had ever whispered into her ear. And what did he say?

HE ANSWERED: I have whispered in her ears and I have said those eight verses of St Bernard, but she didn't want to listen and said that I stank to her.

He was asked why Camillo came with him to the house of maestro Agostino.

HE ANSWERED: Camillo only came once, or twice, there at the bath house at the house of the father of this possessed woman. For we all went to vespers in Santo Stefano. Maestro Agostino begged us to go there for a little while. So we went there. And he never got involved in this business of Maddalena, the possessed woman, save that when he said a few words, the possessed woman said, 'This is your student, because you teach him those words.' And I told her, 'These are the things I taught him.' And I said to her those eight verses of St Bernard that are made for our confusion.[33]

He was asked what is the content of the prayer that he says he composed.

HE ANSWERED: This is the prayer.

Ave Maria, Queen. Intercede, Virgin Mary, daughter of your son who made every thing out of nothing. Bring hope, health, and counsel. Oh guide, or escort of every Christian, who comes to you in every danger. He who comes to you does not strive in vain. He who wishes to do good, washing himself of evil through grace, give him your full breast.

The Lord is always with you, He who wanted from the beginning that you be chosen to carry this celestial God. But, Madonna, who are blessed more than all women, as St Elizabeth said, may that pleasant little face be blessed, the one that St Luke painted in your arms before any other painter in the world, Jesus, who in your belly put on flesh. Thirty-three years he was in this life and then with his death conquered death and, rising again, gave me life. And he sits in Heaven on the right hand of his father, that holy sceptre, the book of life, sweetest holy Mary, exalted above the stars by the son and above all the angelic squadrons. Mary, who are most prompt and ready for your devotions, always praying for all people who are baptized, most Christianly I commend myself to you. Pray for us miserable sinners, that we know not death. Pray to your son, Lord of lords, now and forever virgin Madonna, that we escape eternal pain and that you give us glory. So be it. Amen.

Then there were shown to him various things found by the police in the house of the aforesaid Cassandra and the lord asked him to say what these things were.

HE ANSWERED: Signore, if I've ever seen these things, I pray God that, if I've seen them, the earth may open up and swallow me. And may I be sent to Hell, if I know what these things are.

He was asked whether he had ever an agreement and dealings with any woman named Cassandra.

HE ANSWERED: I have not had dealings with her and I don't know her. If you ever find that I have ever had dealings with any Cassandra, may our Lord be the judge; I've never seen these things and I don't know what is inside them.

He was asked if he has any woman friend or has he had one in the past three years or so with whom he slept.

HE ANSWERED: I have not had dealings with any woman and I have not had a woman for ten or twelve years, except that I have my wife up in the village. *And, turning toward an image of our Lord, Jesus Christ, he said*: Lord, I have had dealings with no woman for the last ten years. If you have ever done a miracle, do this. Let the Devils carry me off so that I may stand before God as judge, and let Him hang me. And let the same be true if I know anything of these goods that have just now been shown to me.

He was asked what persuaded him to tell the possessed woman that he would no longer go hear sung masses.

HE ANSWERED: I promised her in order that it might leave her body and to liberate her and that poor fellow of a husband, but I didn't promise with my heart. And the next morning I went to a sung high mass at San Lorenzo, as I told you above.

He was asked how many times he made a pact with the spirits who were troubling the body of Maddalena about not going to sung masses, as he said above.

HE ANSWERED: Once, as I said, we gave our faith to one another, and then another time, in the bath house, we reaffirmed the pact. And then, later, she said, 'Go as often as you want to sung mass. What is it to me?'

Then the lord ordered him to be put back in his place of detention with the intention of continuing.

23 January 1559
Arraigned in person in Rome in Corte Savelli in a certain room of the upper place of examination before the aforesaid magnificent lord Francesco Salamonio and in the presence of me, the notary: **Cassandra**, *daughter of the late Francesco from Imola, residing in Via Giulia, who swore the oath to tell the truth and touched the scriptures and said as follows.*

She was asked about her name, her family name, and her place of birth.

SHE ANSWERED: My name is Cassandra, daughter of the late Francesco dalle Vigne, from Imola, and my mother was Bolognese.

She was asked if she knows or can presume to know for what reason she was imprisoned and now comes to be examined.

SHE ANSWERED: Signore, no. I do not know for what reason I am in jail nor about what I must be examined.

She was asked where she lives and with whom. And what is her occupation, and from what does she make a living?

SHE ANSWERED: I live in Via Giulia, alone, for my husband is in Venice. I live on the little bit my husband sends me and on the rent I get from a room of the house I have. And so I carry on, looking after myself. And my trade is spinning and sewing. I do the best I can to get by.

She was asked for how long she has resided in Via Giulia.

SHE ANSWERED: It's been eight years; I've always been in Via Giulia. It's true I've changed rooms, going from one house to another, but always on the same street.

She was asked again about the cause of her arrest.

SHE ANSWERED: I can as readily guess the reason I am here as I can think, 'Let the fires of St Anthony burn me!' For I profess to be a good Christian, and as such, this past Christmas, I confessed and took communion. I went to confess at the church of the Aracoeli[34] and then I took communion in my parish along with the gentleman I have as a tenant in my house and with an old woman I also have in the house for charity's sake.

She was asked if she knew or knows a certain Maddalena, wife of maestro Agostino, a cobbler who lives in the Via del Panico.

SHE ANSWERED: Signore, no! I do not know her, and it's been eight months since I was in the Via del Panico.

She was asked who normally comes to visit in her house.

SHE ANSWERED: There is a gentleman named messer Benedetto Accolti and another with him named Francesco. No others spend time in my house.

She was asked whether the watch told her why they were arresting her.

SHE ANSWERED: Captain Ventura arrested me. He didn't tell me why or wherefore, except that ever since Thursday I have been in the dungeon as if I had betrayed Christ.

She was asked if she knew and knows anyone from Visso who is a cobbler by trade.

SHE ANSWERED: Signore, no. Never!

She was asked if she knew or knows any woman currently troubled by spirits.

SHE ANSWERED: The only one I know is that woman who lives up there at the Popolo. It's been some twenty years now that she's been possessed. I have known her for eight years and I've seen her from time to time, but I don't know if they are spirits or not.

She was asked if Ventura searched through her storage chests at the same time as he arrested her and led her to prison.

SHE ANSWERED: My signore, I don't know anything. It's true he asked me for the keys and I told him they were under the cushion of the bed. So I have had neither news nor communications about them.

She was asked what sort of things she had in her chests.

SHE ANSWERED: I had a smock, a bit of velvet, a shirt, and a little bag of writings that the bursar of the cardinal Santa Fiora left me to keep when he departed from Rome.[35] I don't know what kinds of writings they are, for I bought his goods when he went away, and he left me that little bag for safe keeping. It's a little bag of white cloth.

She was asked whether in that chest there is any sort of purse with spices inside it.

SHE ANSWERED: There is a purse that he left me with certain spices inside. There are spices there that haven't been crushed yet. I keep that sachet there for my chests.

She was asked whether that purse left with her by the aforesaid Giovanni was tied closed at the time of her arrest, with the things that he left on his departure inside it.

SHE ANSWERED: The little bag that messer Giovanni left me was inside the bigger bag.

And she was shown a certain bag brought from her house by captain Ventura, the bargello, and the lord asked her whether this was the one that, as she says, Giovanni left her.

SHE ANSWERED: Signore, no. This is a pillowcase that was there in my chest.

And there was shown to her a little book in the bag, which begins, 'Flee from here, thief. This little book stands guard.'[36] She was asked whose book this is.

SHE ANSWERED: Signore, this book and all the other writings in my chest come from that Giovanni. And there are also some letters Giovanni wrote to me from France, though, as for me, I can neither read nor write.

She was asked whether she knows what sort of writings Giovanni had left with her.

SHE ANSWERED: Signore, I do not know. If I had known it was something bad, I would have thrown it in the fire. I kept it, because I thought it was something to be kept.

She was asked whether, in those chests of hers, she has anything that has to do with her.

SHE ANSWERED: Messer, no. It could be that I have some letters sent me by Giulio Vissolo, a Venetian, my husband, and by that Giovanni.

She was asked whether Giovanni left other things with her besides writings.

SHE ANSWERED: He didn't leave me anything besides the writings and that purse which he gave me.

Then she was shown a certain mixture of green colour and she was asked what mixture it is.

SHE ANSWERED: This is green copper, a mixture that my husband used in his jewellery work for making false jewels, which he did with his partner.[37]

Then there was shown to her a certain small cloth in which some material was tied and the lord asked her what is this piece of cloth and the material inside it.

SHE ANSWERED: This is not a bad thing. This is borax, which works in water to make women pretty.

And next in the series, there were shown to her some little sticks wrapped in a certain paper, which she saw and she was asked what these little sticks are.

SHE ANSWERED: Signore, I don't know. They look to me like tooth-picks. I couldn't tell you what they are.

Then, likewise, she was shown some little stones tied in a piece of parchment. They were seen by her and she was asked what this material is and what she uses it for.

SHE ANSWERED: I took them for holy stone, but they aren't, nor can they be, and I don't use them for anything. And this belongs to that Giovanni.

Then she was shown certain almonds having an inscription of several words, wrapped up in hairs in a piece of paper.[38] And they were seen by her, and she was asked what they are and how she uses them.

SHE ANSWERED: The wife of a Venetian named Mariella, who lives in the Via del Pellegrino,[39] gave me a braid of hair because I have little hair, for I wear them on my head, as you can see. And these are fever almonds that messer Giovanni wrote me about and left with me saying that they were good for the fever I had. I ate about ten of them and these few here were left over.

And then a little piece of paper was opened and inside it were found two pieces of white bone. She was asked why she keeps this and what she uses it for.

SHE ANSWERED: This is fish [?] bone, which I think I found in the garden when the river overflowed, for I found it in a skin in the ditch with certain of those big beans women play with.[40] I don't know what sort of bones these are; if I do, may St Anthony burn me.

And there were shown to her certain little dried roots wrapped in a paper and she looked at them diligently. And with them were shown some big beans.

She was asked what these little roots are.

SHE ANSWERED: Signore, I don't recognize them, and these are the beans, as I said.

And she was shown a wrapping of white cloth. She was asked what this wrapping is.

SHE ANSWERED: Signore. This must be mine. You will see that inside there is a little bit of silk.

And she undid the wrapper on the lord's orders and there was found in it a rather thin piece of paper. She was asked about this paper. What was it and what is it used for?

SHE ANSWERED: This is unborn paper that messer Giovanni gave me.[41] He said it was a holy thing to wear it, but he didn't tell me what virtue it had. *Adding*: This paper – I don't think it was from messer Giovanni, but from a friend of his from San Giovanni – I don't remember his name, but he could be called Antonio – and he's dead now – who fetched out spirits.

She was asked if she knew or was acquainted with Antonio and if she had dealings with him.

SHE ANSWERED: I didn't have his acquaintance, except that, two or three times, he came to my house with messer Giovanni. He used to frequent the house of [the cardinal] Santa Fiora and everybody knew him.

She was asked if she knew what were these words and characters on the virgin paper here.

SHE ANSWERED: I don't know. I've never seen them before.

She was asked how long it has been since she had any letters from Giovanni.

SHE ANSWERED: It might be about four months now that I haven't had letters from him.

She was asked whether Giovanni had written her anything about his writings, about which we have spoken above.

SHE ANSWERED: He has only written me once, that is, a letter that I kept. *And to another question she said*: That woman who gave me the hair I told you about is named Mariella, the wife of Giovanni Maria the Venetian, a jeweller who works at Pasquino;⁴² I don't know the exact place, but he has a house and a shop.

She was asked and urged to stop being evasive and to tell honestly where she obtained the things that had been exhibited before her eyes. And let her say what they were and are used for and explain the whole affair without lies.

SHE ANSWERED: Messer Giovanni left me everything except that green copper and the borax, which are mine, and this hair was given to me by that woman, as I told you – I wanted to use it make heavy braids. I can show you their mates, which are in my hair and are the same thing.

And she showed them, saying: These are a little blonder, because I've bleached them. These almonds messer Giovanni gave me, and he also gave me pills that he said were good for fever. And these white bones I found in the garden along with these beans, in the ditch, after the river flooded, and I didn't put them to any use, except for beauty's sake. This virgin paper messer Giovanni left me, and I've sworn seven times, he didn't tell me what it was except that I should use it. Nor do I know what these other things are; he left them here for me. And I can have the people at the house of Santa Fiora come here to prove that messer Giovanni left me these writings, but I don't believe they've seen these other things that are in here.

She was asked if Giovanni told her what these things were used for and what virtue and effect they had.

SHE ANSWERED: He didn't tell me what they were good for, nor what virtue they had. All he did was give me these writings and tell me, ' Keep them safe.' He didn't say anything about bad things, or good ones, but only talked about the writings.

She was asked whether she ever sought out the things in the bag left to her, as she asserts, by Giovanni, and opened it up and saw what things they were and showed them to anybody.

SHE ANSWERED: Signore, no! No one but your Lordship has seen them and I have not spoken about them with anyone.

She was asked again if she has any notice and knowledge of the aforesaid maestro Agostino and Maddalena, husband and wife. And was she also in their house in any way?

SHE ANSWERED: Signore, maestro Agostino, the saddle-maker, kept me company before he took a wife. He had promised to marry me before I took a husband, but I have never seen his wife and I do not know her.

And the lord told her to tell the whole story of the acquaintance and deal-ings she had with Agostino. How long did it last, and from where did the ill feeling arise between them? And why did they break off their accustomed friendship and companionship?

SHE ANSWERED: The first year that I came to Rome I made friends with him because he lived near the Inn of the Bell near Monte Giordano.[43] And he was the first man I ever knew in Rome. I was at his place, because I was living in his very house, that is, where he took lodgings, and we lived there. We lived together there down to the election of Pope Julius III and a few months longer.[44] Then he took a house near San Giacomo degli Incurabili and I stayed four or five months longer at his place over there.[45] Then he began not to want to take care of me[46] and he let me lack bread and wine. And he wanted to kiss[?] every whore he saw. But I wanted to live on my own, so I took a place to live in Via Giulia, where I have been for six years. For, later on, I married this husband, it could be four years ago now. Agostino, as I said, had promised to take me as his wife. And he promised me in Tor di Nona, where he was in jail. I made an effort when he was jailed; I went to the vicario and said that I was not his wife, but that I hoped I would be, because the idea sat well with me [?].

And, on account of the blows that Agostino gave me and then because he went to the whores, I left his company and I've never wanted to see him again, nor have I spoken to him again, nor have I wanted to go where he is.

She was asked if she knows or has heard that Agostino has a wife. And for how long has he had her?

SHE ANSWERED: I have in fact heard that Agostino has a wife, but I don't know when he took her, nor have I tried to find out, because I have my own affairs to attend to.

She was asked if she knows where maestro Agostino lives.

SHE ANSWERED: I don't know, for it's been five or six years that I haven't known where he lives.

She was asked about the name of the wife of maestro Agostino. Does she know or has she heard it said what ill has befallen her?

SHE ANSWERED: I don't know her name because I don't know her, nor have I heard that she is suffering any ill, nor do I know whether she is well or sick.

She was asked specifically whether she knows or has heard that the wife of Agostino is troubled by some spirits or she has gone out of her mind. And how did this illness come to her?

SHE ANSWERED: Signore, I don't know.

She was asked if she had ever asked whom Agostino took as a wife.

SHE ANSWERED: Signore, never, because I never even tried to find out, because Agostino had nothing to do with me.

She was asked how long it has been since she has seen Agostino.

SHE ANSWERED: I don't remember precisely. *Adding*: This past Carnival, it has been a year that I haven't seen him.[47]

She was asked if she sent any gift to Agostino after he married his present wife.

SHE ANSWERED: Messer, no! No such thing! It was never my custom.

She was asked whether she ever gave to Agostino any of the spices and herbs left her by Giovanni.

SHE ANSWERED: No such thing! Not spices, not anything at all ever left my house, because he wanted those spices to be for me, and he never gave me anything, nor did anyone ever know that I had them in my house.[48]

She was asked whether she has persecuted and still persecutes maestro Agostino with hatred and enmity because he broke his faith with her.

SHE ANSWERED: I have never had hatred, either for him, or for any other person. Anyone who confesses and takes communion should not bear any hatred at all.

She was asked again if she has known and been acquainted with Danese of Visso.

SHE ANSWERED: Messer, never!

She was asked about the women with whom she dealt and deals.

SHE ANSWERED: No one visits in my house except respectable women. Sometimes a neighbour from around there comes to ask for water. And for the past month I have kept a poor thing of a woman in the house for the love of God.[49]

She was asked whether she has the skill of making and unmaking charms.

SHE ANSWERED: Messer, no! That's not the sort of thing I do. I don't know how to make them or unmake them in any way at all. For I don't want the practices of the Devil, but those of God.

And the lord said that the very opposite seemed to be demonstrated by the things found in her house in her chests, to wit, that she was accustomed to meddle in just such sorcery.[50]

SHE ANSWERED: I am not afraid that these things found in my house will be held against me because no wrong will be done to me; they are not my things. I could give a surety to present myself every time the court wants to see me. And one could write a letter to France to messer Giovanni and he will justify the claim that it was he who left these things. I have no wish to suffer for this.

She was asked whether she worked or engineered any evil to the detriment of the wife of maestro Agostino. And how did she do it, and how much did she do?

SHE ANSWERED: Messer, no!

And the lord asked how she could say that when the wife of maestro Agostino, when she is troubled by spirits, asserts that every evil that she suffers comes from her [Cassandra] and from Danese of Visso, whom she herself says she does not know.

SHE ANSWERED: She isn't telling the truth, saying it was me. She's lying through her throat. For I don't even know who it could be. You go find the person who did it, because I don't know anything about this.

And the lord added a question. Does she at least know where this illness of the wife of maestro Agostino came from?

SHE ANSWERED: I didn't make it happen. So how do You want me to know who did it? I don't go around looking for these things, for she has done me no harm, and even if she'd killed my mother, I would never have done things like that, which are not done by a respectable woman, but by the Devil.[51] And if I recognized the friar that I went to for confession, I would have him examined about my confession.

She was asked if she knew or at least has heard it said that the wife of Agostino was troubled by spirits.

SHE ANSWERED: I tell you that I know nothing about it.

She was asked if she has any knowledge of this virgin paper found among the other things in her chests when she was arrested.

SHE ANSWERED: Nothing, signore! No, I don't know what this virgin paper and this nonsense[52] was, whether for good or for ill. It is true that I have seen that red [...] thing there but I thought that it was silk, for I never looked at it.

She was asked if she ever fed anyone those almonds left her, as she asserts, by Giovanni. And to whom?

SHE ANSWERED: I repeat, I have never given any of it to anyone, but I ate some of them when he left them to me.

She was asked how long it has been since Giovanni left Rome.

SHE ANSWERED: This March it will have been two years ago that he left Rome.

She was asked what are the facts about this Antonio, the associate of Giovanni, whom she mentioned above.

SHE ANSWERED: I don't know where he came from. I've not seen him more than two or three times, when he came to my house. He might have been French, as far as I know. I don't even know that he was called Antonio; Giovanni called him 'pal.'[53]

She was asked how she knew that Antonio had the skill of casting out spirits.

SHE ANSWERED: I know because I saw him reading over that possessed woman who is at the Popolo, because I was at the Popolo and she was near me.

She was asked how it came to pass that she was present at those readings or adjurations that were practised on that possessed woman by that Antonio. And what were those adjurations?[54]

SHE ANSWERED: I went there with the other women to see, because she was shrieking. And I only went once. Antonio wasn't reading anything, but he was saying something; I don't know what because I couldn't make it out.[55]

She was asked whether Antonio had ever said anything about ejecting spirits from the human body, or putting them in, in her presence, in her home or elsewhere. And what words did he use?

SHE ANSWERED: Oh, no such thing, signore! He never spoke with me about these matters. Never! Never! What he told me I cannot say. He never said these things to me, nor did I even know that he knew how to do these things, except when I went to see that woman at the Popolo with all the neighbour women.

She was asked whether, as she said above, after that time when she saw Antonio adjuring the spirits by which that woman was troubled, she ever saw him again.

SHE ANSWERED: From that time on, I've never seen him again.

She was asked if she had seen Antonio at other times.

SHE ANSWERED: I saw him one other time, passing down the street with messer Giovanni, and I've never seen him again, except one time in my house, because he came with messer Giovanni, and again when he was conjuring those spirits, as I told You above.

Then the lord ordered her to be put back in her place [in jail] with the intention of continuing. And before she left, she said: Signore, I want to make a protest, and I want them to write down that I protest all my damages, expenditures, and interest against all those who make me stay here against reason, because I am innocent of this thing. I am poor, but I protest, as I told You. And I will give a surety, if that too is necessary, for I am poor, because I am as innocent of this as I am of the first shirt that I ever wore.

No sooner had she pronounced this than she was quickly put back under the conditions written here above.

26 January 1559
There was arraigned before the court, in the same place and before the same lord Francesco [Salamonio] about whom see above: maestro **Domenico**, *who swore the oath to tell the truth and touched the scriptures. He was asked if he was disposed to tell the truth about the things about which he was interrogated in his other examination.*[56]

HE ANSWERED: Signore, what I told You the first time I tell You again now. Nor could I say otherwise if I were given one hundred thousand martyrdoms.

He was asked if he knows that Danese was and is a sorcerer[57] *and a person accustomed to deal in incantations and other diabolical actions. And did he himself also become involved in these things as a disciple or associate of Danese?*

HE ANSWERED: In this matter, I can't tell you anything for sure. As for me, I have always held him to be a good man and I have never heard him say anything except holy things. And I have never plotted with Danese, nor with anyone that one could ever find, to get involved with things like that.

He was asked if he knew and knows a certain Cassandra who lives in Via Giulia.

HE ANSWERED: Signore, no, I don't know her except in so far as I have heard her named by the brother-in-law of the possessed woman, who said that she caused her to be possessed. When he mentioned Cassandra, I asked the brother-in-law of that woman who she might be. He said that she was someone who had been a friend of maestro Agostino.[58] That's all I know.

He was asked if he had heard any incantations or adjurations[59] and works of sorcery made by Danese.

HE ANSWERED: Signore, no, I have not heard him say or make any incantations. And if I heard him say it, I don't know if it was in the bathhouse or elsewhere. Danese said to that possessed woman, 'Say Jesus Christ!' She did say it, but she couldn't say it well, so Danese said, 'Ah, traitor! You don't want to say it well.'

Then the lord ordered him to be put in the public part of the jail with the intention of [preparing his defence], etc. And while this was happening [?], he [Domenico] said: I heard Danese tell maestro Agostino, the husband of the possessed woman, the eight verses of St Bernard so that she would not harm him in the night. And he showed him those prayers there in the breviary.

27 January 1559
There was arraigned before the court before the magnificent lord Francesco Salamonio, substitute auditore, and before me, the notary: **Cassandra**, *about whom see elsewhere, who swore and touched the scriptures and said as follows.*

She was asked whether she was willing to lay aside her usual hardness of heart and to stop being evasive and to say for what end she kept those items of sorcery that had been shown to her eyes and for what things and persons had she employed such sorcery.

SHE ANSWERED: I have never kept anything that was a possession of mine, and you will never find I did. Those are things messer Giovanni left me. And if I had known that they were bad things, I would have thrown them in the fire. I love my honour more than all the gold in the world. I have never seen those things, except when your Lordship showed them to me, even if they were in my chest, because I had a chest there that was upstairs. And I never went up there to see what it had in it, way up there where I keep the pigeons. But then I fetched them and put them in my [downstairs] chest.

She was asked if she ever threatened maestro Agostino and his wife to the effect that she would do them some ill so that maestro Agostino would never be able peacefully to keep his wife, whom he took against her [Cassandra's] will and in violation of the faith he had pledged her.

SHE ANSWERED: Signore, You will never find that I threatened him. What pleased him pleased me too, for if he had wanted me, he wouldn't have taken her.

She was asked again whether she ever saw the wife of Agostino. And did she know or does she know what ill befell her, and when?

SHE ANSWERED: I have never seen her, or known her, or talked with her. I may have seen her, but I didn't know that she was the wife of Agostino, and I have never heard that that woman had good or ill fortune. I stay in my house and I don't meddle in the affairs of others.

She was asked again where she obtained that unborn paper with the characters on it, and what it was used for, and likewise, about the other things shown to her in her other examination.

SHE ANSWERED: I never had it in any place. If it is found in those papers, I never saw it. And I never used it for anything. And as for those other things, I didn't use them for anything either. It is true that I ate some of those almonds for fever because messer Giovanni gave them to me.

She was asked whether, in the letters Giovanni sent her, he explained anything about the writings and the items of sorcery which, as she says, he left with her when he departed.

SHE ANSWERED: Signore, no. He never wrote me a word. It is true that when he left, messer Giovanni told me that I should take good care of those writings that he was leaving me, but of the other things he told me not a thing, nor did I know that they were anything.

She was asked if maestro Agostino and his wife had ever visited her in the house where she lives at present.

SHE ANSWERED: Signore, no.

She was asked if she had or has knowledge and acquaintance of any person who had and has commerce and dealings with maestro Agostino and his wife.

SHE ANSWERED: Signore, no.

She was asked again if she knew or knows of Danese the cobbler.

SHE ANSWERED: Signore, no.

She was asked whether she ever had commerce with anyone who was accustomed to deal in sorcery.

SHE ANSWERED: Signore, no. No one will ever find that to be so.

She was asked what things or words Antonio, whom she mentioned in her other examination, used in regards to that woman who was possessed.

SHE ANSWERED: Signore, I do not know. We went to see with the neighbour women. So I found him there and he didn't have anything, except that he was shouting at that woman. And I went out, because I had to go back home and I couldn't stay there to listen.

She was asked how long Giovanni visited in her house before he left Rome.

SHE ANSWERED: Giovanni came by several times because he was a frequent visitor for a quarter of a year before he went away, for he used to visit a neighbour woman next door, so he used to come into my house.

She was asked whether she and Giovanni ever had a conversation together about what had happened with maestro Agostino.

SHE ANSWERED: Signore, yes. For he knew about it, since I told him that Agostino was angry at me because I had left him and didn't want his friendship any more, because he wanted every whore he saw. And Giovanni told me, 'If he doesn't want you and you don't want him, let him go.'

She was asked whether she told Giovanni that Agostino had promised to marry her.

SHE ANSWERED: I told him. And Giovanni knew that was what got maestro Agostino out of jail, making him a surety of five hundred scudi and of my life [?], but it was my visit that got him out.

She was asked who revealed to her that maestro Agostino had taken a wife.

SHE ANSWERED: I heard it from some people and then maestro Agostino told me.

And the lord asked where, and when. And what did maestro Agostino say about the wife he was marrying?

SHE ANSWERED: He said it when I was at the window of a house that I was living in near Santa Caterina da Siena; he said it to a neighbour there. He told her that he had taken a wife. I answered him from the window, 'May it do you good!' I left, and I don't know what they said next, nor do I know when it was.

She was asked if she knows specifically whom maestro Agostino married.

SHE ANSWERED: Signore, no, I don't know and I don't try to find out.

She was asked if she and Giovanni ever spoke with one another about matters of sorcery.

SHE ANSWERED: I have never spoken about it.

She was asked whether it was Giovanni himself who made the characters and signs on the almonds or some other person. And who was it?

SHE ANSWERED: Messer Giovanni himself told me that he had written them.

She was asked whether she ever asked Giovanni if he had any skill in matters of sorcery.

SHE ANSWERED: I never asked him nor even looked into the matter, neither with him nor with anyone. I attend to my spinning and to earning my bread.

She was asked whether anyone, after the marriage contracted between maestro Agostino and his wife, gave either him or his wife a gift or acted in any other way in her name. And who was the person, and what did he give?

SHE ANSWERED: Signore, no!

Then the lord ordered her to be put in the public part of the jail and ordered that she be given a term of three days for preparing her defence and that a copy of the trial be made.

Thursday, 16 February 1559
Arraigned in person before the court in Rome in the court of Tor di Nona before the magnificent lord Francesco Salamonio, auditore, etc., in the presence of me, the notary: **Danese** *di Giovanni Francesco of Visso, about whom see elsewhere, who swore the oath to tell the truth and touched the scriptures and said as follows.*

He was asked if he had decided finally, without evasion, to tell the truth about what sorcery he used with that woman and to reveal the fact because he cannot deny that he was and is a sorcerer. For, if other proof is lacking, it can still be deduced from the faith he gave to those malign spirits about not going to sung mass if they left the body of the woman. Therefore he should dispose himself to tell the rest of the truth, for if he remains obstinate, he will be compelled to tell it by remedies of the law and of fact.[60]

HE ANSWERED: Signore, what I said once to your Lordship, I will repeat forever. And your Lordship can do one thing; send me bound through Rome with the police to talk with all the people who know me and they [the police] will hear the story that they will tell about me and they will say that I am not a sorcerer, nor the sort to do such a thing. And I will have letters come from my village and from the town councillors[61] and the lieutenant that will give information about me and say that I am not a sorcerer, and you will see [?] that I am a respectable man. And what I said to those spirits about not going to high and sung mass, I said for charity, and to do good, and to liberate that woman of such a burden. In the rest, if I have had failings, I throw myself in the arms of Jesus Christ and of your Lordship, that I might suffer any penance for the love of Christ. And I beg your Lordship to let me go because I don't have food to eat and I sleep badly, even though I bear every thing willingly for the love of Christ. And if God gives me the grace to get out of here, I will inform you well about my life and my reputation, for I am not a sorcerer or an evil-doer.

And again and again he was urged and warned to give up his evasions and to say if he was skilled in matters of sorcery. And what sorcery and words did he use in speaking with those spirits who troubled that woman?

HE ANSWERED: I don't know anything about it and I never heard anything more about these incantations and homicides.[62] I never talked to possessed people, except that one, in all my life, and when I talked with her I said in her ear those eight verses of St Bernard; I wanted to see if, by them, I could fetch out that plague of spirits.

Then, in order to have the whole truth, because of the evidence and the suspicions and the conjectures and the confessions of the suspect and the depositions of the other witnesses, the lord ordered him to be brought to the place of interrogation and there to be stripped and bound and, if necessary, to be raised up. And he was brought there and stripped and bound and warned to tell the rest of the truth, whether he had made any kind of pledge in speaking to the woman troubled by malign spirits and whether he is skilled in any such sorcery.

HE ANSWERED: Signore, no, I do not know how to do any incantations.

Then the lord ordered him to be raised in torture and, when he was up, he said continually, 'Oh, Holy Mary of Loreto, Oh, Holy Mary of Loreto, help me, Holy Mary! Oh, my Jesus Christ, help me! I have not done any wrong to the faith. Oh, Jesus Christ! What do you want me to say? I never did any wrong. I did no wrong. I said with my mouth that I would not go to high mass, but not with the heart. I don't understand these things, except that I am being quartered. Let me down a little and then pull me up again. Oh, God, help me! Oh, Jesus! Oh God, help me! I never did any wrong. I never did wrong. Give me the cord around my neck if I have done wrong. No, I'll stake my soul on it. As Jesus Christ gave it to me, so I want to render it back to him. I never ate in the morning, which proves that I didn't have mass.[56]

And he was warned again and again by the lord to say if he was skilled in such an art of enchanting spirits, as above.

HE ALWAYS SAID: Signore, I have never done any wrong. Nor have I ever blasphemed. If I have done incantations and if I know how to do these things, may God make me die by thunderbolt.

And when he had been thus elevated for a quarter of an hour and he persisted in such answers, the lord ordered him to be put down gently and put in the public part of the jail.[64]

THE COMMENTARY

This single trial tells two separate stories. It begins with a tale of lay exorcism, but soon takes up a thread of female magic. Though the two histories seem quite separate strands, the magistrates see them as intertwined. For them, they knot in Maddalena, the wife of the saddler, maestro Agostino, whose body harbours demons. The exorcist, a shoemaker named Danese, has tangled with Maddalena, for he has tried to cure her. Cassandra, the reputed caster of spells, by contrast, seems never to have laid eyes on her. But Maddalena, speaking through her demons, accuses Cassandra, who once was

Agostino's woman, of joining Danese in her bedevilment. The allegation makes sense not only to the saddler's possibly addled wife, but also to the court, for both understand possession often to be the fruit of magic and, indeed, of that league with the devil that jurisprudence defines as witchcraft. The magistrates also spy in Cassandra a likely motive, a spurned woman's envy. Taking Maddalena's demons at their word, the court arrests both Danese and Cassandra as malicious confederates in supernatural dealings.

In this prosecution, the court of the governor takes part in a large enterprise, the suppression of irregular religion. In this trial, as in many such, the state lends the church a hand in its campaign to arrogate to itself alone the task of dealing ceremonially with the realm of the invisible. Throughout western Europe, in the sixteenth century, churches and states labour to control and to reshape the traditional culture of the populace. The authorities hope to replace what seems to them the chaotic heritage of the Middle Ages with what they think to be a safer, straiter, better-disciplined culture. Magic and witchcraft are just one battleground in this wider campaign. One small, related skirmish flares up over the control of exorcism, the rite that casts out devils. To exorcize is to cure, in theory, not a natural illness, but a supernatural accident, the invasion of a body by malevolent spirits who can supplant the victim's own soul and self and put the faculties to their own use. In the minds of Renaissance Italians, one cause for such possession, for which neither nature nor the patient is to blame, is malicious magic. Whatever the condition's etiology, the only remedy is a liturgical practice of venerable antiquity that, in the eyes of the hierarchy, belongs to the clergy alone. Danese thus is a trespasser. In Danese's and Cassandra's trial, as in many such, the judges impose their own reading on behaviour to which the practitioners have given a very different, customary gloss. Thus, they read into Danese's home-made exorcisms and Cassandra's magic the devil-worship described in learned prosecutors' manuals. Indeed, the populace and the learned alike take devils seriously, but, for the most part, it is the authorities alone who reinterpret all magic as witchcraft and witchcraft as demonolatry.

Like the magistrates, Danese the cobbler, Cassandra the seamstress, and Maddalena the possessed woman all have thought or acted in ways foreign to us. Nevertheless, by laying out the facts in good order, one can make some sense of all of them, certainly of the cobbler, the court, and the seamstress, and even of the mad woman, for all these actors have their rationality. Let us begin with the shoemaker.

Danese is not a solid citizen; this homespun exorcist is a marginal artisan. He is only half established in Rome. Although an immigrant of some twenty years, he has kept a wife for ten or more in Visso, a village well north-east of Rome in the high country between Umbria and the Marches. Now and again he leaves the city. He is not a master artisan, for he keeps no shop or household in Rome, but moves about from cobbler to cobbler, working and eating now in one place, now in another. Danese several times tells the court that he is well known and well reputed, both in Rome and in his village. Yet his fellow shoemaker, Camillo, says he has no close friends. Danese's marginality is in no way rare in Rome. It is important for the trial, however, because it renders him more liable to denunciation and to prosecution.

It is not clear how Danese himself defines his curative art. Until his arrest, on 19 January, he continues to visit Agostino and Maddalena, plying them with prayers and counsel and wrangling with the demon. He tries a bargain with it; he would abstain from high mass and the demon would depart. But the spirit forever balks at keeping its half of the deal. Danese says that, like the devil, he has cheated, for the very day after giving faith, he broke his word and attended a sung mass. Neither the shoemaker nor the court calls these labours 'exorcism.'

There is good reason to believe Danese's protestations that he is no conjurer; he does not seem a professional spirit fetcher, like Antonio, whom Cassandra saw with a madwoman at Santa Maria del Popolo, or like Coccio, out at Palestrina, whose reputation reaches some twenty miles to Rome. There is a fine example of one such magician in Cellini's *Autobiography*.[65] That sorcerer draws mystic circles on the ground of the Colosseum, hoists a pentangle, reads spells, lights fires, and throws on spices to draw devils by the legion. The necromancer of the peasants' play in the next trial does much the same to conjure just one demon. Danese has no such arcane science and no such liturgy of gestures or incantations with which to cast out devils, as would a more formidable, more expensive necromancer like Coccio, or, for that matter, would the friar, whose legitimate ministrations have so drained poor Agostino's purse. Rather, the shoemaker relies on a common currency of well-known prayers and pious exhortations. It is Danese's very amateurism, his willingness to improvise, that makes him an interesting subject.

Though Danese claims that he is no regular trafficker with demons, the law strives to convince itself and him that he is. Danese professes to be a novice; Maddalena's, says he, is the only devil he has ever conjured. If so, his career has been brief, for it was only in the week before Christmas, just over a month ago, that he first knew her husband, and only on St Stephen's day, 26 December, that he first laid eyes on her. Shortly afterwards, he and Maddalena's demon made their bargain. Though Camillo volunteers the term, Danese does not readily call this agreement a 'pact.' In his words, it is only a 'promise' or a giving of 'faith.' 'Pact' is the court's demonological term. The prosecutors of witchcraft see the pact with the devil as the central element of that crime. That may be why, in the interrogations, the magistrates readily call Danese a 'sorcerer' [*homo maleficus*], while they only accuse Cassandra of 'acts of witchcraft' [*maleficia*] but do not label her as a 'witch.' Only at the very end of his first interrogation does Danese bend to heavy pressure, echoing the damning legal phrase and calling his promise a 'pact.' As if they have at last snared the elusive word they want, the judges at once end the session.

Before trying to understand him, one must ask if Danese is telling the truth about his exorcism. We have several reasons to believe him. For one thing, what he says jibes well with the reports of the other two arrested cobblers, Camillo and Domenico. True, it is hard to line up the sequence of meetings Camillo cites with the one Danese gives the court.[66] On the other hand, neither Camillo nor Domenico claims Danese is a seasoned exorcist. Furthermore, he blunders in his testimony in ways one would not expect in a habitual necromancer who had had time to reflect on the illegality of his art. For he readily volunteers the story of his deal with Maddalena's demon, the one deed most likely to bring down on his head the ire of the law. If Danese lies, it is probably to omit rather than distort. Thus, it is hard to imagine any truth he might have said that would much change our picture of the quality of his dealings with the supernatural. Quantity is another matter, for why would Agostino so have importuned Danese's help had he lacked a reputation for a certain power over spirits? He thus may well have had a much longer history of amateurish healing.

Danese advertises himself as a good Christian. Indeed, his religion clearly buttresses his self-confidence and fortifies him in his dealings with Maddalena, with Agostino, and with the court. Before all of them, and before the devil, Danese parades his rectitude. He never defers to the magistrates, pleading ignorance and asking guidance. As a Christian, he acts as if he feels he is his own man. Like the courtesan, Lucrezia the Greek, he finds pathways to the supernatural in the realm of writing. But, unlike her, he uses orthodox materials that he himself can read. His literacy may well have stiffened his conviction that his piety was right, for it gave him mastery over words of great protective power, such as his long prayer to the Madonna or those eight verses he attributed to St Bernard. Danese seems content to trust to his own improvisations, rather than to the authority of the institutions of the church. Like many pious laymen, in an age when the Catholic Reformation has not quite yet enforced conformity, he has shaped his own spirituality by culling what he wants from high religious culture. Thus, his dealings with the devil are Christian, but out of bounds and, thus, illegal. What we do not know is whether, as is likely, he stitched together his combinations himself or whether he borrowed them whole from others.

Danese's piety is charitable. It leads him to offer help, though not to Maddalena, for whom he recounts no words of pity, but to the burdened husband, Agostino, that 'poor fellow.'[67] There is no trace of payment. As Danese tells it, on hearing that Agostino intends to go to Coccio, the necromancer in Palestrina, he first steps in, alarmed that the saddler was using 'a demon to chase a demon.' He recommends instead the image of the Madonna at Santa Maria del Popolo, a church built on a spot once haunted by Nero's terrific ghost and thus in Roman legend long linked with the possessed. Danese volunteers himself as a lay spiritual adviser to the troubled couple. By contrast, the other cobblers seem to come along for the show. Because Danese wants to portray himself in court as, not an exorcist, but a mere helpful neighbour, he obscures the pathway to his trafficking with Maddalena's demons. He does not make clear if, through heedless charity, he has slipped inadvertently across a threshold, or if he has come expecting to cross it.

Danese's self-assurance shapes his dealings with the demon. In his story, the cobbler treats him much as, in agonistic Rome, one might any other enemy. Like a human foe, this devil of Maddalena's is no alien; it shares Danese's language and his sense of values. Thus Danese can plead with it, 'You have given this poor maestro Agostino such a working over; look what you've reduced him to! I want you to stop tormenting him.' He can not only entreat the devil, but also cajole and chide and taunt him. The antagonists share a moral language.

Also, like a human enemy, Maddalena's demon can understand the terms of a treaty. In Danese's account, the cobbler is the first to suggest a deal, though it is Maddalena and her demon who propose the terms: that he will absent himself from high mass and the demon will depart. What do Romans do with enemies? Often enough, they deal with them in bad faith. Thus, neither Danese nor the demon keeps his word. Careless of honour and piety, they abuse the pact in mutual treachery. Danese claims in court he could make his promise falsely, without the heart's assent. When the devil's treachery becomes patent, it and Danese fall to trading insults, much as might any Roman adversaries after a pact collapsed. When they fight, Renaissance Italians welcome spectators. In this case Camillo, Domenico, Lazzaro, and maybe other cobblers are there to gawk and thrill and marvel. It is a pity they do not expand on how they felt about the show.

Maddalena and her demon are also worth listening to, for even madness has its methods. Modern medicine would probably find Maddalena seriously ill. But not all cases of Renaissance possession are deeply rooted; some, especially in nunneries, seem rather to be a form of hysteria, brought on by isolation, loneliness, and contagion by example.[68] Such possession is often readily cured, for the sufferers revel in the exorcism and the attention it brings. Maddalena, however, shows no signs of ever having craved the cure. Her illness is well entrenched; she and Agostino have been battling it now for three years. But if Maddalena is truly sick, that does not mean her speech and actions are meaningless, for even the mad still participate in their culture. How might she be making sense? As Camillo remarks, her world offers two competing diagnoses for her troubles; she is either crazy or possessed. By choosing the latter reading of her state, Maddalena can blame others, such as Danese and 'that whore of a Cassandra' for putting her madness in her. Also, she can disavow and yet indulge those impulses that violate common sense or social codes of conduct. Thus, her devil, rather than she, can assert and aggress in ways most women must often deny themselves. The 'demon' unleashes Maddalena's tongue against the males; she can swear with verve and threaten and bully men. She can also set up deals with men, as she does with Danese. At the same time, through her devil, Maddalena sullies whatever tries to make her whole. We never see her describe herself as foul. Rather, she casts all her dirt upon others; Danese and the wafer of the sacrament stink to her. In some ways possession liberates its victims.

In this light, what might the pact with Danese mean to Maddalena? Is it some sort of flirtation with sanity, or a challenge to others to try to make her pure? The deal certainly lets her subvert the sacred, if only in a small way. She may be trying to cleanse herself by casting impurity onto her exorcist. Or the pact may merely let Maddalena defend her madness, as she does when her demon tells Danese that he has thrust a dagger into its heart.

Almost as puzzling as Maddalena is her supposed nemesis, the seamstress, Cassandra. Maddalena and the court both believe that, by some gift of herbs, she must have called in the devil. Of course, we moderns believe that she can have accomplished no such thing. But has she tried? Probably not. But does she at least practise magic? There, finally, the court may well be right, for it has seized from her house the paraphernalia of enchantment. Thus, Maddalena's accusation, for all its madness, has a certain cunning; Cassandra is a likely sorceress. Agostino may have told her so. To Cassandra's great misfortune, the circumstances, too, argue for a spell, for not only was she once Agostino's woman; she has been his betrothed. She might well seem to have repaid his breach of faith by striking him through his wife. Here, like Danese, the court treats Maddalena's misfortune as less hers than her husband's; it imputes to Cassandra anger at the man, not envy of his consort.

Cassandra, like Danese, is no solid citizen. She, too, is only partly settled in Rome, for, like his, her household is incomplete. Like him, she is an immigrant with a spouse in another town, hers a husband of four years' standing, a jeweller, who lives in Venice. She came to Rome eight years ago and quickly moved in with the bachelor, Agostino. Before long, when he was jailed in Tor di Nona, she became engaged to him to help set him free. But things soon soured. Cassandra claims that Agostino kicked her and ran after all the whores. So she broke with him, probably about six years ago, when she first took up lodgings in Via Giulia. Certainly, they must have parted at least five years ago, for since then, she says, she has not known where his house is. Cassandra now ekes out a living on what her husband sends her and on rent from lodgers. She also sews, spins, and keeps pigeons to make a living, and befriends men from the house of cardinal Santa Fiora, who, she claims, pursue the art of magic.

Before the magistrates Cassandra must defend herself against very damning evidence. The court brings out object after dubious object. At first she bluffs with ease, 'This is a pillowcase' for a cushion. But then comes a book that she cannot read. She asserts that it was left her by her friend Giovanni, now conveniently in France. Next comes some paste for making jewellery and then some borax for cosmetics. Next in line are some little sticks wrapped in paper that she can claim, a little implausibly, to be toothpicks. But, from there, the going gets much rougher, as the court deploys, one after another, small, strange packets containing nuts and bones and beans and hair, and a sheet of 'virgin paper' made, in theory, from a caul or the skin of a stillborn child. Cassandra's explanations grow lame or fail her altogether. The bones, she says, she found in a ditch after a Tiber flood, along with 'some big beans that women play with.' But the explanation is compromising, for, as appears in the trial of Camilla the go-between, with beans women played at conjuring. Cassandra in her embarrassment more and more falls back on the excuse that it all belongs to her friend, Giovanni. With good reason, an experienced magistrate would dismiss this apology as a common subterfuge. Lacking a better defence, Cassandra also insists on her total indifference to Agostino's fate, her ignorance of Giovanni's secret science, her respectability, her honour, and her Christian piety. A poor woman on her own has paltry defences. Unlike Danese, she does not offer character witnesses. Perhaps her female friends would do her little good in a male world of justice. Still, her last defiant speech, where she claims damages in the language of the law, proves that, for all her low station, disfavoured sex, and illiteracy, she has some sense of how one deals with courts.

The magistrates are not fools. True, in this case, they seem wrong, even by the standards of the time, about both their suspects; Cassandra, almost surely, has never cast a spell on Maddalena and Danese is no witch. But in their judicial error there is method, which takes counsel from the most learned doctrines of the day. Look with their eyes at Cassandra, in whose chest were found the instruments of magic. Applied magic is not a fable, but a common Italian practice. Though only theology and legal theory see in every incantation a formal pact with devils, vulgar and learned opinion agree that spells have real power. Also, Cassandra has had every reason to wreak vengeance on the man who broke faith with her. Thus, any reasonable judge should try her. But the court's case is imperfect, for it has only

one witness, Maddalena, whose accusation might be mad or diabolical. But the judge seems not to have been too troubled by that fact,
for, it seems, he has neither sought out other witnesses, nor has he
tortured Cassandra in hopes of a confession. He puts her in the public part of the jail to prepare her defence, for he believes that he
already has evidence enough to try her. If he is content to go forward
with so weak a case, it must be because Cassandra's behaviour fits
models offered in Roman folk wisdom, in the court's experience, and
in the science of judicial demonology.

That same demonology also governs the treatment of Danese. At
the interrogation by torture, the magistrates make clear how their
thinking works. Although they take seriously Maddalena's accusation
against Cassandra, in Danese's case they seem less heedful of what
she said of him. He had no motive to bewitch her and, what is more,
no contact with her at the time of her first possession. But Danese
manifestly has been dealing with a devil; he says so himself and the
witnesses agree. At issue is the nature of that commerce. Is Danese a
'maleficent man,' that is, a witch, or only, as he protests, a good
Christian who has stumbled into error. As they must, the magistrates
fasten onto the pact, what Danese calls the 'faith,' between the cobbler
and the demon. For the learned treatises on witchcraft, since the
famous and influential *Hammer of Witches* (1486), have been unani-
mous in insisting on the centrality of the witch's pledge to the devil.
True, Danese's promise was not too dangerous; he did not give over
his soul in bondage. But, as a pledge to the detriment of religion, it
fits perfectly with the practices laid out in the literature. Thus, the
pact is evidence of diabolical arts. But, to the magistrates' frustration,
it is the only evidence. Neither Danese nor his fellow cobblers mention
any other word or deed that fits the descriptions in the books. That is
why Danese must be tortured. But he stands firm in his insistence on
his good faith. It is far from clear who wins the contest of judicial
torture. Eschewing further torture and seemingly content to end the
interrogation, the magistrates put Danese in the public part of the
jail. There is no mention of preparing a defence; what happens next
remains a mystery.

Whatever Danese's lot, Cassandra faces a further trial. She faces
punishment, but probably not death, for, unlike many other Renaissance tribunals, those in Italy seldom send witches to the gallows or
the stake. Her predicament is emblematic; her misfortunes and

Danese's are shared by many men and women of the latter sixteenth century in Italy, where, ever more, church and state reach out to police popular traffic with the supernatural.

CHAPTER EIGHT

The Village Play

🜋

THE TRIAL

[In response to a denunciation by a local cleric, the Cardinal of Montepulciano prosecutes some villagers of Aspra, who during Carnival have put on an unseemly play. Having sent his notary to the village to interview other clergy, the cardinal then summons five villagers before the court in Rome, where for two days a judge investigates the words and gestures in the spectacle.]

For Information [Here begins the notary's copy of several documents pertaining to the case.]

[First comes the letter of denunciation, here unsigned.]

Most Reverend Monsignor,
For the exaltation of the Catholic faith and the oppression of heresy; they say that on Sunday of the past Carnival, in Aspra,[1] in the diocese of Sabina, those named below put on a play that was prohibited and contrary to the holy Catholic faith, because of its action and its words. For, in it appeared, among others, a person dressed like a monk, with a habit, and a bell above his hermitage. Furthermore, they represented him as calling nymphs with his bell. At the end of his speech, he pulled off the habit. Also, there was a necromancer with his conjuring, and someone dressed like the Devil who did conjuring, and one who sacrificed a lamb to the god Pan, or rather, to the gods, with most horrid words. And there was a notary who, at the beginning of his speech, invoked the Devil in the place of the One we are accustomed, with such reverence, to call 'God.' Whatever else was done

against every holy and human law also displeased the public, which desired to repress the audacity of men so little Catholic, by forbidding the play to be recited. Then they had the audacity to boast they would do it, even though it was forbidden, for they feared no punishment. Furthermore, they railed at many worthy elders. In order best to remove the beginnings of such a plague, one needs a cure. It is a public matter. Some of them went singing and dancing around the village, just as they would have done in Carnival, on the first day of Lent.

Their names:

Orazio, son of Giovanni Camillo, a cobbler. Many times he was investigated about sacrilege with a nun, as one might recall. The nun was hanged. Now he has been pardoned, we don't know how. He spoke the part of the Monk.
Stefano di Adamo
Tiberio [di ser] Famiano Albertini
Emilio di Giovanni di Marco
Ovidio Fedele
Penicchio
Britio di Giovanni Battista Vasellaro and
three others, boys who are minors[2]

9 March 1574

[Here the notary reports on his mission to pursue these complaints.]

The Signori sent a commission to arrange matters.
In the name of God, Amen. Since it is evident, be it known that in the year 1574, in the second indiction, the fifth day, Sunday, the twenty-first of March under the most holy father in Christ, Gregory XIII, by divine providence Pope, in his second year. I, the notary, by virtue of the letters of the most illustrious and most reverend Cardinal of Montepulciano and Bishop of Sabina, departed and went to the village of Aspra to carry out the several things contained in the said letters.[3] *And I was prevented from giving said letters to signore Flaminio Iacobelli de Collevecchio, the podestà of the said village of Aspra, forbidden by the most illustrious signore Onorio Savelli.*[4] *They were read and registered by me, the notary. They go as follows:*

[The cardinal's letter, carried by the notary, to the podestà of Aspra.]

On the back:
To the magnificent signore podestà of Aspra, who is like a brother, with seal and address.

From the most illustrious and most reverend cardinal.

On the inside:
Magnificent signore podestà, like a brother. May your Lordship be content to grant to the present bearer, who is a substitute for messer Giovanni Paolo Magni, our notary, whom we send on matters of importance at the behest of the superiors, the same credence in everything he will say to You in our name that You would grant to us ourselves. And in particular, do not neglect to call at once to your palace all the persons he will name to You and to constrain them to give whatever surety You and the said notary deem to befit the business, to pledge that within two days they will appear before us here in Rome. And as for those who do not have a surety and cannot or will not give it, your Lordship should have them held under good custody at our command, and let us know right away what happened so that we can take care of matters here. And, because You hold dear the love of our Lord, do not fail to carry out all that is written. We commend ourselves to your Lordship and wish You health.

From Rome, 20 March 1574

From his Lordship, as a brother, the Cardinal of Montepulciano.

[The notary reports on how he sent out summonses.]

When these letters had been registered in fulfilment of my commission, I, the notary, at once sent out a document to each and every one of them, who, having seen it, were to appear in person in the palace of the lord podestà at the court of the diocese, before me, the notary of the episcopal court of the aforesaid most illustrious, most reverend lord cardinal for information about some matters regarding the most illustrious and most reverend lord and his court, under penalties that appear in the said injunction.

[The Cardinal's injunction.]

The tenor of the said injunction:
From Giovanni Riccio, his most reverend excellency the Cardinal of Montepulciano, also Bishop of Sabina.
To each and every one in Christ, greetings, in accordance with our office [?], by the contents of the present letter we commission and expressly command in the name of holy obedience that, having seen the present instrument, under penalty of one thousand ducats in gold, if anyone of these men does not appear in the court of our bishopric of Sabina or other appropriate places, he will suffer automatic excommunication. And each and every one

must appear personally before us in the court of the palace of the Lord Podestà of the diocese of the village of Aspra or before our commissioner, but without a procurator or an excuser or a defender of any sort, to inform us and our episcopal court about some things that regard us and our court. Otherwise, after the said time has elapsed, by the authority vested in us, by virtue of the present document, we cite, require, and warn you and whomsoever else on the first day thereafter, and for single days and hours for as long as applicable, that you will be declared to have incurred the aforesaid penalties, and the injunction will bear on both your person and your property.

Given in Aspra, Monday, 22 March 1574.
[signed] *Silvestro Amonio, deputed commissioner*

For the most illustrious and most reverend lord Cardinal of Montepulciano.

[Persons who were notified of the injunction.]
Frate Franco Spagnolo
Pietro Petruccio
Latino Cecio
Paulo Emilio Festo
Daniele Tomasolo
clerics of the village of Aspra

Orazio di Giovanni Camillo, cobbler
Stefano di Adamo, who appeared and gave faith
Tiberio di Famiano Albertini, who appeared and gave faith
Britio di Giovanni Battista Vasellaro
Emilio di Giovanni di Marco
Ovidio Fedele and
Penicchio

On the day aforesaid the injunction was executed as above by Sante, public castaldo[5] *of the said village of Aspra, as he informed us.*

[Interrogations of three witnesses, conducted by the notary in Aspra, interspersed with pledges which guarantee that other witnesses will appear in Rome.]

Monday, 22 March 1574
Examined in the village of Aspra in the palace of the lord podestà, by me, the notary, for the information of the court: **Daniele***, the son of the late Ascanio Tomasolo of Aspra, a witness, who, having sworn to tell the truth was asked*

by me if he knows or presumes to know the cause of his present examination and why he was summoned to inform the episcopal court.

HE ANSWERED: I have no idea why you want to examine me, nor can I even imagine it, except that yesterday evening, in the night, when your Lordship arrived, many people said that it was on account of the priests.

He was asked why he said that the arrival of me, the notary, was on account of the priests.

HE ANSWERED: Signore, in truth I can only tell You what I told You. They said, 'He came on account of the priests.'

He was asked of what profession, parentage, and age he is.

HE ANSWERED: I am about twenty-three years old, and I am from Aspra. So far, I have studied the humanities and I want to become a priest, God willing.

He was asked what holy orders he already has.

HE ANSWERED: I have the four minor orders and first tonsure.[6] I believe it has been about a year now, but I don't remember exactly.

He was asked what companions he has here in Aspra with whom he most often associates.

HE ANSWERED: I keep the company of many young men of my profession, such as Latino Cecio, don Pietro Petruccio, and Paulo Emilio Festo, and a fair number of others, but because I don't have a father and I don't live at home, I also see to my affairs outside the house.

He was asked whether, two months ago, he left the village of Aspra and went to another village. And, if so, where and with whom?

HE ANSWERED: Signore, the first day of Lent I went to Magliano with Don Giacomo, Archpriest of Aspra. In the evening we went to Collevecchio. The next morning, which was the second day of Lent, we came to Aspra at the time of the midday meal. And about fifteen days before Carnival, I went to Terni with my brother-in-law, Giacomo di Simeone. We stayed about two hours and then came to Aspra.[7]

He was asked whether, in the village of Aspra, in the first days of the most recent Carnival, there had been presented, acted, or recited any sort of comedy, eclogue, or pastoral play. What does he know or has he heard about it?

HE ANSWERED: Signore, yes. Here in Aspra this past Carnival a comedy was put on.

He was asked whether the comedy was put on in the day or in the night. And in whose house, and by whom, and on what day, and who helped them? And at whose expense it was recited, and who was the author, and what was the plot, and who were the actors?

HE ANSWERED: Signore, the comedy was presented in the daytime. It was the last Sunday of Carnival, in the piazza of the Menili here in Aspra. It was called 'The Comedy of Crapino.' Who the author was I cannot tell you, but they say that it has been printed, for I have read it several times, because it is in print. There must have been eight or ten actors who recited it. And it was put on at the expense of the actors. The whole village was there to hear it, and there were many outsiders too, from around here. The comedy itself contained pastoral matters, for there were two shepherds. One of them was Ovidio Fedele and the other was Emilio di Marco. And two nymphs came along; one was played by Cesare di Troiano, who must be twelve years old, and the other nymph was played by Tarquinio, son of Tullio, who is from Collevecchio, but he lives here. There was a God of Love, who was played by a labourer named Silverio. There was a peasant, who was played by Stefano di Adamo, and Britio di Giovanni Battista Vasellaro played the part of the other peasant. Penicchio was his nickname.[8] And Massimigliano did the prologue. Tiberio di ser Famiano played the part of a necromancer. Then there was also one Orazio di Giovanni Camillo, who wore on his head a big hood made out of a gray cape, and he was girded from the belt down by a covering, but I don't remember what colour it was, and he had no other mask than that. And there was ser Giovanni Battista Varoni, who drafted a notarial document, because one of those peasants wanted to take a wife. I don't remember if there were any other parts in it.

He was asked what actions, what words, and what examples and signs the players made and manifested in the comedy they recited. And how did it end?

HE ANSWERED: Signore, I know that the comedy was called 'Crapino.' There were no interludes at all. And I saw that those two shepherds whom I told you about fell in love with those two nymphs. What else happened I cannot tell you. I did not pay all that much attention.

He was asked whether, in the comedy, Orazio, dressed with the aforesaid hood, made any gesture befitting a monk. And, if so, what was it?

HE ANSWERED: Signore, in truth, I did not see him make any gesture befitting a monk.

He was asked if Orazio, who was playing a monk, did not hold a bell in his hands. And did he not ring it to make the nymphs come, and at the end of his conversation with them did he not tear up his habit?

HE ANSWERED: Signore, a bell was attached to a tree in the middle of the piazza. And little boys were ringing it and the nymphs were strolling in the piazza. I know that he took off those clothes that he had wrapped around him, but if he tore them or not, I cannot tell You. The bell was on a tree. And there were also some bundles of branches, but that was all the hermitage there was. *Adding to a question of me, the notary:* Tiberio, who played the Necromancer, made some signs on the ground with a stick and along came a fellow dressed as a Devil. Some people say it was Mutio di Giovanni Mariano, but I couldn't recognize him. He went two or three times around that circle the Necromancer had made and then ran away without reciting a single thing. And it is true that Britio, dressed as a peasant, sacrificed a lamb in the middle of the piazza, on the ground. And he said that he wanted to make a sacrifice of that lamb, but the precise words he said, I don't know at all, to tell You the truth. It is true that when ser Giovanni Battista Varoni wanted to make the document, I heard him call on the Devil, but what for I cannot tell You.

He was asked if the comedy was recited by any others besides the aforesaid, and by whom.

HE ANSWERED: Signore, so far as I can remember, no other persons took part in the recitation of the comedy, besides the ones I have already told you.

He was asked whether the players were told by any men of the village of Aspra that in no way should they put on, say, or recite the comedy. And who said this?

HE ANSWERED: Signore, I don't know anything about this. I don't know that anyone from the village forbade them to recite the comedy.

He was asked whether on the first day of Lent in Aspra there was cavorting and singing and dancing, just as on the first day of Carnival. And who did it?

HE ANSWERED: Signore, I have told You the truth, that I had gone to Magliano and heard nothing about this. Nor have I heard afterwards that they played music and danced in Aspra on the first day of Lent, the way they do on the first day of Carnival.

Then I, the notary, terminated the examination and dismissed the witness with an oath to silence and to the effect that he had spoken the truth.

I, Daniel, witness as here above have made my deposition as the truth.

[There then follow notarized pledges to appear in Rome. In summary:

In the palace of the podestà, before the witnesses Ceccho Giovanni Colesanti and Fausto Sante, the gardener, maestro Cicchantonio di Bernardino Antonio Angelo of Aspra pledges that Stefano di Adamo will appear in Rome before the court of the cardinal within two days under a forfeit of two hundred scudi.

Before the same witnesses, ser Fabbiano di Albertini, the father of Tiberio di Albertini pledges that his son will appear within three days in Rome before the Cardinal of Montepulciano, under the forfeit of two hundred scudi.]

There was examined in the same place, by me, the notary, etc., for the information of the court: messer **Latino***, son of Battista Cecio of Aspra, another witness, as above, who, having sworn to tell the truth and touched the scriptures, was asked by me whether he knows or presumes to know the cause of his present examination.*

HE ANSWERED: Signore, unless You tell me why I am being examined, I know no way of telling You.

And I, the notary, asked what was his profession and his age.

HE ANSWERED: I am from Aspra. I must be about twenty-five years old. I am a student, and a deacon; I am ordained in minor orders.

He was asked who were the participants in the comedy recited here in Aspra the past Sunday of Carnival. And what did the comedy contain?

HE ANSWERED: The comedy, which was recited the last Sunday in Carnival here in the piazza of the Menili in Aspra, was recited starting at midday. These were the participants. Massimigliano, alias Penicchio, was the one who did the prologue. He is a fieldworker, but he is poor and has many daughters.[9] Stefano di Adamo and Britio di Giovanni Battista Vasselaro played two shepherds, or two peasants who were servants of two shepherds who had fallen in love. One of them was Ovidio Fedele of Aspra, a tailor; the other was Emilio Guielmi, also of Aspra, a cobbler. There were also two nymphs with whom the shepherds were in love. One of them was Cesare di Troiano, a lad of about fourteen or fifteen years.[10] The other nymph was the son of Tullio di Collevecchio, whose name is Tarquinio, a lad of the same age as Cesare; I think he goes to school in Collevecchio. There was the hermit, and his part was played by Orazio di Giovanni Camillo, a cobbler of Aspra. Then there was a necromancer, and his part was played by Tiberio di ser Famiano Albertini. There also took part in the comedy someone dressed like a devil, whose name is Mutio di Giovanni Mariano, of Aspra. There was a little boy who played the God of Love, who said some verses, and his name is Silverio, son of Pietro Sacchetti, who is the same age as Tarquinio and Cesare. There was also a person who played a notary, whose name is signore Giovanni Battista Varoni, from Aspra, and there weren't any others, so far as I can recall. The comedy bore the title 'Crapino.' It is an old play and in print, but I can't tell you anything about the plot.

He was asked what clothing the players wore, and first of all Tiberio Albertini and Orazio and Mutio.

HE ANSWERED: Tiberio wore a long gray cloak, and on his head he had a black hat and he had a stick in his hand. Orazio was dressed like a hermit, and around his neck, in place of a rosary, a string of balls of skin of the sort that make *querza*,[11] which he ripped off when he saw that the nymphs had duped him at the dinner he had prepared. For he had invited them to his villa, which he had made as a hermitage in the middle of the piazza. And he rang a bell, which was hanging from a pretend tree at his cell.

Mutio, who played the Devil, was dressed all in black skin. And on his head he had a devil's head, that is, two very big horns – I think they were deer's horns – and he invoked Pluto. And he threw pitch on the fire to make incense for Pluto in the middle of a circle that Tiberio, who played the Necromancer, had drawn on the ground with a stick. And he had written certain letters, but I don't know what they were. *And to a question he said*: It is true that Britio, one of the ones who played a peasant, sacrificed a big lamb that he wanted to eat all by himself. He sacrificed him to the god, Pan, saying, 'My master told me to do this sacrifice to the god Pan, but I want to sing the tarantella[12] and make the sacrifice to my teeth.'

He was asked if it is true that the aforesaid participants had been warned by many old, discreet men not to recite the comedy, and yet went on contemptuously to hold and recite it in the piazza.

HE ANSWERED: Certainly, I cannot tell You anything about this, about how they might have been warned by the old men of this village, because, maybe, it wouldn't have taken place if this warning had occurred.

He was asked at whose expense the comedy was staged and recited.

HE ANSWERED: It didn't cost much, but I believe that the players covered the costs.

He was asked what intermezzi were in the comedy. And into how many acts was it divided?

HE ANSWERED: I believe that there were five acts in the comedy, and the intermezzi were music.

Then I, the notary, terminated the examination and imposed a vow of silence.

I, Latino, witness, deposed as the truth as above
[signed in a wavering hand.]

On the same day
[Giovanni Battista, ex-bookseller and Britio's father, and Marco Antonio, his brother, both of Aspra, stand pledge before witnesses for two hundred scudi that Britio will come before the court of the bishop of Sabina in Rome within three days.]

Tuesday, 23 March 1574
*There was examined by me, the notary, in the same place, for the information of the court: messer **Pietro**, son of the late maestro Francesco Petruccio di Aspra, a witness, age about twenty-two, having first tonsure and four minor orders, who swore to tell the truth, touched the scriptures, and answered questions as follows.*

To tell the truth, concerning this thing You are asking me about I can tell You only that the last Sunday of last Carnival here in Aspra they recited a comedy, so I've been told, because I wasn't there to hear it.

Rather, I had gone out of the village in order not to hear it, because the archpriest Giacomo of Aspra said that for us priests it was prohibited to hear comedies. So then I went to Montàsola[13] for my pleasure and I came back home here late, maybe around the five in the evening. They told me that it had been recited in the piazza of the Menili in Aspra and that those who took part were those who had planned it, that is: Orazio di Giovanni Camillo, Stefano di Adamo, Emilio Guielmi, Cesare di Nardo, Mutio di Giovanni Mariano, Tiberio di ser Famiano, Silverio di Pietro Sacchetti, Tarquinio di Tullio da Collevecchio, Britio di Giovanni Battista, Ovidio di Fedele, all of them from Aspra except that boy called Tarquinio.

He was asked to tell and narrate what parts in the aforesaid comedy Orazio and Stefano played and what clothing they wore.

HE ANSWERED: I have heard it said that Orazio played the part of a friar and that he had on a cape with a hood on his head and he had a little bell that he rang, but I don't know why. As for what Stefano did, I couldn't tell You what part he played, because I haven't asked.

He was asked, likewise, if he knows or has learned what parts all the other participants named above played. And how were they dressed, and what actions and gestures did they make and show in the comedy?

HE ANSWERED: Signore, about all the others, I cannot tell You what part they played, nor what dress they wore, nor what actions they made in the comedy, save that I have heard that Mutio had the part of the Devil. I can't tell You anything else.

He was asked what was the title of the comedy and what was in it.

HE ANSWERED: Signore, I don't know, for I've never seen or read the play and I don't know what is in it.

He was asked who was the organizer of the play. And at whose expense was it put on and recited?

HE ANSWERED: Signore, I don't know who organized the play, but as for at whose expense it was done, I think that they collected money going through the village masked, taking it from the outsiders who came.

He was asked if he knows that the participants were asked by some of the elders not in any way to put on the play.

HE ANSWERED: Signore, I have no knowledge that those who put on the play here in Aspra were prohibited by anyone in our village from putting on the play. But I can tell you that, the very next day, they wanted to go to Roccantica[14] to recite the same play, but the court here didn't want them to, but why not I do not know, and in the end they didn't go.

He was asked who might be informed about this play. Who would know what it was like and remember the deeds and gestures contained in it?

HE ANSWERED: Signore, I couldn't tell you who might have information about the comedy, in truth, because I wasn't there, but the participants themselves will be able to tell You everything if You examine them. And also the podestà will be able to tell You because he had to have been there to hear it recited.

Then I, the notary, terminated the examination and dismissed the witness with an oath to keep silence.

 I, Pietro Petruccio, who deposed the above as the truth.

[There follow more pledges to appear in Rome. In summary:

Cola Giacobo, son of the late Angelizzi of Aspra, pledges that Emilio Guielmi will appear in Rome, under forfeit of two hundred scudi. The witnesses are Giacobo Sante, the gardener, and Stefano Reni, the rope-maker.

Maestro Tullio di Collevecchio of Aspra pledges for his son, Tarquinio, aged twelve or about, under a forfeit of one hundred scudi. The same witnesses.

Pietro, son of the late Giovanni Battista Sacchetti of Aspra, pledges for his son aged about eleven years, under a forfeit of one hundred scudi. Witnesses Antonio Nardo and Captain Aenea Silvestro of Aspra.

Troiano, son of the late S[...] Nardi of Aspra, pledges for his son, aged twelve or about, under a forfeit of one hundred scudi. The same witnesses.

Antonio, son of the late Dominico Lucarelli of Aspra pledges for Giovanni Battista Varoni, under forfeit of two hundred scudi. The same witnesses.

For Mutio di Giovanni Mariano, under forfeit of two hundred scudi. No guarantor is named.]

[The rest of the document, below, reports hearings in Rome.]

25 March 1574
Arraigned in person, in Rome, in [the prison of] Corte Savelli before the magnificent doctor of both laws,[15] *signore Aloigi Drogho, a judge delegated by the most illustrious and most reverend Cardinal of Montepulciano and Bishop of Sabina, and before me, the notary:* **Britio***, son of Giovanni Battista Vasselaro of the village of Aspra, who swore the oath to tell the truth and touched the scriptures and was asked by the lord why it is that he appears before the cardinal.*

HE ANSWERED: I don't know why I am in jail, except that messer Francesco Petruccio brought me here and told me that I should do obedience to my masters. But I believe that it is on account of a certain pastoral comedy that was put on this Carnival in Aspra.

He was asked whether any others came with him to Rome from the village of Aspra. And who were they?

HE ANSWERED: There came with me from Aspra Tiberio di Famiano, Emilio, Stefano di Adamo, Mutio di Giovanni Mariano. There are five of us in all and the others are here in jail, too.

He was asked when he and the aforesaid others came to Rome. What did they do after their arrival?

HE ANSWERED: We came to Rome last evening, around eight at night, and we slept in the house of messer Francesco Petruccio, and then, this morning, we went to find the notary, who is here now, to show obedience, because in Aspra they put us under surety to appear in Rome before the most illustrious Cardinal of Montepulciano.

He was asked what work and profession he has and whether he knows how to read.

HE ANSWERED: I am a potter, and I know how to read and write a little.

He was asked just to tell what day the aforesaid comedy was put on, and in what place in particular in the village of Aspra.

HE ANSWERED: The comedy was put on in Aspra the last Sunday of Carnival, after eating-time; it began after the midday meal and lasted about two hours. And it was put on in the piazza, where there was a fair crowd, both citizens and outsiders.

He was asked what the title of the comedy was.

HE ANSWERED: The comedy was called 'The Comedy of Crapino.'

He was asked whether he knows who it was who arranged the said comedy.

HE ANSWERED: I don't know who was the first who arranged the comedy, except that one day I was called by someone named Massimigliano, alias Penicchio, and by Orazio di Giovanni Camillo, and they took me to a house where they were practising the comedy. They asked me if I wanted to take part and recite. I said yes, and they gave me the part of a peasant called Sorbo. About a month later, we performed it in the piazza, as I have said. Before we recited it, we practised it in Penicchio's house about fifteen or twenty times.

He was asked what other persons took part in the recitation of the comedy. And let him say in particular the parts recited by each.

HE ANSWERED: The participants were as follows: Britio, that's me, who played the part of the peasant called Sorbo; Stefano di Adamo, who played the part of Crapino; Tiberio di ser Famiano, who played the Necromancer; Orazio di Giovanni Camillo, who played the Hermit; Mutio di Giovanni Mariano, who played the Demon; Giovanni Battista Varoni, who played the Notary; Ovidio Fedele played the Lover; Silverio di Sacchetti, a boy, played the God of Love; Cesare di Nardo played a Nymph; Tarquinio di Tullio played the other Nymph; Emilio Guielmi played the Lover; and Massimigliano, alias Penicchio, did the prologue, so that in all there were twelve of us, and each of us played the personages I have already told to your Lordship.

He was asked to tell the plot of his part.

HE ANSWERED: I was the servant of the Lover, who ordered me to make a sacrifice to the god, Pan. So I took a lamb and I cut its throat and I let it lie. Then I pretended to eat the lamb, but I was really eating a little bread and cooked meat.

He was asked precisely what words he said when he sacrificed the lamb. And let him also say what actions and gestures there were in this sacrifice.

HE ANSWERED: I had a knife in my hand and the lamb on my shoulder and I said these words, or lines:
    Here I'm come, I want to do
    Just what my master told me to,
    To make a sacrifice to this god

Of this lamb I'd rather eat.
And should my master happen by
In God's faith, I'd not ask him in,
Because this is little for my body
I'd rather stuff down a cow.
The bones I'll give to this dog,
And the marrow, that's for me to eat
And I'd like to sing you the tarantella.

After I said these lines, I put the lamb down under me and cut its throat. And there were lines before and after that, for in my part there were more than ninety lines.

He was asked also to tell the parts that the others he named recited, and to tell their actions.

HE ANSWERED: Stefano played the part of another Peasant. This was his part. He wanted to imitate the Necromancer, who was using a big stick to make a circle on the ground, where there was a bonfire on which he put shreds of cloth and broken bits of shoes and made a lot of smoke. As for the words he said, I don't know, but he will be able to tell You better. Tiberio played the Necromancer, as I told You, and in that same bonfire, beforehand, he had put rags of shoes and had said certain words, but I don't know them. His costume was a long cape; I don't remember what colour it was. On his head he had a big hat of rough felt, coloured black. Mutio Mariano played the part of the Devil. On his head he had a head, like a mask, with the figure of the Devil, with horns. And on his back he had a raincape of cloth and a pair of long hose. I don't remember what he said.

Emilio Guielmi played one of those Lovers. He was dressed as a shepherd. What he said, I do not remember. Ovidio Fedele played the other Lover and was dressed the same as he. Penicchio did the prologue. He had a cape on. Orazio played the Hermit. He had two capes on, one from the belt downwards that it seems to me, was of white wool, and he wore the other from his shoulders. And he had a hood on his head made of cloth of Terni, and he carried a stick with a point[?] and around his neck he had a rosary of balls of *querza*[?] that came down as far as his belt. When he wanted to invite the Nymphs to eat with him, he rang a bell that hung from a tree under which was the hermitage where the Hermit sheltered. When the Nymphs didn't want to come at the sound of the bell, the Hermit tore the rosary into several pieces, but what words he used I do not know. But he will tell You if You examine him.

Giovanni Battista, who played the part of the Notary – he's the one who made the contract between me and my master – he promised to give me the Queen of France, for me, and Ovidio, who played the part of the Lover promised to give the Empress as wife to Stefano, his servant. Anyway, Giovanni Battista issued the two contracts, and I don't remember the words he said when he issued the contracts, but I know for certain that he named the Devil. Those three boys, Cesare, Tarquinio, and Silverio: as I told you, two of them played nymphs and one the God of Love.

He was asked whether he knows that some citizens of the village of Aspra ever spoke with the participants, or with him himself, either before or after the recitation of the comedy. And what did they speak of?

HE ANSWERED: No citizen of Aspra has ever spoken with me. But if they spoke with my companions, or with any one of them, I couldn't tell You. *Adding on his own*: I didn't want to go recite my part because a kinsman of my father had died, but my companions urged me so much that they made me recite. And they also had me asked by a citizen of Aspra called Nicola di ser Morello and by Felice di Lorenzo and by others, I don't remember who, and I was asked by ser Famiano too.

He was asked whether in the comedy there was anyone dressed in clothing that monks and persons dedicated to God usually use.

HE ANSWERED: In the comedy there was no one dressed as a monk except the Hermit and the Necromancer, as I told You before.

He was asked what intermezzi were put on in the comedy.

HE ANSWERED: The intermezzi of the comedy were two or three in number, if I remember rightly; they played the guitar and the lute. It was two villagers, Ovidio and Felice di Lorenzo.

He was asked and warned just to tell the truth; did any citizens of the village of Aspra protest against this comedy, which was recited so indecorously and which set so bad an example, and were they [the players] reproached by them?

HE ANSWERED: Signore, I tell You that nothing was said to me, but whether anything was said to my companions, I do not know.

He was asked who those were who on the first day of Lent went playing music and dancing in public.

HE ANSWERED: The morning of Lent, two hours before daybreak, I went out to hunt pigeons, and when I came back home in the evening, around the first hour of the night [seven in the evening],[16] I heard it said around the village that in the daytime, certain youngsters of Aspra went around playing the lute and the guitar. But I don't know who they were, nor do I remember from whom I heard it, but I never heard that they went dancing.

He was asked at whose expense the comedy was put on by the participants.

HE ANSWERED: The expenses of the comedy were covered by us participants. This is how. I'll tell You. Penicchio, Orazio, and Emilio, as principals, went along with the others in masks, begging money from the outsiders, and also from the citizens who were in Aspra. I did have a mask on, but I didn't go around begging. Almost every day they did it this way; they carried a cup of raisins and sweets and a jug of wine and people gave them whatever they wanted to. *He added in answer to a question:* I don't know which one of them kept that money, nor how much it amounted to.

Then the magnificent lord terminated the examination and ordered him to be put back for now in his place of imprisonment, with the intention of continuing.

Saturday,[17] 26 March 1574
*Arraigned in person, in the same place, before the same magnificent lord deputy, and before me, the notary: **Stefano**, son of the late Adamo, of Aspra, who swore to tell the truth and touched the scriptures and was asked by the lord why he is appearing before the cardinal.*

HE ANSWERED: I am here in jail because messer Francesco Petruccio brought me here yesterday, along with four others. We all came from Aspra, where we were obligated to present ourselves here in Rome before the Cardinal of Montepulciano.

He was asked for what reason he came to Rome and why was he enjoined to appear. Let him tell the names of the four who came with him to the cardinal.

HE ANSWERED: I do not know the reason I came to Rome along with those four others, unless it is for a comedy that we performed on the Sunday of Carnival. The four who came with me are called Tiberio, Britio, Mutio, and Emilio Guielmi.

He was asked what trade he practises in the village of Aspra and if he knows how to read and write.

HE ANSWERED: I am a cobbler and I know how to read and write, but not much.

He was asked whether he was one of those who took part in the aforesaid comedy.

HE ANSWERED: Signore, yes. I was one of the players in the comedy.

He was asked to tell who were the others who took part in the comedy.

HE ANSWERED: One called Massimigliano, alias Penicchio; Britio, the son of Giovanni Battista Vasellaro; Orazio di Giovanni Camillo, a cobbler; Ovidio Fedele; Emilio, the son of Giovanni di Marco; Silverio Sacchetti, a boy; Cesare di Troiano and Tarquinio di Tullio, youths who played the Nymphs; [and] Tiberio di Famiano, Giovanni Battista Varoni, and Stefano, who played music. In all, we are twelve.

He was asked what the title of the comedy was. And who was it who arranged to do it?

HE ANSWERED: The comedy was called 'The Comedy of Crapino.' All of us agreed to recite it, so I couldn't tell You who was the first.

He was asked what person he himself played in the comedy.

HE ANSWERED: I played the part of Crapino.

And the lord said that he should tell all the things he said in the comedy, with all his actions.

HE ANSWERED: The part that I played in the comedy had me be a servant of a shepherd who was in love. And I pretended I wanted to take the Empress to wife. This gave rise to a conflict, or a disagreement, with another Peasant. And messer Giovanni Battista Varoni played the Notary and he issued this document. And I and that other Peasant came to blows with clubs, because we had made some things out of rags that looked like clubs. And that was my part.

He was asked whether, when he recited the comedy, he ever did so in a secret place, and in which.

HE ANSWERED: We practised the comedy more than twenty times, always in Massimigliano's house, and sometimes Felice Sano came to hear it, for we invited him to come and see if it was going well.

He was asked what actions Tiberio di ser Famiano made in the comedy when he recited the part of the Necromancer and how he was dressed.

HE ANSWERED: Tiberio, when he played the Necromancer, made a circle on the ground with a stick. Then he lit a bonfire and on that bonfire he put some Greek pitch. And he was wearing a cloak of cloth, but what colour it was I don't know. And he had a hat on his head, but as for the words he said, I don't know them.

He was asked whether there also took part in the comedy a Hermit. And what words and actions did he make and what clothes did he wear?

HE ANSWERED: The Hermit – Orazio di Giovanni Camillo played him. He was wearing a cape from the belt downwards and another cape over his shoulders and a hood on his head. And he rang a bell, like the ones the cows wear, to catch the attention of the Nymphs. And because they wouldn't come, he got mad and threw his stick to the ground. The rosary of balls of *querza* that he was wearing on his neck, he tore off and threw on the ground.

He was asked in what place the comedy was recited and at whose expense.

HE ANSWERED: The comedy was recited in the piazza of the Menili. It must have lasted two hours, more or less. It was after the midday meal and there were others from the village present when it was recited.

He was asked whether, at the reciting of the comedy, any sort of objection was raised in the village of Aspra. And who did it, and for what reason?

HE ANSWERED: I am not aware that any sort of fuss arose in Aspra on account of this comedy.

He was asked whether he knows whether this comedy was and is permitted[18] *and whether it can be recited without any scruple.*

HE ANSWERED: I don't know that this comedy was prohibited. For, if I had known, I wouldn't have taken part.

He was asked at whose expense and outlay the comedy was recited.

HE ANSWERED: In putting on the comedy, there was no expenditure. It is true that, along with others, two or three times, we went masked through the village begging money with a cup of fruit and sweets, and both the citizens and the outsiders gave us something. With this money, we paid the musicians for celebrating Carnival, but for the play we didn't spend anything.

He was asked if in the comedy there were any intermezzi. And what were they?

HE ANSWERED: Signore, yes. In the comedy there were intermezzi, where one Domenico played the harp.

He was asked to say what words Giovanni Battista Varoni used when he pretended to exercise the office of Notary in the comedy.

HE ANSWERED: When Giovanni Battista wanted to begin to say the words of the document, I remember, he said, 'In the name of one hundred demons, amen.' And in the other parts I do not remember what he said.

He was asked whether in the comedy there were any vestments of monks. Let him tell the truth.

HE ANSWERED: In the comedy there was no vestment of a monk, except the one the Hermit wore, as I said. There were two capes, and the hood that he used on his head, and a lay person's cape[?], and he carried a little bell and a rosary, as I said above.

He was asked and warned to tell if anyone from the village of Aspra took ill the recitation of the comedy and whether before or afterwards they were warned not to recite the comedy.

HE ANSWERED: To me nobody ever said anything to the effect that we shouldn't recite the comedy. If the others were warned, I don't know it.

He was asked if the aforesaid Hermit had a hermitage. And what sort, and in what place?

HE ANSWERED: There were two bundles of sticks there in the piazza, with some thatch. And that served as his hermitage.

He was asked whether, on the first day of Lent, in the village of Aspra some of those who took part in the comedy went strolling, playing music, and cavorting through the village of Aspra.

HE ANSWERED: I don't know. I haven't heard that anyone, on the first day of Lent, went playing music and dancing through the village of Aspra, because that day was a holiday and almost all of us were out hunting birds with crossbows.

Then the lord terminated the examination and ordered him to be put back in his place of detention with the intention of continuing.

Brought in person before the court, before the same persons, for the information of the court, as above: **Mutio**, *son of Giovanni Mariano, of Aspra, who swore to tell the truth and touched the scriptures and was asked by me, the notary, what part he recited in the comedy and what actions he made.*

HE ANSWERED: In the comedy that was put on this Carnival in Aspra I recited the part of the Devil. I was dressed in a pair of long sailor-style hose of black cloth, and a rough shirt of black cloth and on my head I had a big head, like a mask, with two big horns, and I had my whole face painted and I didn't say anything, except these three lines:

My graces will not suffice
To help what you are asking for
Because your sins are too cocky.[19]

When I had said these lines, I left, I took off my costume, and I went out to the fields to guard the herd. *Adding to a question*: I do not know how to read or write, but rather I learned these three lines by heart.

He was asked whether in the comedy he saw any vestments that monks habitually use. And what were they?

HE ANSWERED: In the comedy, there was only the Hermit, who had two capes, one from the belt downwards, the other on his shoulders, with the hood half on his head, and around his neck he had a big necklace of balls of *querza* and he rang a bell, which invited the Nymphs to his cell, or his hermitage, which was made in the piazza with two bundles of sticks. And when he saw that the Nymphs wouldn't come, in anger he ripped off the necklace and threw the stick to the ground, but I didn't see him when he did this act because I had left to take off my costume.

He was asked whether a necromancer took part in the play and what his actions were.

HE ANSWERED: Tiberio di Famiano played the Necromancer, but I don't know what actions he made because I had such tiny holes in the mask that I couldn't see them.

Then, the text having been accepted, the lord terminated the examination and ordered the suspect to be put back in his place [in jail] with the intention of continuing. And then he ordered to be called and brought forward: **Emilio di Guielmi** *of the village of Aspra, who swore the oath to tell the truth and touched the scriptures and was asked by the lord why he found himself before the cardinal.*

HE ANSWERED: I came from Aspra by order of Silvestro, the notary, *indicating me, the notary,* because this past Carnival I joined with some other youths to put on a comedy.

He was asked what the title of the comedy was and what person had he played in it.

HE ANSWERED: The comedy was called 'The Comedy of Crapino,' and I played the Lover.

He was asked to recount in substance all the actions he did in the comedy.

HE ANSWERED: The part I played in the comedy was that of a Shepherd. And a Nymph pretended to be in love with me, so I fell in love with her. And we met and talked together, and I asked her to love me and cherish me with these words:
    Don't show yourself cruel, because you are beautiful
    Because Love has made me subject to you.
But before these, and after them, I recited up to thirty-five or forty lines.

He was asked whether in the comedy there were any vestments of monks, and what they were.

HE ANSWERED: In the comedy there was no monk's habit. And the Hermit did not have anything besides two capes, with a hood on his head, because he was pretending to be a friar, and he rang a bell that was attached to his hermitage, made of bundles of sticks, and he invited the Nymphs. And when he saw that the Nymphs didn't come, he threw the stick on the ground and tore off a necklace that he had on his neck that was of balls of *querza.*

He was asked whether in the comedy there was anyone who exercised the office of Notary and what words he used.

HE ANSWERED: Giovanni Battista Varoni played the Notary and

two Peasants who were in the comedy pretended to take a wife. One of them wanted to have the Queen of France and the other took the Empress. And he [the Notary] told the master [of the servants], on his part, 'Say it in the name of one hundred demons, amen' and other words that I didn't pay attention to. *Adding to a question*: It is true that the bit of money that helped us put on the comedy was collected by us in the village, from outsiders and from citizens, and we put on masks and we went with raisins and fruit [as a token offering(?)] and with that little money we made do. In the comedy we didn't pay musicians because Domenico di Leonardo played his harp only two times; rather, with that money we wanted to pay the Carnival musician.

He was asked whether, on the first day of Lent in the village of Aspra, he and some others went playing music and dancing, not without great scandal. And by whom had he been persuaded to do this?

HE ANSWERED: I didn't go through the village on the first day of Lent, playing through the village, nor do I know that anyone else did, *etc.*

*Then the examination was terminated and he was put back in place [in jail] with the intention of continuing. And then was called: **Tiberio**, son of ser Famiano of Aspra, who swore to tell the truth and touched the scriptures and was asked by the lord how it is he finds himself in this prison and when he came here.*

HE ANSWERED: I am in jail because I have had an order to bring myself to Rome before the most illustrious Cardinal of Montepulciano. I came here yesterday evening with four or five other fellow villagers.

He was asked if he can imagine the reason he was summoned to appear in Rome before the most illustrious and most reverend lord Cardinal of Montepulciano.

HE ANSWERED: I don't know for what reason they gave us that order to come to Rome.

He was asked if in last Carnival in Aspra a comedy was put on. And what was it?

HE ANSWERED: Signore, yes. In this past Carnival in Aspra they put on 'The Comedy of Crapino.'

He was asked who the participants in the comedy were. And had he had any part in it, and what was it?

HE ANSWERED: In the comedy there took part: Stefano di Adamo,

Britio, son of Giovanni Battista, Mutio Mariano, Ovidio Fedele, Orazio di Giovanni Camillo, Penicchio, Giovanni Battista Varoni, Tarquinio di Tullio, Cesare di Troiano, Silverio di Pietro, and Tiberio Famiano, that's me; so in all they make twelve.

He was asked to tell and narrate the part that he recited with all his actions.

HE ANSWERED: I played the part of the Necromancer, or rather of the astrologist, who with a stick made two circles on the ground. And I put a bonfire in it and I put pitch on it and I called the Devil or Pluto, who had to shake a tree under which there was a nymph. And he said these lines:

   I command, O Pluto, that without a shovel
   You shake down this tree
   And deliver the shepherd his beloved.

With these words, the tree fell to the ground and the Nymph escaped. And this was what my recitation consisted of.

He was asked if anyone took part in the comedy dressed as a monk. And who was he?

HE ANSWERED: I wore a cape of black cloth and a hat. There was also a Hermit, who was dressed in two capes, one from the belt down, and the other across his shoulders. And he had a hood on his head, and he had a string of balls of *querza* around his neck, and he rang a bell that hung from a [...] of his hermitage, which was made in the piazza out of bundles of sticks. And he rang that bell. And I don't know why he did it, but he broke the string he had around his neck and threw the stick to the ground, because he was furious.

He was asked whether in the comedy there was a Notary. And what did he say and what words did he use?

HE ANSWERED: He made out a document for those two Peasants. One of them was marrying a woman and the other was marrying another. And Giovanni Battista called them the Queen of France and the Empress, but I can't tell you the exact words he used.

He was asked whether Giovanni Battista in doing so named any devils. And which ones?

HE ANSWERED: I didn't hear Giovanni Battista mention the devil otherwise.

He was asked who was the instigator and the organizer of the comedy.

HE ANSWERED: We were all agreed to put on the comedy. I couldn't tell You who was the first one.

He was asked how much it cost to put the comedy on.

HE ANSWERED: There was no expense at all. It is true that we went masked through the village with the musicians. What little money we begged we paid to the musicians. *Adding to a question*: When we put on the intermezzi in the comedy, one Domenico from Aspra played the harp.

He was asked in whose company he had on the first day of Lent gone through the village of Aspra playing music and dancing. He should tell the truth about this.

HE ANSWERED: I didn't go around Aspra on the first day of Lent playing music, nor do I know that anyone else went, for all that day I was outside Aspra.

He was asked whether he or the other participants had been reprehended by anyone who said that they should not perform such a ridiculous comedy and put on a prohibited festivity.

HE ANSWERED : Signore, no! No one from Aspra ever told us that we shouldn't put on the comedy. If they had, we wouldn't have done it, nor do we know that the comedy is prohibited.

Then the examination was terminated by the lord and he ordered Tiberio and all the others aforesaid to be placed in the public part of the jail with the intention of continuing.

Saturday, 27 March 1574
[A notarial act to the effect that under penalty of confiscation and perpetual imprisonment in the galleys the arraigned should come back to the prison in two days.]

THE COMMENTARY

The commentary for this trial takes the form of a playbill. It presents not just the lost comedy, 'Crapino,' but the entire drama, first of the production of the Carnival play and, then, of the cardinal's Lenten inquiry.

Crapino

A Pastoral Tragicomedy in Three Acts Aspra and Rome, 1574

Dramatis Personae

ACT ONE: Carnival time in the village of Aspra
The cast of the pastoral *'Comedy of Crapino'*

The Reader of the Prologue	Massimigliano, alias Penicchio a poor peasant
A Necromancer	Tiberio di ser Famiano Albertini
A Notary	Ser Giovanni Battista Varoni probably a notary
The Devil	Mutio di Giovanni Mariano a herdsman
A Hermit	Orazio di Giovanni Camillo, a cobbler
An Amorous Shepherd	Emilio di Giovanni di Marco Guielmi a cobbler
Another Amorous Shepherd	Ovidio Fedele a tailor

Sorbo, a Crafty Servant of a Shepherd	Britio di Giovanni Battista Vasellaro a potter
Crapino, another Crafty Servant of a Shepherd	Stefano di Adamo
A Nymph	Cesare di Troiano (or di Nardo) a boy of about 12
Another Nymph	Tarquinio di Tullio di Collevecchio also a boy of about 12
The God of Love	Silverio di Pietro Sacchetti a boy of 11
The Musicians for the Intermezzi	Ovidio Fedele; Felice di Lorenzo
Harpist	Domenico di Leonardo

An audience from Aspra and other towns

ACT TWO: The palace of the podestà in Lent in Aspra, Sunday through Tuesday, 21 to 23 March 1574

The cast of this act in order of appearance

The Denouncer of the play (Off-stage)	Don Giacomo, Archpriest of Aspra
The Cardinal who makes inquiries (Off-stage)	Giovanni Riccio, Bishop of Sabina and Cardinal of Montepulciano
The Bishop's Emissary to Aspra	The Notary, Silvestro Amonio
The Official who tries to keep the Notary out	The Podestà, Flaminio Iacobelli de Collevecchio

The Official who registers the Bishop's letter	Sante, Castaldo of Aspra
Three young Clerics who testify before the Notary	Daniele di Ascanio Tomasolo of Aspra, who sees the play
	Latino di Battista Cecio, who sees the play
	Pietro di Francesco Petruccio, who leaves town in order not to see the play

ACT THREE: Rome, in the prison of Corte Savelli, Thursday and Friday, 25 and 26 March 1574

The cast of this act in order of appearance

Host to the Five Suspects in his house in Rome	Francesco Petruccio
Judge delegated by the Bishop	The magnificent Doctor of Both Laws, Signore Aloigi Drogho
The Notary	Silvestro Amonio
Five Suspects	Britio the cobbler (Sorbo the Servant)
	Stefano di Adamo (Crapino the Servant)
	Mutio the herdsman (The Devil)
	Emilio Guielmi the cobbler (An Amorous Shepherd)
	Tiberio di Famiano (The Necromancer)

The Cast
(major players in alphabetical order)

Britio di Giovanni Battista Vasellaro (Sorbo) has not wanted to take part in the production, he tells the magistrate, for a kinsman of his father has died. But his companions have urged him so much, as have other townsmen, that eventually he has relented. As a witness, he gives far more detail on the mechanics of the production, such as how to pretend to eat a sheep, than on the words and motives of the plot. On the first day of Lent, he is out of town hunting pigeons and thus cannot attest to dancing in the streets. He comes to Rome.

Emilio di Giovanni di Marco Guielmi (an Amorous Shepherd) is literate, but only a little. He is active in organizing the play and in collecting money for the Carnival musicians. As a witness, he can give the magistrate a good account of the words and motives of the players. For the play he has memorized thirty-five or forty lines. He comes to Rome.

Ser Giovanni Battista Varoni (the Notary), to judge by his title, is the social superior of the rest of the cast. At one point in the transcript he appears as 'signore.' He may well have been in real life what he plays in 'Crapino,' a notary, for in the play he has to write out contracts. We know little else about him, as he does not have to testify.

Orazio di Giovanni Camillo (the Hermit), the cobbler, has a bad reputation, says the letter of denunciation, because of some scandal with a nun, who was subsequently hanged. As a principal of the play, he is active in the players' questing for money for the Carnival musicians. Nevertheless, despite his bad name, his sacrilegious role in the play, and his efforts to bring the project off, he is not among the five men examined in Rome.

Massimigliano, also known as Penicchio, (the Reader of the Prologue) is a poor peasant with many daughters still to marry off. Despite his hardships, he is clearly one of the organizers of the play, for it is he who brings in Britio and who lends his house to the players for fifteen or twenty rehearsals. He has been active in the players' masked quests for money. He is not called to Rome.

Ovidio Fedele (another Amorous Shepherd) is a tailor who also plays music in the intermezzi. He is not among those who quest for funds. He does not have to come to Rome.

Stefano di Adamo (Crapino) plays the scamp from which the play takes its name. Nevertheless, when before the judge, the actor shows no sign of cleverness. When asked to explain the plot, he sees the story as a series of physical actions, such as the Necromancer's throwing pitch, or his own thrashing another peasant with a mock club. His seeming naiveté might be that of a wily peasant before the bench. On the first day of Lent he is out of the village, hunting birds with his crossbow. He comes to Rome.

Tiberio di ser Famiano Albertini (the Necromancer) is an evasive witness who pretends not to understand much of the plot or to remember the words of most interest to the judge. He seems to have only a few lines in the play. He comes to Rome.

A SYNOPSIS OF THE PLOT

Act One

In January 1574, in Aspra, today Casperia, a fortified village high in the Sabine mountains north-east of Rome, twelve villagers undertake to produce a play, 'The Comedy of Crapino.' Scheduling it for the last Sunday before Lent, they take to rehearsing it in the house of one of them, Massimigliano, alias Penicchio, a poor peasant and one of the promoters of the project. In the course of the month that follows they meet some fifteen or twenty times, sometimes under the eyes of other townsmen. In that same month, the players more than once go out masked, with music and food and wine, in quest of money to pay the Carnival musicians.

All does not go smoothly, for at some point before the day of the play itself, one or more elders of the village lodges with someone a protest against the work. That is all we know for certain, save that the senior priest in the town, don Giacomo, prevails upon at least one of the younger clerics to leave town for the day so as to miss the show. But, despite the archpriest's efforts, the play itself is successful enough. On Sunday, 14 February, after the midday meal, local folk and outsiders crowd the piazza, a hemicycle just below the parish church atop the town. Among the onlookers are the podestà and at least two clerics.

Just how does the story of the play itself go? We know many of the incidents, but we cannot easily put the plot in order, for the magistrate who eventually investigates the play never asks and none of his witnesses tries to tell the tale from beginning to end. Of course, since 'Crapino' is in print, the judge could easily enough satisfy his curiosity by reading it. But, so far as we can tell, it does not today survive under that name. Still, one can try to rewrite it. The testimonies offer all sorts of Lego-blocks of narrative, but it is hard to know how they fitted together. Here, in random order, are the pieces of the puzzle. *Item*: Two shepherds fall in love, at least one of them with a haughty, elusive nymph, whom he courts in the elevated language of love. *Item*: One nymph is hidden inside a tree. To fetch her out, a necromancer draws circles on the ground, lights fires in them, burns pitch to make foul incense, and calls on Pluto to knock down the tree. A devil with huge horns obliges, rushing in and prancing around the magic circle and hurling insults at the great sinner who has called him. The tree then topples, flushing out the nymph. The rascally servant, Crapino, apes this magic, stoking a fire of his own with bits of cloth and old shoes to make an awful smoke. *Item*: While the shepherds yearn for the nymphs, their servants, Crapino and Sorbo, also cast their sights on women. One shepherd promises Sorbo the Queen of France, while Crapino covets the Empress of Germany. The notary makes out a marriage contract for both servants, invoking not the name of God but a hundred devils. Somehow, these marital ambitions bring Crapino and another peasant, probably Sorbo, to a quarrel that ends in cudgel blows. *Item*: Sorbo's master wants his servant to sacrifice a lamb to Pan, but greedy Sorbo takes the animal, kills it, and sacrifices it not to a god but to his teeth, gobbling it down raw on the spot. *Item*: The hermit too has designs on the nymphs, planning to invite them to a dinner at the hermitage. To summon them, he rings a bell suspended from a tree above his hut. When they demur, he flies into a rage, pulls down the bell, throws down his staff, and tears from his neck a garland or rosary of great beads. That is all we know. Clearly, this is a play about the disappointment of fools who hanker after what they cannot hope to have. The prologue, the nymphs, the God of Love, the wily servants, and the amorous shepherds all have their ready models in ancient mythology, drama, and pastoral literature. On the other hand, the devil, the notary, the necromancer, and the hermit are cut from the homespun cloth of popular street theatre. Thus, even before the villagers lay hands on it, 'Crapino' is a jovial parody, a Renaissance pastiche of several classical genres.

Act Two

The first act thus ends with a stage-play within the play of life. With the second act, we move from Carnival to Lent. Normally, in Renaissance Italy, the contrast between the revelry, pranks, foolery, and general disorder of the first and the solemnity, continence, and austerity of the second is stark. But in Aspra, in 1574, some villagers fail to observe the change, for some persons, we know not who, go playing and dancing through the village on 24 February, Ash Wednesday. Just under two weeks later, on 9 March, someone else, again we know not who, sends a letter to Giovanni Riccio the cardinal of Montepulciano, who, as Bishop of Sabina, has jurisdiction in Aspra. The letter denounces the play, claiming that it is prohibited and against the Catholic faith, both for its actions and its words. The monk who pulled off his habit – so says the letter – and who called nymphs with his bell gave offence. So did the notary, who invoked demons, and the necromancer and the devil, both of whom did conjuring. To make things worse, 'many worthy elders' had prohibited the play, but the players had defied them, boasting that they feared no punishment. The letter recalls the bad reputation of Orazio, the nun-suborner who played the monk, and names as well six others of the principals.

This Lenten missive stirs up the bishop. Eleven days later, he writes a letter to the podestà, asking that the miscreants be brought at once, under caution, to his court in Rome. The next day, Sunday, 21 March, the notary, Silvestro, arrives in Aspra to do the cardinal's bidding. The podestà, says the letter, is to bring the suspects to his palace, to arrange sureties against their appearing in Rome within two days or, lacking a pledge, to jail them for the meantime. In Onorio Savelli, the local lord, the notary meets an obstacle, for he does not want his podestà, who himself has watched the play, to register the letter. The magnate's motives are not on record, but he probably resents the prelate's meddling and the implicit condemnation of his official's discretion. On Monday, the cardinal replies with a second missive thundering with threats of excommunication and thousand-scudi fines. That does the trick.

It is probably still Monday when Silvestro, the notary, examines two young clerics, Daniele and Latino. Both have seen the play. The notary may have singled them out because, as churchmen, they should be allies in the campaign for rectitude. On the other hand, he does not call in their senior colleagues. Their interrogation may thus seek as much to make the junior clergy toe the line as to gather information. The two witnesses do seem more loyal to their fellow villagers than to the intrusive cardinal. Daniele does his best to protect the players, saying he did not pay much attention to words and gestures. He did not consider the hermit a friar, that is, a proper churchman, nor did he see him call a nymph with his bell or rend his garments, though he did take them off. Nor, for that matter, was the hermitage much of a hermitage. Daniele's good memory for costumes does not extend to incriminating words. He forgets both Sorbo's to Pan at the sacrifice and the notary's invocation of the devil. The second witness, Latino, is not much more useful to the prosecution. He claims not to know the plot. While he informs the notary at length on the names and occupations of the players and is quick to explain costumes and actions, he is not very forthcoming with descriptions of sacrilegious deeds. He claims never to have heard that any village elders had warned against putting on the play. The next day, the notary brings in yet a third cleric, Pietro di Francesco Petruccio, who can help him little for, unlike his two colleagues, taking to heart don Giacomo's warnings, he left town to miss the show.

Act Three

The third act takes place in the chambers of the Corte Savelli prison in Rome. Five of the players – Britio, Emilio, Mutio, Stefano, and Tiberio – have come to Rome on Wednesday. Having slept in the house of one Francesco Petruccio, probably a kinsman of the cleric Pietro's late father of the same name, on Thursday morning they have come to find the notary, 'to show their obedience.' The court claps them in jail. Over the next two days, the notary and the bishop's judge examine all five and then set them free under penalty of the galleys if they fail to return.

Under questioning, the five captive actors describe their play concretely. That is, most of them, as narrators, choose to recall not words and motives but gestures, deeds, and costumes. The cobbler, Britio, who played the part of Sorbo, comes first. He is full of circumstantial details about how to pretend to eat raw sheep. Though he himself is adept enough with language to have memorized more than ninety verses, and while he has a ready memory for all sorts of acts and gestures, he has, he protests, none for the words of the other players. There are other things he does not recall, for he claims to have no knowledge of the names of the Lenten dancers nor any of warnings against staging the play. On Friday, the court calls a second cobbler, Stefano di Adamo. Crapino's actor is even less a man of words. His testimony, too, is all about clothes and deeds. Thus, he describes how he cudgelled a fellow actor with a mock club made of rags and dwells on how the Necromancer drew his circles and stoked his fires. Like Britio, he knows of no protests raised against the play beforehand. Having been out hunting on Ash Wednesday, he cannot incriminate any Lenten dancers. The third witness, Mutio, the devil, contrives to know as little as can be. He claims to have seen hardly any of the play, first because the eye-holes in his mask were too small, and second, because, having said his lines, he went off to tend the cows. Emilio di Guielmi, the Lover, has a slightly greater skill at explaining plot. Like the others, he tries to paint the hermit as less than clerical; he was only pretending to be a friar. As for what the notary said, Emilio did not pay attention. The final witness, Tiberio, who played the necromancer, claims not to know why the hermit rang his bell. Like Britio and Stefano, he too says that, had he been warned, he would not have put on the play.

There ends the third act of the play outside a play. As often with trials, there is no tidy dénouement. One wants to know what happened to the cast of the comedy, but the documents do not tell; there is no sentence. One knows only that, by the end of the first round of testimony, the court is of no mind to desist or settle. It would seem, from the insistent questions on the matter, that the villagers' putative disobedience to the elders' warnings could weigh heavily in the balance.

It is hard to say which of the other transgressions, those inside the comedy, most mattered. There were the invocation of the devil and sacrifices to Pan and Pluto, all three of them God's rivals. There was necromancy, less threatening as parody than in Danese's trial, where it seemed in earnest. But none of these would have loomed so large as the portrayal of a sacrilegious hermit in the travesty of a friar's habit. Survey his offences. A man who should fast in chaste solitude, he has consorted with nymphs, inviting them to feast with him at his holy retreat. Instead of showing mildness, in a fit of pique he has cast down four symbols of his religious life: his bell, his rosary, his habit, and his staff. But if the hermit has so affronted, why has its actor, that Orazio of dubious repute, not been called with the others to Rome?

The third act, the testimony of the actors, is a precious document, a handsome supplement to the rehearsal scenes of the menials in *A Midsummer Night's Dream*. The villagers of Aspra, like Shakespeare's artisans and like the exorcist Danese, have tried to appropriate some of the culture of the élite, transforming it in the process. Where Danese turned the published prayers of St Bernard and liturgical formulae into tools for dealing with the supernatural things around him, the peasant actors have adapted a printed play to amuse a local festival. The boundaries between high and popular are porous. All sorts of matter passes over, but changes in the crossing. Here, as with Danese, sensing danger and sacrilege in the deformation, the church, through the law, has stepped in to reclaim its own. The authorities strive to fortify the élite as the arbiter of culture; popular inventiveness must be guided and channelled. Court and church together haul the five defendants all the way to Rome, the font of authority, for·chastisement.

Seldom can one see how a Renaissance play looked to its players. As critics, the village thespians seem to lack a sense of the shape of their work of art. For them, it seems, words counted for less than dress and gesture and the parts weighed more than the whole, which they seem either disinclined or unable to discuss. But one must ask if the fragmentation of their narrative is due to their vision of their art or to the strained circumstances of their account. The judge sets his sights on details, not on the whole; his pinched questions invite a narrow response. Furthermore, the reticence about words and plot and motives may also represent the mask that wily countrymen often don in the face of the city's law. The testimonies are in such accord on so many points that the five defendants must have plotted their strategy before going to court, perhaps on the road south to Rome. The villagers seem to have a cagey sense of where their weak points are. Maybe that is why the five are so ready to give an account of deeds, as if they want to offer the semblance of cooperation without giving anything away. A director who staged a modern version of Act Three would have to ponder the spirit in which they give their testimony. As they recount their actions and recite their lines, should they seem cowed, or circumspect, or should they rather appear to brave the law's grim machinery with a little of an artist's pride in a job well done?

Notes

✺

CHAPTER ONE

1 The manuscript, a fragment, lacks the usual date and does not indicate the identity of the accused.

2 The Salviati palace, today Palazzo dei Penitenzieri, stands halfway between Castel Sant'Angelo and Saint Peter's.

3 In 1541, the bishop of Ancona is Gieronimo Vitelli-Ghianderone. He has until 1530 been archbishop not of Melfi, as the men say, but of Amalfi. He has also, between 1534 and 1538, been absentee abbot of San Galgano and then passed the Sienese abbey to his 'nephew,' in fact his son, Giovanni Andrea Vitelli-Ghianderone. Gieronimo will hold the see of Ancona to his death in 1550.

4 Rione Ponte lies close to the bridge to Castel Sant'Angelo. The Altoviti palace stands on Piazza Altoviti, on the Tiber side right at the end of the bridge.

5 Il Riccio means 'the hedgehog' and il Corvatto is reminiscent of 'the crow' (il corvo).

6 The manuscript has rather 'La Spiaggia.' But there was no such recorded place in all the Province of Siena. La Staggia is a far better reading. There are several such places, only one of which, near Montalcino, south of Siena, fits the geography of this account.

7 Montepulciano is in Florentine territory, across an international border from the Sienese village of the peasants. The killers will make a dash back there after they draw blood.

8 Cortona, like Montepulciano, is under Florentine rule. Città di Castello is over another frontier, under papal jurisdiction. In the sixteenth century it is a Vitelli town where the Bishop and the Abbot have family connections.

9 The Borgo is the neighbourhood between the river and Saint Peter's.

10 The killers thus stay with kinfolk of their masters.

11 *Per amor della inimicitia che havevamo.* That is exactly what the manuscript says, unambiguously. Could the scribe have meant to write *amicitia*, 'friendship'? We suspect so. But it may mean, 'Because we had enemies.'

12 Notice that Ancona is another town where the lords have connections.

13 The words in brackets are inadvertently left out of this good copy.

14 'Disfigure and lame them': *storpiati*. No single English verb catches the sense of the Italian *storpiare*, which, in the Renaissance, means not only to lame but also to disfigure. A wound to the ears would be especially efficacious because, damaging the face, it would steal honour. See the commentary on 'Paolo di Grassi and His Courtesans' for further discussion of honour and faces.

15 'Piazza of the Duke': the great square now known as Piazza Farnese

16 The name may well be blank because the scribe, making this good copy from an earlier, rougher draft, found the name illegible or impossible to reconstruct from phonetic shorthand notes.

17 Pozzo Bianco: A neighbourhood near the market of Campo dei Fiori. In the fifteenth and early sixteenth century, it is known for its inexpensive prostitutes. It is not too far from the house of the Bishop.

18 The chronology here is unclear. Corvatto seems to have been arrested and examined once before, and this second time to have let his patrons down by implicating them.

CHAPTER TWO

1 Camilla lives near the Santa Fiora palace and the church of Santa Lucia, probably on the street of the Banchi. Where she lives is important for this trial.

2 Paolo, too, lives near San Luigi. Giulia and Beatrice, whom Chierico calls a courtesan, also figure in the next trial, the story of the brawl.

3 Paolo Giordano Orsini, a great nobleman and prominent figure in Rome. He would become infamous for two later murders, one of his unfaithful wife, the other of his own beloved's husband. He appears in Stendhal's story of Vittoria Accoramboni in his *Italian Chronicles*.

4 The Piazza della Dogana is just to the south of the church of San Luigi. Pacheco lives at Sant'Apollinare, about five blocks away.

5 The court is interested in the source of turpentine that might have been used to set a door afire.

6 'To be brought in': *adduci*. Here, Camilla is not labelled as 'arraigned'

(*constituta*). Nevertheless, the interrogation, which treats her as a suspect, elsewhere uses the term.

7 Later testimony shows that Giulio Cestini lives on the street of the Banchi, near the Tiber bend.

8 This Paolo is Paolo Giordano, not Paolo di Grassi.

9 'I don't know where she's from': that is, I do not know her whole name. Courtesans very commonly drop the patronymic or lineage name and adopt a geographic second name, as in 'Camilla the Sienese,' 'Pasqua the Paduan,' and 'Lucrezia the Greek.' Their profession does not suit names of husbands and fathers, words that bear male honour.

10 Probably San Salvatore in Lauro, near the Tor di Nona, rather than other Salvatore churches

11 The hospital and church of Santo Spirito stand nearby, on the far side of the river, between the Tiber and St Peter's. The little girls are wards of the hospice.

12 Farfa is an ancient abbey in the Sabine mountains northeast of Rome.

13 *Trionfetti*: a card game

14 The court is again interested in turpentine.

15 Roman prostitutes often curl their hair. Camilla is using a resinous medicinal gum. A small coin, the baiocco would not buy much of it.

16 'It was burned on me'; 'It was burned on her.' These grammatical structures do not translate into proper English. They are datives of aggression. This passage refers to an earlier burning of a prostitute's door. At the time, in 1557, the court had suspected Camilla. For more on Lucrezia, see 'Lucrezia's Magic,' chapter 6 below. For the next several questions, the court pursues the matter of the earlier burning and then returns to the more recent fire.

17 Monte Giordano is a square, in the twentieth century enlarged and renamed Piazza dell'Orologio. A little to the north of Camilla's house, it is on an easy detour from a route from her house to Paolo's. The court will return to questions of urban geography when it calls Camilla to a second hearing.

18 Though the notary here treats Chierico as a witness rather than as an arraigned suspect, by the end of the interrogation he will classify him differently. Chierico, in less trouble than Camilla and Giorgio, answers only to a notary, not to a judge and a prosecutor.

19 The Ave Maria bells ring around six in the evening.

20 This is not the modern Via dei Chiavari, but a street near Piazza Sant'Apollinare.

21 San Luigi, Palazzo Madama, and Paolo's house by the Dogana are all

very close. The men are coming from the north.

22 No Italian could mistake Florentine dialect for Venetian. This inconsistency in identifying the speakers thus casts doubt on the whole story.

23 Banchi: The street of the bankers is not far from Monte Giordano, where Pasqua lives.

24 Jacobo Jacobacci, like Paolo di Grassi, lives by the Dogana.

25 The Pellegrino: Santa Maria dei Pellegrini is a church one block inland from the Ponte Sisto.

26 Via Giulia is the long, straight street running parallel to the Tiber to the Ponte Sisto.

27 Jacobo Jacobacci is a Roman gentleman of some substance. It is he, it seems, who scratches Pasqua the Paduan in the face.

28 Via dei Pontefici: A street near the Tomb of Augustus, in a district known for its many courtesans

29 It is not clear what a *traversa* is.

30 Second indiction: The second in a fifteen-year cycle starting at the time of Constantine, a calendrical flourish

31 Cardinal Crispo's house stands on the east side of a small piazza facing the church of San Luigi. Paolo lives about a block to the south. The stables may be between the two.

32 For the special role of the caporione during Vacant See, see the commentary for this trial. The church of San Salvatore [alle Coppelle] is just a few blocks north.

33 Paolo, who is very much alive, of course has not been 'assassinated.' He means that he has been treacherously assaulted.

34 We have the magistrates of three rioni on the scene. Paolo's own rione is Sant'Eustachio. Ponte is to the west. 'San Stefano' is not a standard rione name. The swordsman witness says rather that the third to come was the caporione of Colonna.

35 Gioanbattista Vittorio is caporione of Sant'Eustachio.

36 The court here threatens the witness with judicial torture.

37 Sixteenth-century barbers often double as surgeons and routinely treat wounds.

38 The Massimi, a noble family of the neighbourhood, have two palaces there.

39 'With the girl.' The term is casual; Camilla is no child.

40 Cardinal Santa Fiora, also known as Cardinal Sforza, lives by the church of Santa Lucia della Chiavica, on the street of the Banchi.

41 The light arquebus (*archibugetto*) is a long flintlock gun, ancestor of the musket.

42 'I am crying because the shame of being in jail hurts': *Io piango perche mi sa* [*sic*] *male di questa vergogna d'esser pregione*.

43 Jean Bertrand, bishop of Sens, is appointed cardinal in March 1557.

44 Coltello is a lawyer.

45 Levant is the eastern Mediterranean; Barbary is North Africa. The Sauli are a Genoese patrician family. As a Corsican, born under Genoese rule, Chierico might have Genoese connections.

46 The Romans conceive of the week as having seven days and eight nights.

47 The Count of Santa Fiora, the cardinal's brother, is a great noble of the Sforza family, far above Paolo in station.

48 The church of San Luigi is only a few yards to the north of Paolo's shop at the Dogana. It stands between the Pantheon and Piazza Navona.

49 Since all these place names remain, a modern map of Rome will let one trace their steps. The Column is the victory column of Marcus Aurelius still standing in Piazza Colonna. Montecitorio, in 1559, is not yet a palace, but a piece of slightly higher ground.

50 The *Banchi*, 'the banks', are both a street and a district near the castle bridge. Money-changers, bankers, and goldsmiths, often Florentine, live there.

51 These buildings bear the same names today. The men must have come south along the street now called Via della Dogana Vecchia.

52 Like Paolo di Grassi, the governor has his dwelling at the Dogana.

53 Those who flee toward Piazza Navona head west, the others south. Pirro Tari is, in the fall of 1559, one of the three *conservatori* of Rome, heads of communal government.

54 By *Popolo* ['people'], Paolo means not the common people, but rather, the collectivity of well-born Romans. For the politics of Paolo's utterance, see the commentary for this trial.

55 'Justice is the master': *Padrone è la Giustitia*. There are two possible translations. The less likely: that abstract justice is the master, or patron of Rome. The better: that the law is in charge. In common parlance, the magistrates and the police were *la giustizia*. 'Master' in all this passage translates *padrone*.

56 Giulio [actually, Giuliano] Cesarini, a wealthy baron, has a palace a little east of Paolo.

57 'They fuck us our wives': *Ci fottero le moglie*. Here we have a dative of aggression. 'They strike at us fucking our wives.' The grammatical structure mirrors the indirectness of the aggression.

58 The castle is a major strong point that dominates the city. In a Vacant

See it is a more secure place for what remains of papal government than are the jails.

59 Paolo is name-dropping. Cencio Capizucchi belongs to a famous old Roman family. A soldier notorious for his duels, he has risen high in the military service of Paul IV, but, during the violent Vacant See, has sided with the rioters who attack the pope's works and memory.

60 Literally, *non te stimarei*: 'I would not respect you'; in the familiar.

61 *Serra qua, serra qua*: Possibly, 'Close ranks with me!'

62 Storto has come to the boundaries of his rione, where his authority lapses.

63 A *canna* is roughly two metres.

64 The caporione has no direct authority over soldiers of the governor.

65 'The time of the other governor': Probably this refers to the time of the previous tenant, Antonio Paganelli, who held office only briefly, from 7 March to 18 August 1559.

66 By this, Paolo means that in Vacant See the power of the governor is suspended and the policing of the streets falls to the magistrates of the commune.

67 'To strike back by word and deed': *bisognaria fare et dire*, literally, 'It would be necessary to act and to speak.' This is the standard expression for strong retaliatory action. Paolo picks the phrasing of the question up in the next line, *se havessi voluto far' i fatti*: 'If I had wanted to do deeds ...'

68 'Castello': Città di Castello

69 Many months have gone by. There is now a new pope, so the Vacant See is only a lively memory.

70 'A slap in the cheek': *sguanciata*. This is a special word for such a blow, a conventional affront to the face.

71 The very riotous Vacant See begins with the death of Paul IV on 18 August 1559 and ends with the election of Pius IV on 26 December 1559.

72 This is almost certainly the friend of Camilla's whom Ferdiano di Ricchi accuses of attacking Agostino Bonamore. See the commentary on 'Agostino Bonamore and the Secret Pigeon.'

73 The doggerel on the note: *Camilla senese magra | Est locanda per li sbirri | per le hosti et per le poltroni*

74 The Ortaccio, a newly built-up part of town where many of the courtesans live, is by the tomb of Augustus some distance to the north of Camilla's house.

75 Hortensia is the Hortensietta of the preceding testimony.

76 Courtesans are not allowed to ride in coaches.

77 This is the Cardinal del Monte whom Giacobo Malatesta is rumoured to have thrashed. His misbehaviour is notorious. See the Introduction.

78 'Whip with stirrup thongs': *dare delle stafilate*. The form of blow is in the sixteenth century common enough to have a name of its own.

79 Governatore, Tribunale Criminale, Registri di Atti, Busta 36, f. 129v (29 November 1559)

80 Governatore, Tribunale Criminale, Registri di Sentenze II, 3 August 1560

CHAPTER THREE

1 'Bargello of Rome': actually, of the governor

2 The clavicembalo is an ancestor to the harpsichord.

3 'My people.' Here, Ottavia slides from indirect to direct discourse. Thus it is not clear if by 'my people' she means Bernardino's friends or, as is more likely, her family.

4 Gaeta is a coastal town on the border with the Kingdom of Naples. Documents from 1563 place an Inn of the Chain in the Pescheria district, between the Capitol and the Tiber. On the southern edge of the inhabited district of Rome, such a hostelry would be well placed for an escape toward Naples.

5 The Porta San Sebastiano opens upon the Appian way, which leads south from Rome.

6 The towns of Velletri and Cisterna lie to the south, on one of the roads to the Kingdom of Naples. The frontier, halfway between the two capitals, would have protected the fugitives from pursuit.

7 'Rough shirt': *buricchia*

8 'In the same place as above': Bernardino is thus, like Ottavia, at the house of the bargello. He has not yet been jailed.

9 A square not far from the bridge to Castel Sant'Angelo, Monte Giordano has many cheap lodgings. Pasqua, the courtesan whose door is burned in the first of the Paolo di Grassi trials, lives there.

10 'As heatedly as could be': *con tutta la furia del mondo*. *Furia* has a wide range, covering anger, impatience, haste, and sexual excitement.

11 'He had intercourse with me one time': *Hebbe a fare una volta con me*. The expression is unambiguous and rather matter of fact.

12 'The [bed]-clothes': *Li panni* might also mean the clothing.

13 The word is missing in the transcript. This is a good copy, which can skip words from the original.

14 'I had sexual relations with her': *Hebbi usato con lei*. This is a neutral expression.

15 'You didn't do anything to me': *Non mi fecesti niente*. In the fluid spelling of the sixteenth century, the verb could go with either *tu* or *voi*. In this whole exchange, the rapid alternation of second-person pronouns mirrors the shifting feelings of the two speakers.

16 'I've been keeping her company': *che la trattengo*. The expression can also mean 'keeping her' or 'entertaining her.' Context suggests 'keeping her company.'

17 'With the bishop or with the bishop's son,' that is, 'with any Tom, Dick, or Harry.' These are not real people.

18 The nunnery on the Tiber Island also turns up in the trial of Camilla the Go-Between, where the servant has a daughter, a nun there, who receives gifts of food.

19 'A pledge': *una fede*, literally a 'faith.' In the Renaissance, the word is used for promises, for guarantees, for trust, and, as here, for things of value, such as wedding rings, accepted as hostages, or 'pledges,' to secure reliable behaviour. The letter pledges Ottavia's willingness to shoulder responsibility should things go wrong.

20 The court keeps several concurrent registers of Investigations. Although there remain books covering this date, unfortunately, none mentions Ottavia.

21 San Salvatore in Lauro stands near the Tor di Nona jail, by the river, just upstream of the castle bridge.

22 We should read Curzio's deposition as reassembled from individual answers to a list of questions that have not been recorded here.

23 'Cops': *sbirri*. The Italian word is informal and unflattering.

24 Orlando: A hero of various chivalrous romances

25 A vague passage. It seems most likely that each sister is telling about the loves of the other. 'Who gave her money to do it to her': *che li dava che li faceva*. This phrase is also obscure, but Bernardino's general sense of improper love intrigue is plain.

26 Piazza of Sant'Angelo: either the square also known as Piazza del Castello, which stands at the city end of the castle bridge, or, less likely, the space by the church of Sant'Angelo in Pescheria, by the theatre of Marcellus.

27 Cardinal de la Cueva is governing Naples until the new viceroy comes. This Alfonso Gelito must be the same Alfonso who appears earlier as courting Ottavia.

28 From here on, the manuscript is in a bad state, for, as the scribe has tired, his handwriting has coarsened. To make matters worse, over the centuries, the ink has leached through from the other side of the page.

Thus, there are gaps and guesses in the translation.

29 'Do me justice, Signore.' The same term, *signore*, means both 'Lord God' and 'your lordship.' In his pain and distress, Bernardino mingles two kinds of supplication, to a mortal and to the deity.

30 The text is very degraded and obscure here.

CHAPTER FOUR

1 Ferdiano's family name is Di Ricchi.

2 A later trial (Busta 49, case 4, [1559]) shows that Agostino's shop is in Piazza Giudea, just outside the newly walled ghetto.

3 One of several Santa Croce palaces stands on the Vicolo de' Catinari, on the left bank just upstream from Tiber Island and a few streets in. It is there, a few blocks from his shop, that Agostino is wounded.

4 Ferdiano lives across the river, some distance from the site of the attack.

5 'Io non la potevo vedere perche per questa causa mi cascò d'adosso.' Does Agostino mean that he did not want to look at her or, as is less likely, that he was not allowed to go see her? The ambiguity of this passage runs through the whole trial.

6 By 'his daughter,' it is not clear whether Agostino means his wife or her sister, Caterina.

7 According to Ferdiano in the trial of 1559, Agostino's mother is in 1558 living in the house at his expense.

8 This passage is in the familiar, informal '*tu*' form.

9 'His dowry' (*la sua dote*) could also mean 'her dowry.'

10 'Punished': *lo farria castighare*. In the Renaissance, the term has a wide semantic range, from 'punish' or 'chasten' to 'rough up.' The expression thus does not always presuppose possession of legal or moral right.

11 When Margarita marries Agostino, she no longer needs to be in the charge of a woman servant. Note that there is no mother in the house. But what of the sister, Caterina, who seems still unmarried, but has no servant over her?

12 'With willing permission': *con bona licentia*. In 1559, in the later trial, Ferdiano tells the court he had had her jailed for stealing handkerchiefs.

13 'Because I was a member of the family': *perche io havevo fatto parentado*. It is probably best to take this expression figuratively. Literally, it means to be a god-kinsman, having sponsored a baptism, or to become related by marriage, but the term has a looser sense meaning alliance and good friendship. Bartholomea probably means that she is on good terms with the Di Ricchi.

14 Six weeks have passed.

15 'Strolagho' means 'astrologer,' but there is no indication that Francesco
is one. Like his brother, Francesco should be called Di Ricchi. Sixteenth-
century names are unstable.

16 Marforio is a name Romans give to a huge Roman statue to which in the
Renaissance they often affix derogatory verses. The statue, which today
shelters in a museum, in Agostino's day lies near the foot of the capitol.

17 'Don't get fancy ideas': *non te incantar l'anima.*

18 Claudio della Valle is the chief notary for the governor's tribunal.
Agostino's first testimony, above, is in his house. Camilla the go-between,
in the adultery trial in the next chapter, is pleased to drop his name.

19 'Insisted': *fecit instantiam.* This is a legal term echoed in Agostino's reply.

20 Ludovico Mattei's palace is halfway between Campo dei Fiori and the
Campidoglio. Agostino is just one block from his shop in Piazza Giudea.

21 In Agostino's time, this square, at the foot of the Capitoline hill, lies near
his shop. Mussolini's catastrophic urban improvements have now
effaced both the piazza and much of its neighbourhood.

22 The Minerva: the church of Santa Maria sopra Minerva, by the Pantheon

23 The Piazza del Castello is in rione Ponte, at the city end of the castle
bridge. It no longer exists.

24 The most prominent Santa Cecilia church is across the river, in
Trastevere, where Ferdiano's family live.

25 'The duke': The Duke of Paliano, a papal kinsman and man of great
influence in the state. He figures in the story of Malatesta and the
Hatter.

26 The church of Santo Stefano del Cacco is two streets southeast of the
church of the Minerva, where Barthelomea testifies. There is a Strozzi
palace not far away.

27 Ferdiano, in the 1559 trial, confirms the thrashing.

28 Cecco, a nickname for Francesco, here designates Francesco the fish-
monger.

29 Excepting a few formulae, the document ends here.

CHAPTER FIVE

1 The testimonies are not filed in chronological order. We have rearranged
them.

2 This loggia or *loggetta*, a porch that faces not the street, but a closed
yard, figures importantly in the story. It may be on the ground floor, but
it is high enough that from it madonna Giulia can throw letters into her

neighbour's yard. The house seems to have had three upstairs rooms. Camilla appears to have slept at one end of the house and the couple at the other. The middle room, the trysting place, which Camilla also calls hers, lies between the two bedrooms.

3 Camilla seems to be under questioning upstairs, in sight of the top of the stairs.

4 'Went in,' presumably into the middle room

5 *Orsù*: Well!

6 'Here from the window.' If this interrogation takes place on the second floor of the house, the window is one flight above the ground, perhaps directly above the loggia.

7 The fiscale of the Campidoglio is a prosecutor for the court of the commune of Rome. Claudio della Valle is a notary of the governor's court. Camilla here is dropping legal names for safety's sake.

8 There is an airspace between the ceiling and the roof ample enough for cats and nimble lovers.

9 *'Grande errore.'* The term is stronger than the modern English 'error.' It covers gross violations of social ethics. Notice that, though moral, the term is not especially Christian.

10 *Ohimè*: Oh dear!

11 'From the *loggetta*' is ambiguous. Most likely, Camilla is out back, on the Piccardi *loggetta*, and Camillo is speaking to her from a window of his house. Were he on a porch of his own, Giulia would probably say 'from his *loggetta*.'

12 'Ruin ... Good fortune': *ruina ... ventura*. These are rhetorical opposites.

13 'Entertainment': *spasso*

14 The magistrates have already gone up to inspect the hole.

15 To draw beans (*tirare le fave*) is a cross between magic and fortune-telling. Do the beans declare of jealousy, or do they cause it? In magic, the line is seldom clear. Giulia says that Camilla wants to use the beans to *dar martello* to Camillo, that is, to drive him into the jealous passion that the Renaissance thinks typical of ardent lovers.

16 'Assassinated' is figurative. It means 'destroyed, done in.'

17 'The same place': the house

18 'Embassies.' In the Renaissance, love messages and other delicate communications through intermediaries are called *ambasciate*.

19 Giulia and Camilla have been going to the convent where the mistress's sisters live, Santa Maria in Campo Marzio. Montecitorio, today the Italian Chamber of Deputies, in the sixteenth century is a street and hill northeast of the Pantheon, not far from the nunnery.

20 'Spell-casting': *fattochiaria*. Witchcraft, with its intimations of diabolical alliances, is too strong a term. See the notes to chapter 7, 'The Exorcist and the Spell-Caster.'

21 As its name indicates, this is the monastery on the Tiber Island.

22 The Renaissance *pizza* is a round bread, sometimes sweet, which has none of the modern toppings. The tomato, an American vegetable in the sixteenth century, has yet to arrive in Italian kitchens.

23 Giulia has a guardian because her parents are no longer living.

24 *Suor*: 'Sister,' a nun's title of address

25 'Under the altar' or perhaps 'under the altar cloth'

26 Notice that Camilla is now in jail.

27 Three thousand scudi, would be a sizeable dowry for a person of Gieronimo's station.

28 'Rigorous examination and extraordinary measures': that is, torture

CHAPTER SIX

1 Because water damage has faded the document badly, there are many gaps in the translation.

2 For the text of a prayer to Saint Daniel, see the commentary after this document.

3 'Servant': *Scalco*, a domestic with ceremonial duties. In status, he is far below some of Lucrezia's customers.

4 The Ripetta is the upstream river port of Rome, near the tomb of Augustus.

5 'She called her a whore to her face, though she is a respectable woman': *gli ha dato della putana per la testa essendo donna da bene*. Not easy to translate. *Gli ha dato* can be read as 'she hit her' *per la testa* 'in the head' with the term 'whore.' As always, the head is the seat of honour.

6 Another Lucrezia, not the courtesan but her servant

7 24 August 1557

8 'A jug of oil': *una foglietta dolio*. A *foglietta* was about half a litre.

9 *Cameriere*: One of any of a number of high officials of the papal court, either lay or ecclesiastical. In this case, a 'gentleman,' he must be a layman.

10 'Cloths': *veste*. Could these be primitive diaphragms of cloth to prevent conception or venereal disease?

11 'Tightened': *strette*

12 'Syphilitic traces': *taroli*, usually, are the boils of syphilis. It is not clear how sperm could have them.

13 Santa Maria della Pace is just northwest of Piazza Navona.

14 Sant'Ivo is just southeast of Piazza Navona.

15 The embassy of the king of France lies just south of the straight street that leads to the Trinità dei Monti (today, the Spanish steps).

16 Santa Maria dei Miracoli is near the Piazza del Popolo, then a poor neighbourhood. There are major demolitions in the zone in the fall of 1556, when the state lays an earthen redoubt as defence against the Spanish armies.

17 A large syphilitic hospital, San Giacomo lies between the river and the Corso (Via Lata). Imperia imagines herself walking north on the Via Lata, toward the Popolo.

18 'We slept together': sharing a bed is a social, not a sexual, act. Like sharing a table, it seals and signals friendship.

19 The church still stands, three blocks north of the Pantheon.

20 Not all a courtesan's clients are her 'friends.' 'Friend' here means steady client and protector.

21 'Used anything for magical love craft': *usa fuit aliquibus ad artem amoris.*

22 A. Bertolotti, *Streghe Sortiere e Maliardi nel Secolo XVI in Roma* (Florence 1883; reprint, 1979), 77. 'Jealous love sickness': *martello.* The author does not cite his source for the prayer.

CHAPTER SEVEN

1 'Without my cape.' This is often said in court, especially, as here, in the colder months. Camillo, like other suspects, wants to show the magistrate that his visit is impulsive, not premeditated.

2 Camillo's narrative is confusing. He describes how he is in his shop in the Via del Panico, near the bridge to Castel Sant'Angelo, when there appears the saddler, Agostino, who lives in the same street. A shoemaker exorcist, Danese (whose name is pronounced somewhat like 'dan-Ay-say'), is also present. The two visitors persuade Camillo to accompany them to Agostino's house.

3 'To call up spirits': *scongiurare*

4 'The captain': Captain Ventura Troscitti, bargello of the governor's court, has come to make arrests.

5 'Adjurations': A technical Latin term of the court's that means pressing requests that have the force of an oath. Camillo, in response to the question, uses the Italian term *incantazioni*, 'incantations' or 'spells.'

6 The church of Santa Maria della Consolazione is in 1559 on the edge of the settled part of Rome, on the forum side of the Capitoline hill.

7 'You scoundrel, you bastard!': *forfantaccio, manigoldio.* The original sense

of *manigoldio* was 'executioner,' but the term has by the sixteenth century taken on a looser sense. Antique invective is especially hard to translate, for it presumes old codes of values.

8 Visso is just north of the mountain town of Norcia. In Benvenuto Cellini's *Autobiography*, there is a necromancer from the zone. Cellini remarks, 'The peasants of Norcia were trustworthy people with some experience of the black art' (Penguin edition, p. 124).

9 Campo dei Fiori is a large square, the site of a major market.

10 Via Giulia, one of the longest streets of the city, runs parallel to the Tiber from the castle bridge down to Ponte Sisto. Santa Caterina, near Cassandra's house, is toward the downstream end. Note that Camillo soon tells the court that Danese often slept at his brother's, by Ponte Sisto. To the magistrates, proximity might argue for acquaintance between the two main suspects.

11 'The man-waker': *svigliauomo*. We have not been able to trace this expression. Is it an owl?

12 'It's not worth writing down what they say, for those who say it never speak the truth': *Non se vol pigliar copia et quel che dicano non dicano mai verità.*

13 'Sung mass': high mass, with a choir

14 Renaissance Romans go to the church of Santa Maria del Popolo, at the northern gate of the town, to pray for the possessed. 'Il Popolo' denotes both the church and the big square it stands on.

15 San Giovanni is the great Lateran basilica.

16 Palestrina is a town about twenty miles south-east of Rome.

17 'Coccio is the master there': *Coccio ci e padrone.*

18 'And I have gone broke': *e mi so rovinato.*

19 'Oh good Jesus, illumine my eyes': *O bone Iesue illumina oculos meos.* The attribution to Bernard is in error.

20 'Fra Perusino, his shop assistant': This must be a jocular nickname.

21 In Maddalena's discourse, as Danese reports it here, the words of the demons alternate with those of their host and victim. Sometimes one demon speaks, sometimes several.

22 In 1559, monthly communion is still rare. Most Romans go only at Easter.

23 'Needs': *mancanze*, literally, 'lacks.' The expression is puzzling.

24 'And the husband said, "Would that it were the will of God that I do this thing and she would be free!"': *Et il marito disse volesse Dio che io havessi a fare questo et fusse libera.* The translation treats 'io' as denoting the husband and so puts the sentence in direct discourse, with quotation

marks. Another reading, in indirect discourse, has '*io*' mean Danese: 'The husband said that it might be the wish of God that I did this thing and that she be free.' But the words of the possessed woman immediately following suggest the first reading.

25 There are six churches by that name.

26 Isn't it a disgrace to God that he doesn't give you licence?' : *Ne disgrazia dio che non vi da licentia.*

27 'Strip this sorcerer': *Spogliate questo huomo malefico.* In the language of the law, the term *maleficus* attaches both to witches and sorcerers and to other serious malefactors. Nevertheless, in context, the bargello, as quoted, could have had no other meaning than 'sorcerer,' for the legal term had no other common sense in everyday speech.

28 'A picture' : *una tavoletta*

29 Santa Caterina da Siena is on the Via Giulia. Danese is not contradicting himself, but merely making the address more precise.

30 'Lady': *madonna*

31 'Charms': *facturas*

32 In demonology, *carta vergine*, virgin paper, is made from a birth caul or from the skin of a stillborn baby.

33 'Are made for our confusion': The text is very clear here, but the words make little sense. The scribe of this copy may have slipped, misreading an abbreviation for 'consolation.'

34 The Aracoeli, or 'Altar of Heaven,' is a prominent Franciscan church on the Campidoglio.

35 The Cardinal Santa Fiora is Guido Ascanio Sforza. See the note on him in the first trial about Paolo di Grassi.

36 '*Hinc fuge fur moneo presidis manet iste libellus.*' The Latin is flawed, as can happen in popular works aspiring to more learning than they command. Good grammar would expect *preside*, not *presidis*.

37 'Green copper': *Rameverde*, as here, or *verderame* is copper carbonate.

38 Both hair and inscribed almonds are used in popular magic.

39 Via del Pellegrino runs parallel to Via Giulia.

40 On 14 September 1557, the Tiber jumps its banks and inundates much of the lower city inside its bend, including the Via Giulia. The flood does great damage, breaking an ancient bridge across the river and sweeping away almost all the floating mills that grind the city's grain. The catastrophe leaves a strong impression. Bones and beans are standard paraphernalia of magic; for an example of divination with beans, see chapter 5, 'Camilla the Go-Between.'

41 'Unborn paper' (*carta non nata*) is another term for 'virgin paper.'

42 Pasquino, one of Rome's 'talking statues' to which one pasted scurrilous notes, still stands near the southern end of Piazza Navona.

43 Monte Giordano is both a square and a district near the bridge to Castel Sant'Angelo. The inn, in an alley between the Via del Panico and the Via dei Banchi, is just around the corner from Agostino's eventual house.
· For other lodgers at Monte Giordano, see chapter 2, 'Paolo di Grassi and his Courtesans' and chapter 4, 'Ottavia and Her Music Teacher.'

44 Julius III becomes pope in 1550.

45 San Giacomo degli Incurabili, a big syphilitic hospital below the Popolo, is in a neighbourhood crowded with prostitutes like those Cassandra says Agostino fancied.

46 'To take care of me': *governarmi*

47 Traditionally, Carnival starts with the feast of St Anthony, on 18 January, just a few days before the present testimony, which takes place on 23 January. Thus, Cassandra probably means she saw Agostino a little over a year ago.

48 'And he never gave me anything': *et a me non ha donato mai niente.* A puzzling passage; the text in the manuscript is very clear. Either Cassandra or a scribe seems to have reversed the intended meaning, that she never gave anything to anyone else.

49 'For the love of God': as charity, without payment

50 'Sorcery': *maleficiis.* The term could also mean 'evil deeds.' Notice that here the court labels the deeds, but not the person. A common Latin term for witch is *malefica*, but the court does not use it here.

51 'By a respectable woman': *da donna da bene.*

52 'This nonsense': *questa baglia*

53 'Pal': *compare*, literally, God-kinsman

54 'Adjurations': the scribe here twice writes erroneously *abiurationes.*

55 'I couldn't make it out': *Non sapeva intender.* It may also mean 'I didn't know how to listen to it,' or 'I couldn't understand.'

56 'His other examination.' There is no earlier examination of Domenico in this transcript; it may have been recorded elsewhere.

57 'Sorcerer': *Homo maleficus.* Only at this point does the court label Danese himself as a sorcerer, rather than just calling his actions sorcery. From here on in the trial, the term appears more and more often.

58 'A friend of maestro Agostino': *amica di maestro Agostino.* The term here means that she had been a sexual partner.

59 The text has *abiurationes.*

60 This is a standard formula refering to judicial torture.

61 'Town councillors': *priori*

62 'Homicides' is a figure of speech connoting monstrous deeds.

63 'I never ate in the morning, which proves that I didn't have mass.' That is what the manuscript says, but the sense seems backwards. Danese should have wanted to say that he fasted and so must indeed have gone to mass, despite his promise to the demon.

64 This ending is ambiguous. It lacks the usual phrase about 'three days for preparing his defence.' Danese is still in prison.

65 Cellini, *Autobiography*, 120–4

66 Camillo sees the madwoman and the lay exorcist together five times, at the first of which the two renew their pact. The fifth meeting is cut short by the arrival of Captain Ventura, the bargello, and his police. Danese mentions the first and last of these encounters but passes over the other three.

67 'Poor fellow': *poverhuomo* is one word.

68 Aldous Huxley's famous devils of Loudun are a case in point.

CHAPTER EIGHT

1 Aspra is today called Casperia. It is a fairly remote town in the Sabine mountains north of Rome.

2 Renaissance names have several components and in use often appear in a variety of shortened forms created by omitting one or another part. For a full guide to names of the characters in this trial, see the list of 'Dramatis Personae' in the commentary below.

3 The same man is at once cardinal of Montepulciano, in Tuscany, and Bishop of Sabina, the diocese to which Aspra belongs. Because he lives and works in Rome, the latter part of the trial takes place in the city. The 'second indiction' is a calendrical flourish that adds no meaningful information to the date.

4 Aspra belongs to a branch of the noble Savelli family. Onorio himself is notoriously high-handed.

5 *Castaldo*: bailiff

6 Daniele has taken minor orders in expectation of becoming a priest. He is thus legally a cleric.

7 These are local trips. Magliano to the west, is down in the Tiber valley, not far from Aspra. Collevecchio is between Magliano and Aspra. Terni, a district town to the north, is a little further away.

8 The witness seems mistaken here, for it is Massimigliano who bears this nickname.

9 'Many daughters': A mark of poverty, since girls were expensive to

marry and less productive than sons of earnings for the house.

10 The pledges to ensure these boys' appearance in Rome give their ages as around twelve years. The sponsors must have known the boys better than the present witness and thus their information is probably more accurate.

11 *Querza*: A puzzling term. The word can be a dialect version of *quercia*, oak, but then why is it made of skin?

12 *Tarantella*: Originally the trance dance of Calabria, but here just a peasant air

13 Montàsola is village just north of Aspra.

14 The village of Roccantica lies very close by.

15 The judge has a degree both in canon and in civil law.

16 The manuscript says, erroneously, 'the first hour of the day,' but must have intended the first hour of the night.

17 'Saturday': actually, Friday

18 'Permitted': The court has in mind the Index of Forbidden Books.

19 'Cocky': *gagliardi* – spirited, fresh, 'feisty.' The word applies mostly to males.

Bibliography

ARCHIVAL SOURCES

Archivio di Stato di Roma, Governatore, Tribunale Criminale, Processi
(XVI secolo): Busta 8, trial 4 (1542) ('The Abbot's Assassins'); Busta 38, trial
8 (1558) ('Agostino Bonamore and the Secret Pigeon'); Busta 48 (1559–60),
trials 4 and 19 ('Paolo di Grassi and His Courtesans'); trial 8 ('Ottavia and
Her Music Teacher'); trial 13 ('The Exorcist and the Spell-Caster'); trial 15
('Camilla the Go-Between'); Busta 60, trial 6 (Introduction: 'Malatesta and
the Hatter'); Busta 155, trial 3 (1574) ('The Village Play'); Investigazioni 62
(1559) ('Lucrezia's Magic')

SELECT BIBLIOGRAPHY
FOR BACKGROUND AND FURTHER READING*

Works on Renaissance and early modern Rome

Ceen, Allan. *The Quartiere de' Banchi. Urban Planning in Rome in the First Half
of the Cinquecento.* New York and London: Garland 1986
Cellini, Benvenuto. *Autobiography.* Harmondsworth: Penguin 1956; or any
other edition. A Renaissance goldsmith's adventures, many of them in
Rome. The tales are often tall, but the social attitudes are real.
Cohen, Elizabeth S. 'No Longer Virgins: Self-Representation by Young
Women in Late Renaissance Rome.' In *Refiguring Woman: Perspectives on
Gender and the Italian Renaissance,* ed. M. Migiel and J. Schiesari, 169–91.
Ithaca: Cornell University Press 1991

* With one exception, only works written in English are listed.

– 'Honor and Gender in the Streets of Early Modern Rome.' *Journal of Interdisciplinary History* 22 (1992): 597–625

Cohen, Elizabeth S., and Thomas V. Cohen. 'Camilla the Go–Between: The Politics of Gender in a Roman Household (1559).' *Continuity and Change* 4 (1989): 53–77

Cohen, Thomas V. 'The Case of the Mysterious Coil of Rope: Street Life and Jewish Persona in Rome in the Middle of the Sixteenth Century.' *Sixteenth Century Journal* 19 (1988): 209–21

– 'The Lay Liturgy of Affront in Sixteenth-Century Rome.' *Journal of Social History* 25 (1992): 857–77

Delumeau, Jean. *Vie économique et sociale de Rome dans la seconde moitié du XVIe siècle.* 2 vols. Paris: De Broccard 1957–9. Fundamental and without peer in English

Hughes, Steven C. 'Fear and Loathing in Bologna and Rome: The Papal Police in Perspective.' *Journal of Social History* 21 (1987): 97–116

Ingersoll, Richard. *The Ritual Use of Space in Renaissance Rome.* Ann Arbor: University Microfilms 1986

Krautheimer, Richard. *Rome: The Profile of a City: 312–1308.* Princeton: Princeton University Press 1980. On physical evolution from antiquity.

– *The Rome of Alexander VII.* Princeton: Princeton University Press 1985. On city planning in the age of the baroque.

Nussdorfer, Laurie. *Civic Politics in the Rome of Urban VIII.* Princeton: Princeton University Press 1992

Partner, Peter. *Renaissance Rome: 1500–1559.* Berkeley and Los Angeles: University of California Press 1976. An introduction, available in paperback

Pastor, Ludwig von. *History of the Popes.* London: J. Hodges 1923–53. A very solid, comprehensive political history, but often helpful for other issues as well. Vols 11–20 cover the period of these trials.

Stinger, Charles L. *The Renaissance in Rome.* Bloomington: Indiana University Press 1985. On humanistic culture

Works on early modern Italy dealing with court records

Brown, Judith C. *Immodest Acts: The Life of a Lesbian Nun in Renaissance Italy.* New York: Oxford University Press 1986. Available in paperback; a trial-based tale about how a nun mingled sexuality and religious theatrics in a play for power

Brucker, Gene. *Giovanni and Lusanna: Love and Marriage in Renaissance*

Florence. Berkeley and Los Angeles: University of California Press 1986. The story, told from court records, of a woman's attempt to hold a husband of higher station

Burke, Peter. *The Historical Anthropology of Early Modern Italy*. Cambridge: Cambridge University Press 1987. Essays on magic, healing, insults, language, and ritual, with a particularly lively introduction

Ginzburg, Carlo. *The Cheese and the Worms*. Baltimore: Johns Hopkins University Press 1980. Available in paperback; a canny reading of the interaction between the magistrates and their suspect, a miller of very irregular religious opinions

Kuehn, Thomas. *Law, Family, and Women: Toward a Legal Anthropology of Renaissance Italy*. Chicago: University of Chicago Press 1991

– 'Reading Microhistory: The Example of *Giovanni and Lusanna*.' *Journal of Modern History* 61 (1989): 514–34. A trenchant, subtle critique of the claims and methods of those who try to write history out of judicial records

Martin, John. 'A Journeymen's Feast of Fools.' *Journal of Medieval and Renaissance Studies* 17 (1987): 149–74

Muir, Edward, and Guido Ruggiero, eds. *Sex and Gender in Historical Perspective*. Baltimore: Johns Hopkins University Press 1990

Ruggiero, Guido. *The Boundaries of Eros: Sex Crime and Sexuality in Renaissance Venice*. New York: Oxford University Press 1985. A very useful survey of the boundaries of sanctioned sexual conduct in a society that lives by honour

Some additional readings on Renaissance Italy
that treat issues arising in the trials

Chojnacki, Stanley. 'Dowries and Kinsmen in Early Renaissance Venice.' *Journal of Interdisciplinary History* 4 (1975): 571–600

Klapisch–Zuber, Christiane. *Women, Family and Ritual in Renaissance Italy*. Chicago: University of Chicago Press 1985

Masson, Georgina. *Courtesans of the Italian Renaissance*. London: Secker and Warburg 1975

Romano, Dennis. *Patricians and Popolani: The Social Foundations of the Venetian Renaissance State*. Baltimore: Johns Hopkins University Press 1987

Weissman, Ronald. *Ritual Brotherhood in Renaissance Florence*. New York and London: Academic Press 1982. Chapter 1 has an excellent discussion of the tension between the dictates of honour and those of Christian brotherhood in an urban community.

Some works on social history outside Italy that make use of court records

Bossy, John, ed. *Disputes and Settlements*. Cambridge: Cambridge University Press 1983. On the social functions of law in pre-modern Europe

Davis, Natalie Z. *Fiction in the Archives: Pardon Tales and Their Tellers in Sixteenth–Century France*. Stanford: Stanford University Press 1987. On how to read the stories told to secure judicial pardons

Farr, James R. *Hands of Honor: Artisans and Their World in Dijon, 1550–1650*. Ithaca: Cornell University Press 1988. See especially pp. 150–95.

Kagan, Richard L. *Lucrecia's Dreams. Politics and Prophecy in Sixteenth–Century Spain*. Berkeley and Los Angeles: University of California Press 1990

Levack, Brian. *The Witch-Hunt in Early Modern Europe*. London: Longman 1987.

Sabean, David, W. *Power in the Blood: Popular Culture and Village Discourse in Early Modern Germany*. Cambridge: Cambridge University Press 1984

Readings on the role of honour in Mediterranean societies

Gilmore, David, ed. *Honor and Shame and the Unity of the Mediterranean*. Washington: American Anthropological Society 1987

Peristiany, J.G., ed. *Honor and Shame: The Values of Mediterranean Society*. Chicago: University of Chicago 1966. An anthology of excellent essays, especially that of Julian Pitt-Rivers

Index

Illustration Credits

🙟

CHAPTER OPENINGS

Ritratto di tutti quelli che vanno vendendo per Roma (details)
Istituto Nazionale per la Grafica, Rome
Chapters 1, 4, 7

Henrik van Cleve, Saint Peter's Square (detail)
Istituto Nazionale per la Grafica, Rome
Chapter 3

Cesare Vecellio, *Habiti Antichi et Moderni di tutto il Mondo*. Venice: Sessa
[1598]
Metropolitan Toronto Reference Library, Special Collections, Toronto
Chapters 2, 5, 6

View of Aspra, Frontispiece, *Statutum Terrae Asprae* (reprint, 1981)
Jean de Bonnot, Editeur, Paris
Chapter 8

ILLUSTRATIONS

Van Aelst, Conclave for the Election of Paul V
F. Ehrle and H. Egger, *Die Conclavepläne* (Vatican City, 1933). Avery
   Architectural and Fine Arts Library, Columbia University in the city of
   New York

Polidoro Caldara di Caravaggio, Women Sewing
Cabinet des Dessins, Louvre, Paris

Silvestre, The Madonna of the Popolo
Foto Bibliotheca Hertziana, Rome

Du Pérac, Forum with the Arch of Septimius Severus
Istituto Nazionale per la Grafica, Rome

Lafréry, Castel Sant'Angelo
Foto Bibliotheca Hertziana, Rome

Van Cleve, Colosseum
Istituto Nazionale per la Grafica, Rome

Wyngaerde, Panorama of Rome (detail)
Metropolitan Museum of Art, New York

Du Pérac, Rome from the roof of the Cancelleria
Foto Biblioteca Vaticana